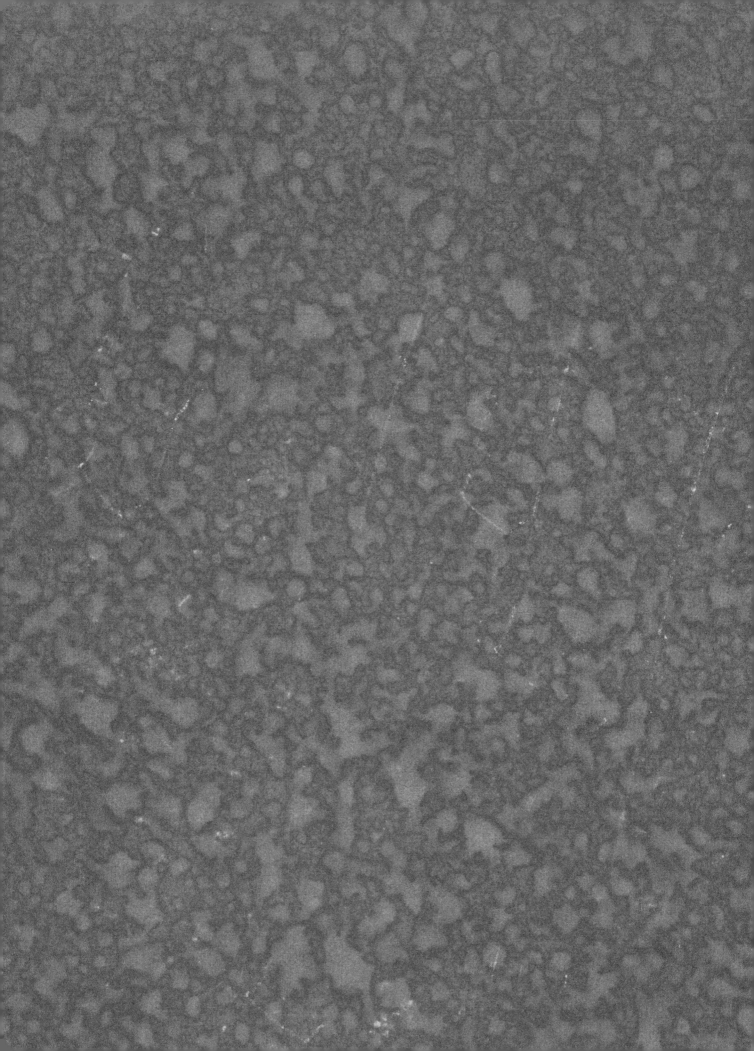

FRATERNITY

WRITTEN BY
JUAN DÍAZ CANALES

ILLUSTRATED BY
JOSÉ-LUIS MUNUERA

COLORS BY
SEDYAS

Foreword Text by Alex Romero
Translation by Jeremy Melloul
Localization, Layout, and Editing by Mike Kennedy

LION FORGE™   THE MAGNETIC COLLECTION™

ISBN: 978-1-941302-51-4

Library of Congress Control Number: 2018941030

Thank you to my dear Toñi who, for my entire life, has helped me with my work.

    — Juan Díaz Canales

To James Whale, Terence Fisher, and Morris.

    — José-Luis Munuera

"That man can never attain a state of superior and permanent happiness until he shall be surrounded by those external circumstances which will train him from birth to feel pure charity and sincere affection toward the whole of his species, to speak the truth only on all occasions, and to regard with a merciful and kind disposition all that has life."

Robert Owen

The Book of the New Moral World:
Containing the Rational System of Society, Founded on Demonstrable Facts,
Developing the Constitution and Laws of Human Nature and of Society

1836

The Seventeenth Law of the Universal Rational Constitution for the Government of the Human Species Collectively or for Any District Taken Separately.

We were going to recreate the world with our own hands.

We had already torn down the world of our forefathers, first with the Enlightenment and later with the steam engine and the irredeemable guillotine. We left behind the fields, our wedding trousseaux, the inquisitive looks from the neighbors, and the viscous morality of the village priests. We left our destinies behind us, the cradle that was to become our grave, and we engaged upon our own path, the one at the end of which we would find ourselves.

But there were many things that we could not leave behind: our passions, our hatred, our deadly love for humanity, the labyrinth of words with which we deceived ourselves and others, and perhaps that is precisely why we eventually found ourselves.

This was the case for Robert Owen, son of blacksmith Robert Owen, who should have learned his father's trade and forged the cage of his own life imprisonment. But he was born at the end of time, in the Wales of 1771, itself a nation and a half, an arm of the sea, eighteen years distant from the French Revolution. He enlarged his succinct education and, as a child, went to London to seek his fortune, that of a man who himself had nothing to do either but to be a blacksmith or to die on the very piece of land where he had been born.

He went from one haberdashery shop to another and ended up failing in the thick forest of Manchester chimneys with but a hundred pounds, three spinning machines, and a dazzling vision of the future of humanity: the indispensable materials that would weave the future for Robert Owen.

Subtly guided by the invisible hand of Adam Smith, several associates helped him in his business with the impeccably rational goal of helping themselves: they called their textile empire Chorlton Twist Company and expanded its territory not by violence and the plunder of war, but by the mutually beneficial exchange of commerce, buying land and mills from anyone who saw more interest in the money they offered than in the judicious exploitation of their property.

New Lanark, the small industrial town on the banks of the Clyde River, was one of those nonviolent conquests. The result of David Dale and Richard Arkwright's designs, this production was fueled by the energy of the waterfalls and the blood of the two thousand unfortunate souls crammed into their hives. Perhaps anxious about his future epitaph, Dale tried to bleed the children a little less, and in the fall of 1799, when he knew that Owen was ready to assume care of them, he sold him the village with all his machines and gave him the hand of his daughter Caroline. Drunk with a strictly rational and enlightened romanticism, the crown prince consort Robert Owen saw the opportunity to govern according to his own well-understood interests: why limit himself to the care of children when he could improve the living conditions of all his new subjects? He gave them larger and cleaner work stations, built schools and a shop where they could buy necessities at cost, strictly monitored the consumption of alcohol, and was the stern but caring father that was at no doubt needed by these unfortunate ones, all children whatever their age.

But forgive me, I do not do proper justice to a man who has striven to be just within the limits of his judgment. I could tell you that, as a clever businessman, he took care of his subordinates so as to increase their interests in the work and thus drive out any dream of emancipation.

I would then create confusion between his true purpose and the lesson he learned from other more calculating philanthropists. Owen, imbued with the ideas of the Scottish Enlightenment, sincerely believed that he had repaired the errors of St. Augustine and Campanella, Moro, and Bacon: New Lanark was to be the first citadel of New Atlantis. It was the perfect model of a rational system for the development of capabilities inscribed by human nature.

But that was the very problem: human nature.

New Lanark prospered, but Owen's associates were unwilling to invest in his more expensive projects or share their earnings with the workforce, so the experiment remained little more than an attempt at what would inevitably happen. And Owen, in want of lands to build paradise, went to seek them on the other bank of the ocean, in the new world. Where else could he have gone? That's where he and I met, and that's when we discovered that, while the world may be new, man is still old. Or, more exactly, human nature is old. But we will overcome.

His quest led him to Indiana, to the last establishment of George Rapp's Harmony Society. Another visionary, Mr. Rapp was of German origin, a self-proclaimed prophet who fled the authorities of the old continent in 1803 with almost a thousand followers. They founded a community in Pennsylvania—the original Harmony—where the first principle stated that all belonged to all and the second principle declared all obeyed Rapp. I leave you to find the conclusion that follows. After ten years, Rapp sold the community with considerable profit to the Mennonites and guided his flock to Indiana where he founded the second Harmony. This lasted another ten years until Robert Owen appeared with his plans for earthly paradise in one hand and one hundred and fifty thousand dollars in the other. Rapp took the money and returned with the community to Pennsylvania. What interested his family, they who knew the imminence of the apocalypse, was not an earthly paradise but the purification and rejection of material goods that Rapp so zealously sacrificed.

In 1825, Harmony became New Harmony.

I do not remember exactly when I heard about Owen for the first time, but I can say that he changed the course of my life. If my life has any value for myself or for others, I owe it to him. No one has ever heard me utter a word that lacked respect, and, although it costs me, in these intimate diaries, to share the errors and answers of his glorious march, I have the right to think that no man will be more pleased with my success than Robert Owen himself.

My first vocation was music: it fed my wife and myself when, as newlyweds, we settled in Cincinnati around 1819. I also earned a little money by selling an oil lamp that I patented, as well as other inventions of modest ingenuity. Perhaps I would have made a fortune with these ideas, but I stopped caring about them when I knew the project of New Harmony. I can attest, with a certain melancholy pride, that I was a member of the first group that met to founder the pooling of property, that I participated in the drafting and approval of the first constitution in February 1826, and that I directed the orchestra of New Harmony, to which I finally devoted my soul and talent. I lived in the colony with my wife and my little girl for a little over a year, which was more time than it took to see it fail.

One colony after another, we were going to recreate the world with our own hands. If life is a theatrical performance that we all give together, what prevents us from rewriting the text of this comedy, choosing our own role, changing the scenery? The new world was the backdrop on which we would paint our garden of delights, where everything would be as we would like. Adepts of Rapp, Anabaptists, Methodists, Socialists all claimed to rewrite the social contract in terms that would be more favorable to them. Myself, I was involved in another community project in Cincinnati before leaving for New Harmony. Unlike Plato, we did not need to seduce the tyrant of Syracuse to execute our plans: we were self-sufficient. Like Plato, we ended our utopian adventure reduced to slavery: for that too, we sufficed ourselves.

At New Harmony, we would all participate equally in the work and the division of benefits, so the vast majority lay in the shade of a tree waiting for the common benefits of the work of others. Gradually, it seemed that the variety of opinions, tastes, and intentions was more than the requirement of conformity could bare. Most members of the community were discouraged by our reforms, and conservatism returned after we had tested all forms of government possible within our miniature world. We had restaged the French Revolution with, on the passive side, ravaged hearts instead of corpses. It was as if the natural law of diversity had vanquished us itself: our "united interests" came into direct conflict with the individuals' eccentricities and circumstances, and also with the instinct of self-preservation. It was self-evident that by the very fact that people and interests came in contact, concessions and compromises were unavoidable.

Robert Owen thought that in a promising environment, human nature could flourish in its purity prior to any society. He was so convinced that New Harmony was this environment that he did not even stay to oversee the operation of the social machinery he had started.

Perhaps he had been right despite himself, and the poisonous vine that blossomed in every nook and cranny of New Harmony was human nature. Perhaps human nature, like a weed, manages to thrive in any soil, be it earthly paradise or graveyard.

And, although human nature may be a beautiful and delicate flower, if, as Owen says, it is education that determines its growth, how can educators transcend the education they have themselves received? If we found Rousseau's noble savage, how could we instruct him without transmitting our perversity to him? How could we teach him our language, the meaning of words such as "man," "woman," "master," or "slave" without sowing in his mind the structure and order in which these words make sense, without creating a man, a woman, a master, or a slave?

If this were true, humanity would be condemned to stray from its own nature until the end of time, because of the original sin of generational indoctrination.

We were going to recreate the world with our own hands, and for a while it seemed like we were going to get there, that we were all going to escape from our cells. We realized that the body of Leviathan was made up of our own intertwined bodies, that society was not an entity separate from ourselves, and that for that reason it could be all we wanted.

But what did we want it to be?

At the end of his life, Owen took refuge in the spirit world and looked for ways to build the future. Fortunately, the spirits had nothing to say, for if they spoke they would only make us even more prisoners of their designs and traditions. In fact, the dead already speak through our mouths and manifest themselves through our bodies since we speak the language they have bequeathed to us. We think the ideas they have passed on to us and we wander dressed in their clothes by the paths that they have drawn. We can change the form of Leviathan, and baptize it with another name, but it remains Leviathan.

Sometimes I wonder if things could have happened differently, if it happened that we had the slightest opportunity to escape.

What would have happened if we had been others, if I had not been, I, Josiah Warren the individualist and if he had not been Robert Owen, the socialist. If the colony had not been called New Harmony, if it were other settlers who had populated it, in a world that would have looked a lot like ours without being identical to it.

Would we have known then true human nature? Maybe that would not even be enough. Maybe to be free it would be necessary to imagine a nature much different from that of humans.

So these words I write will not serve much, as these, like all words, are human, too human.

Josiah Warren *
Boston, 1872

* Josiah Warren was an American inventor, printer, and author greatly influenced by Robert Owen. He is widely considered the first American anarchist. This text, however, is a fictional essay speculating Josiah's experiences in the real-life settlement of New Harmony, Indiana. The story that follows is an imaginary tale set within a fabricated version of that scenario.

FRATERNITY

PART I

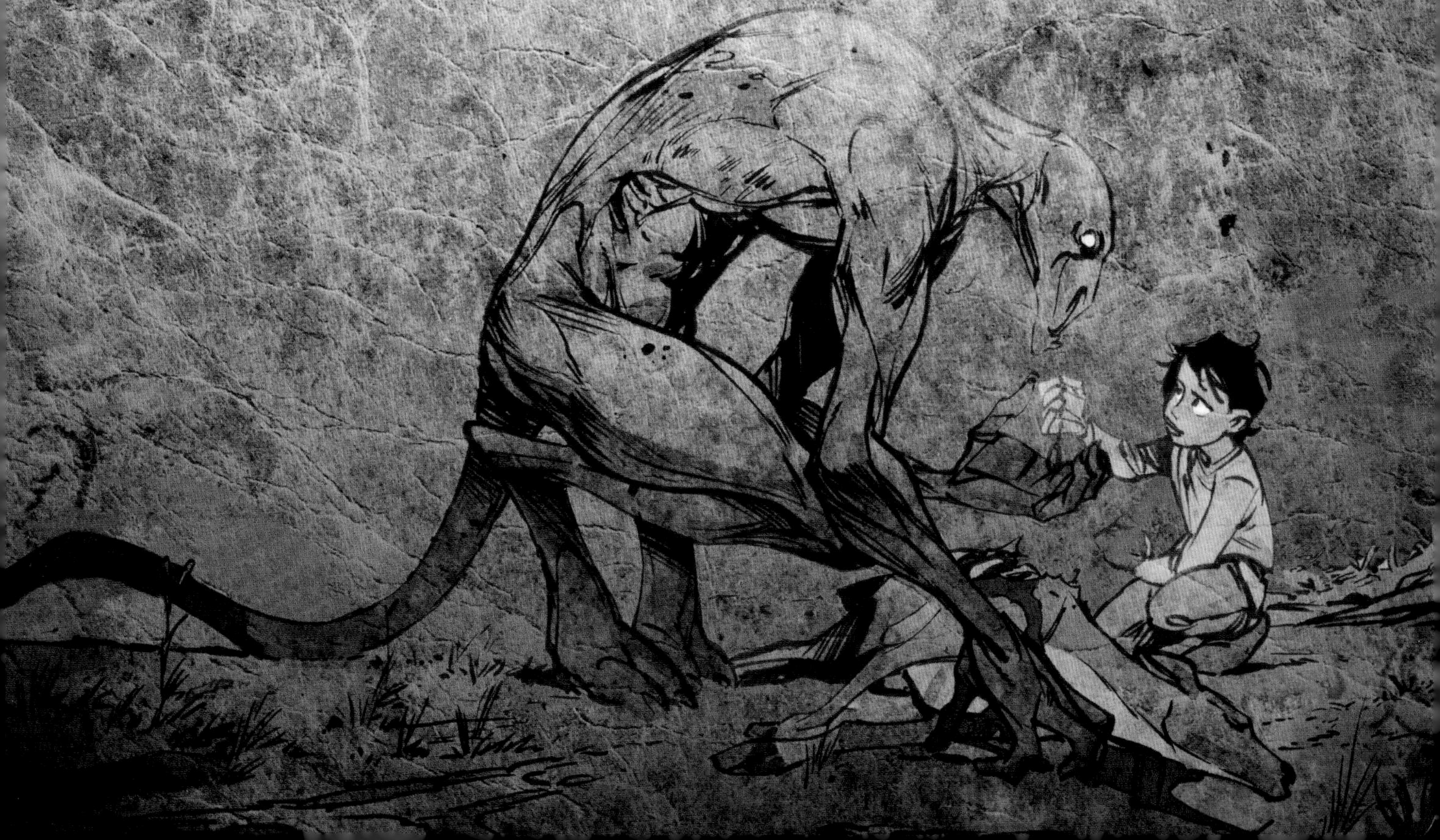

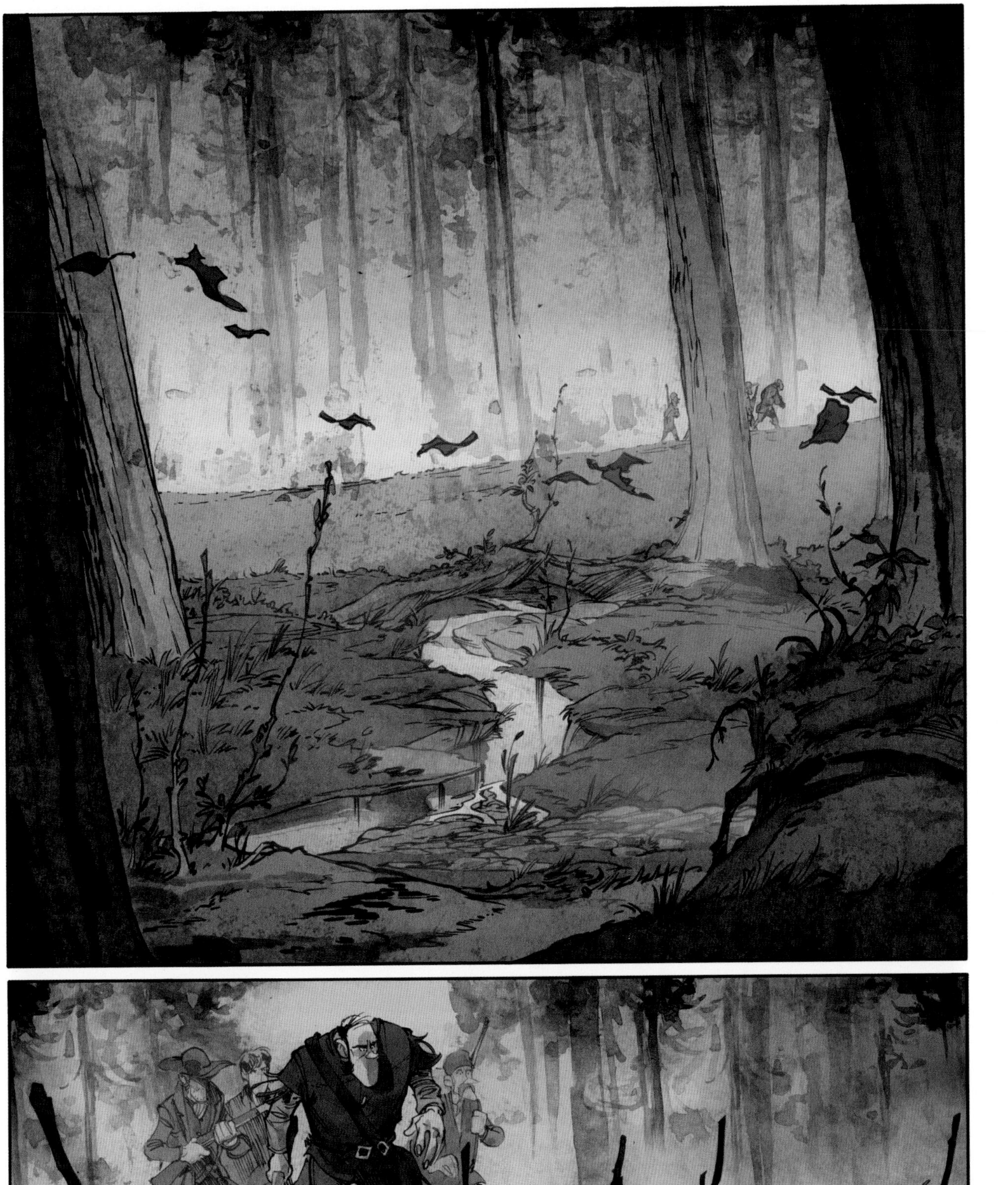

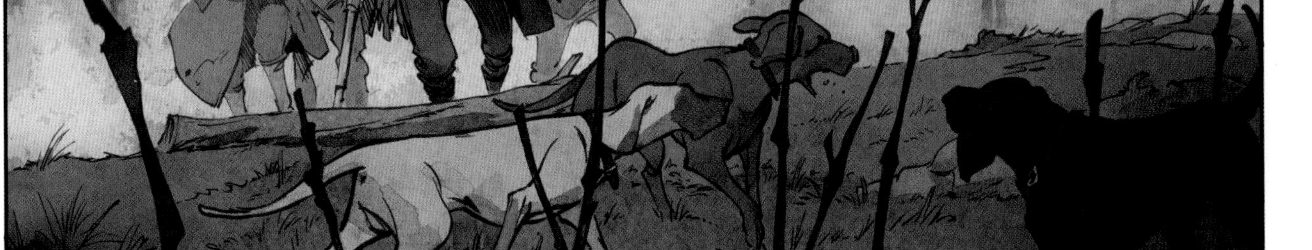

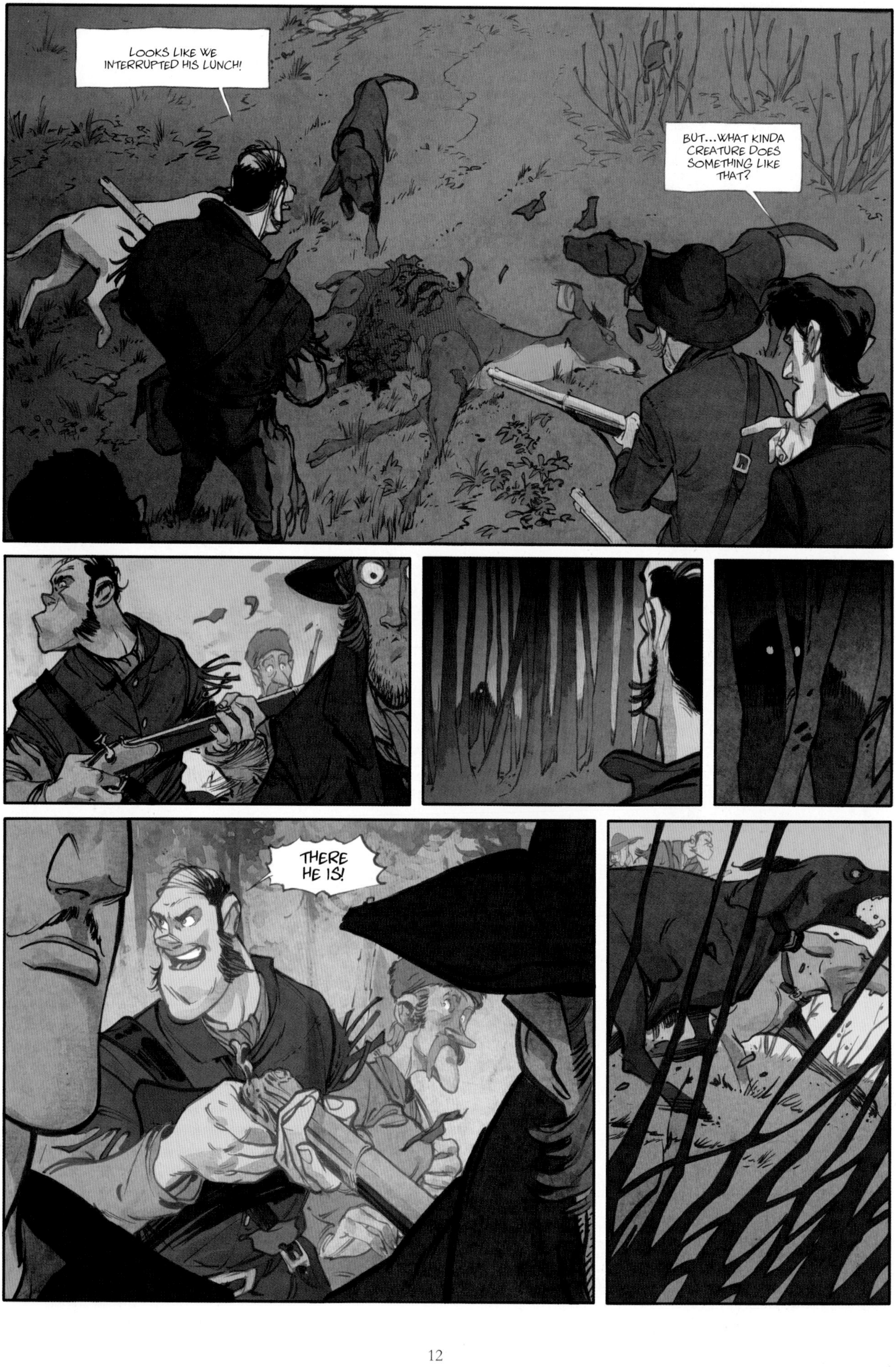
LOOKS LIKE WE INTERRUPTED HIS LUNCH!
BUT...WHAT KINDA CREATURE DOES SOMETHING LIKE THAT?
THERE HE IS!

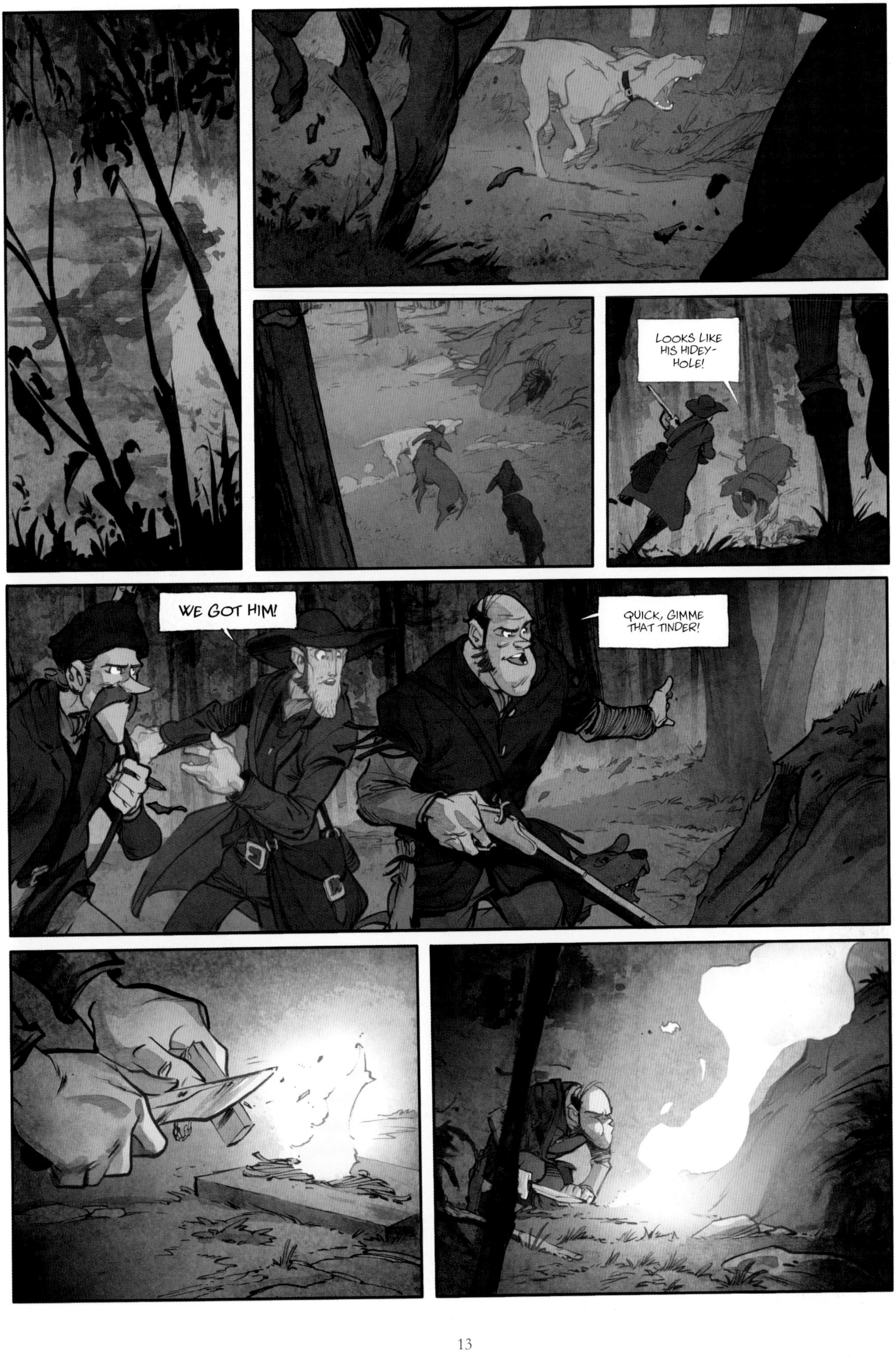
LOOKS LIKE HIS HIDEY-HOLE!
WE GOT HIM!
QUICK, GIMME THAT TINDER!

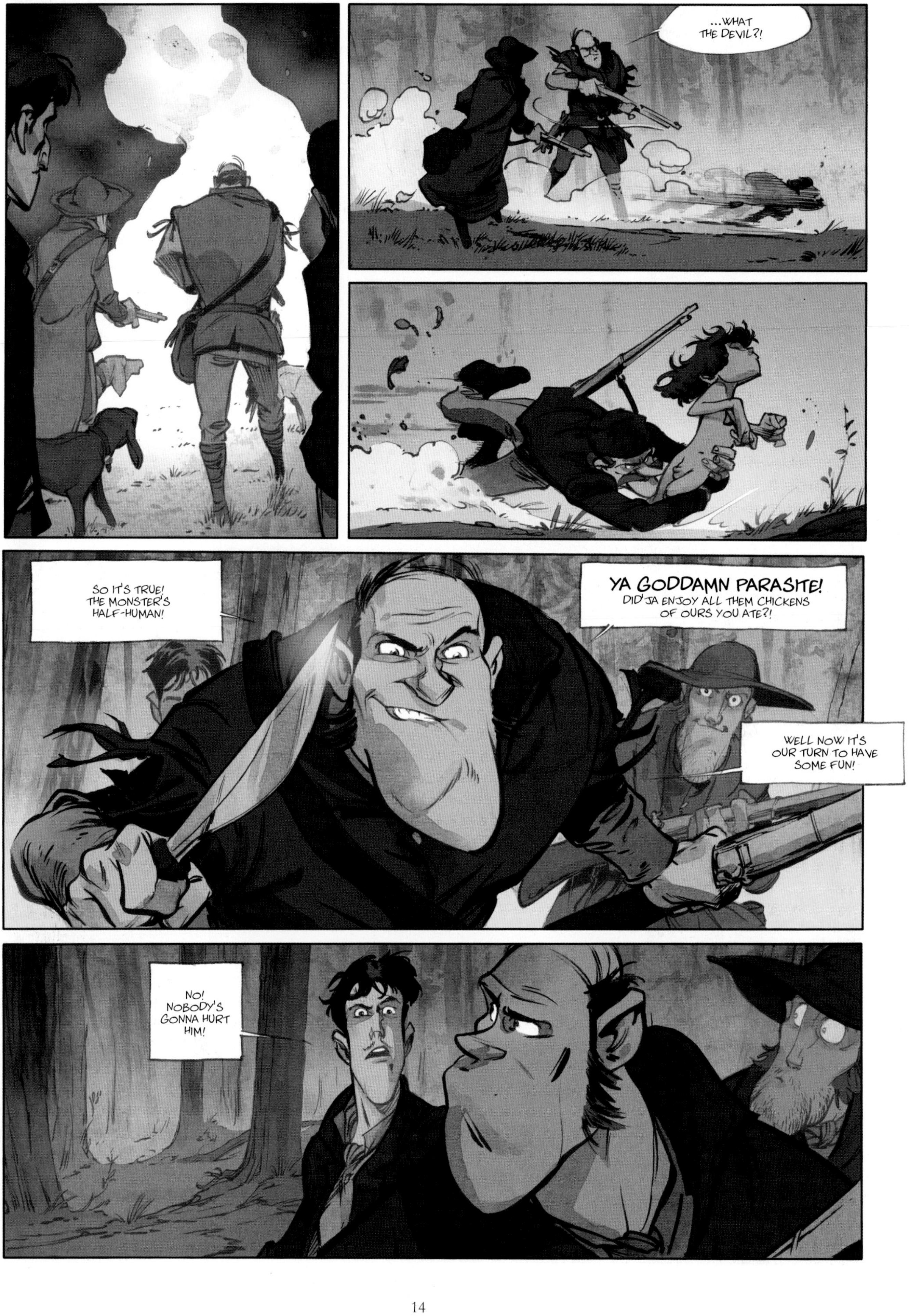
...WHAT THE DEVIL?!
SO IT'S TRUE! THE MONSTER'S HALF-HUMAN!
YA GODDAMN PARASITE! DID'JA ENJOY ALL THEM CHICKENS OF OURS YOU ATE?!
WELL NOW IT'S OUR TURN TO HAVE SOME FUN!
NO! NOBODY'S GONNA HURT HIM!

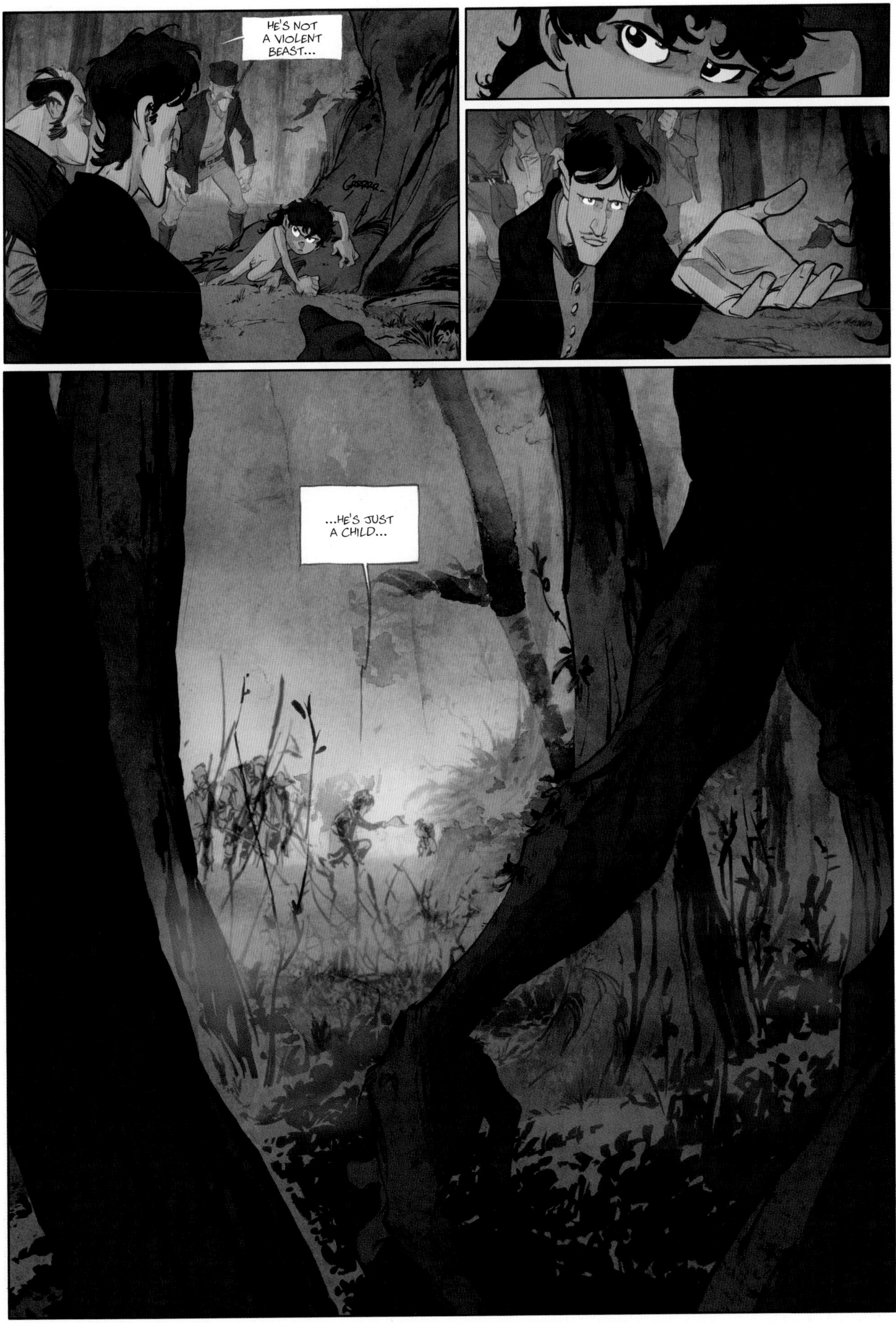
HE'S NOT A VIOLENT BEAST...
...HE'S JUST A CHILD...

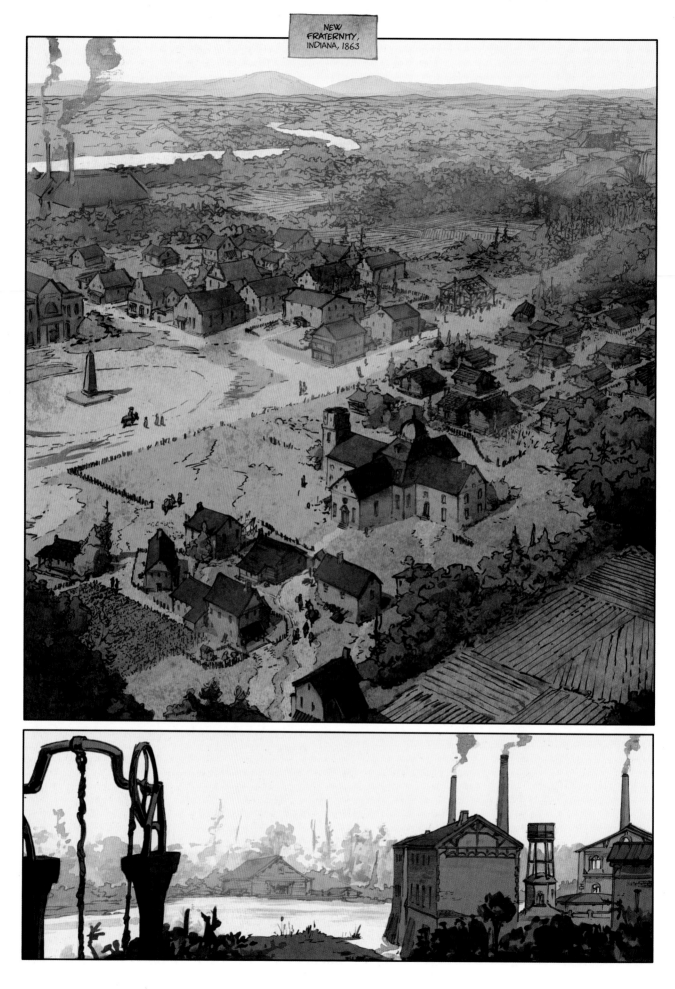

NEW
FRATERNITY,
INDIANA, 1863

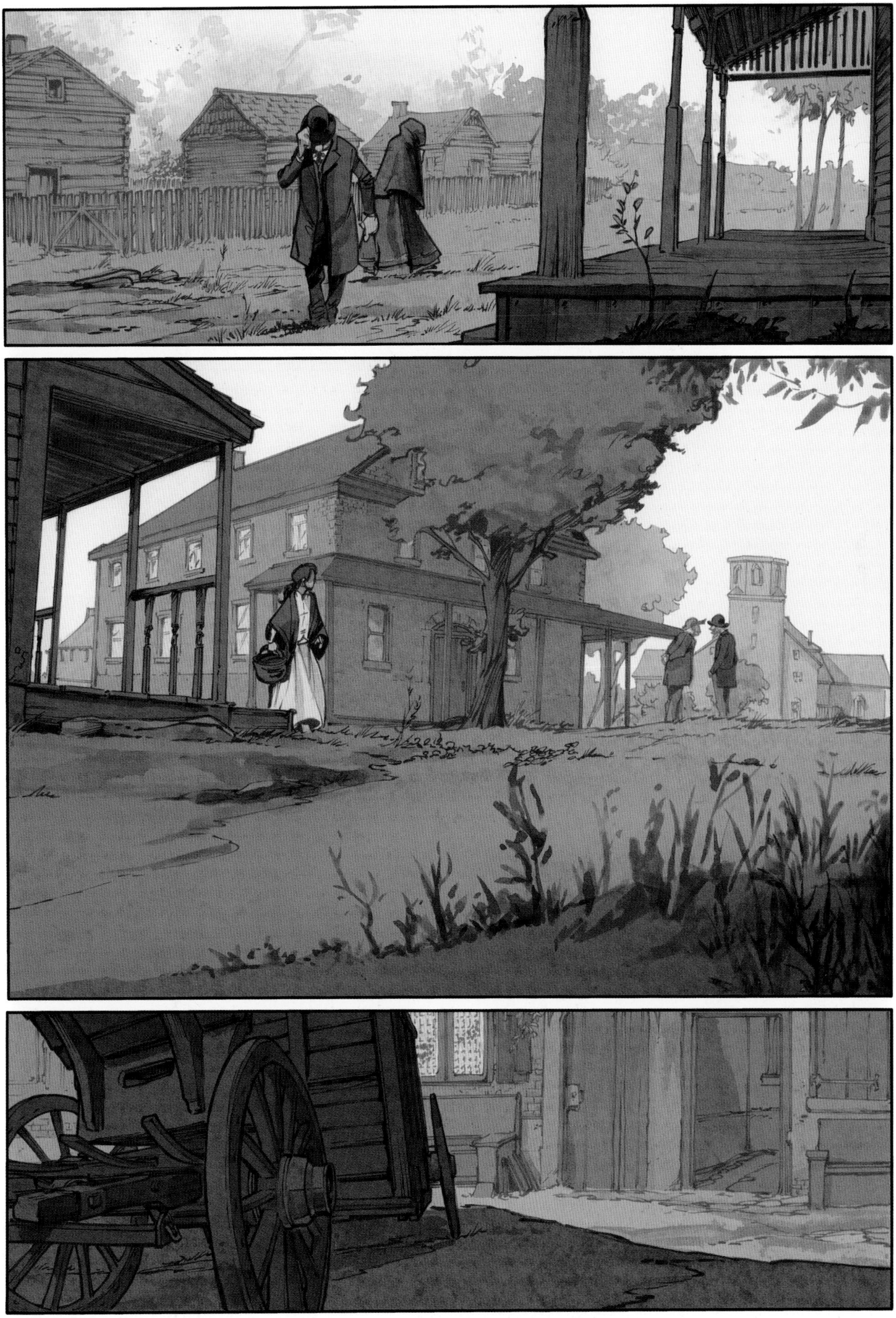

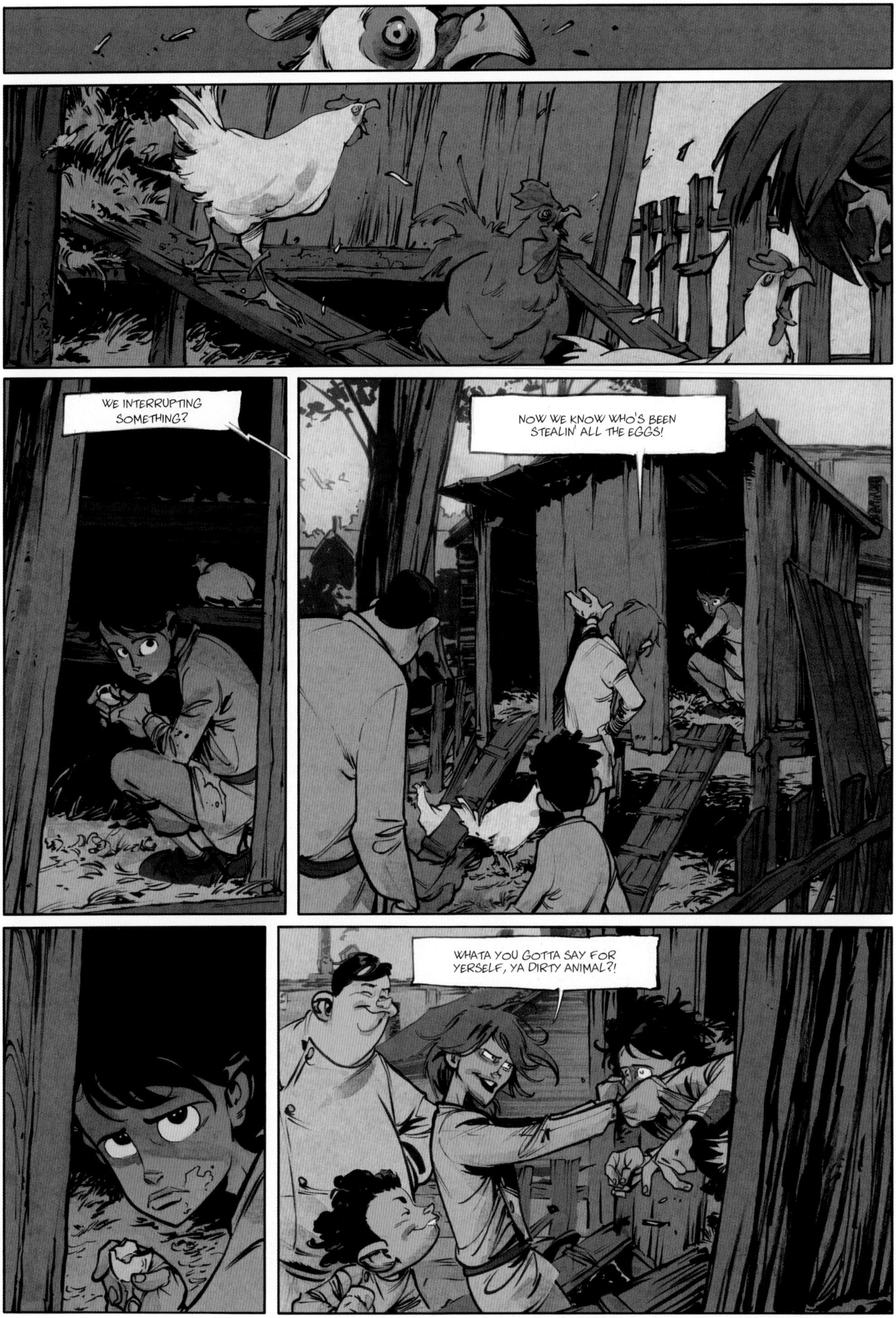
WE INTERRUPTING SOMETHING?
NOW WE KNOW WHO'S BEEN STEALIN' ALL THE EGGS!
WHATA YOU GOTTA SAY FOR YERSELF, YA DIRTY ANIMAL?!

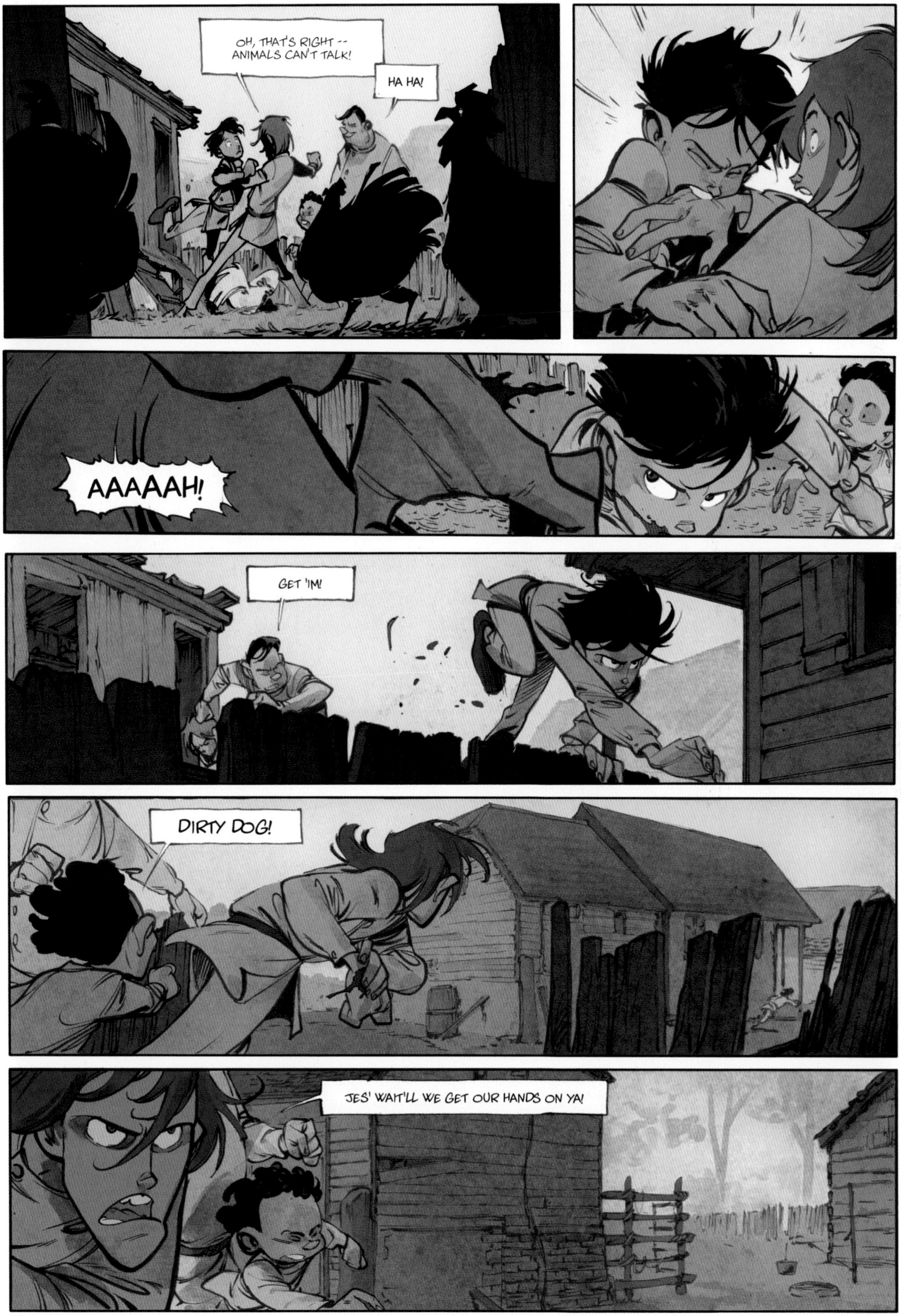
OH, THAT'S RIGHT -- ANIMALS CAN'T TALK!
HA HA!
AAAAAH!
GET 'IM!
DIRTY DOG!
JES' WAIT'LL WE GET OUR HANDS ON YA!

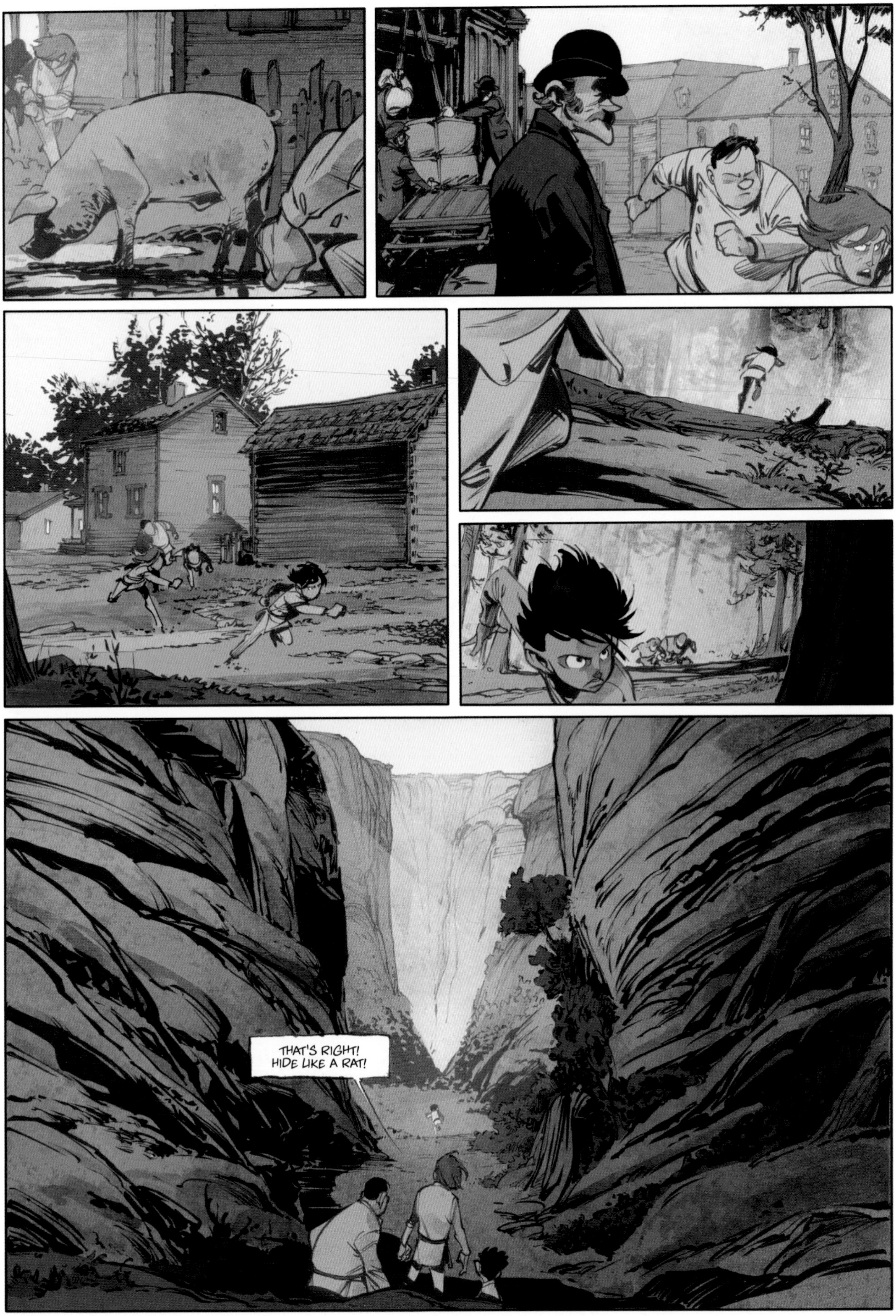
THAT'S RIGHT! HIDE LIKE A RAT!

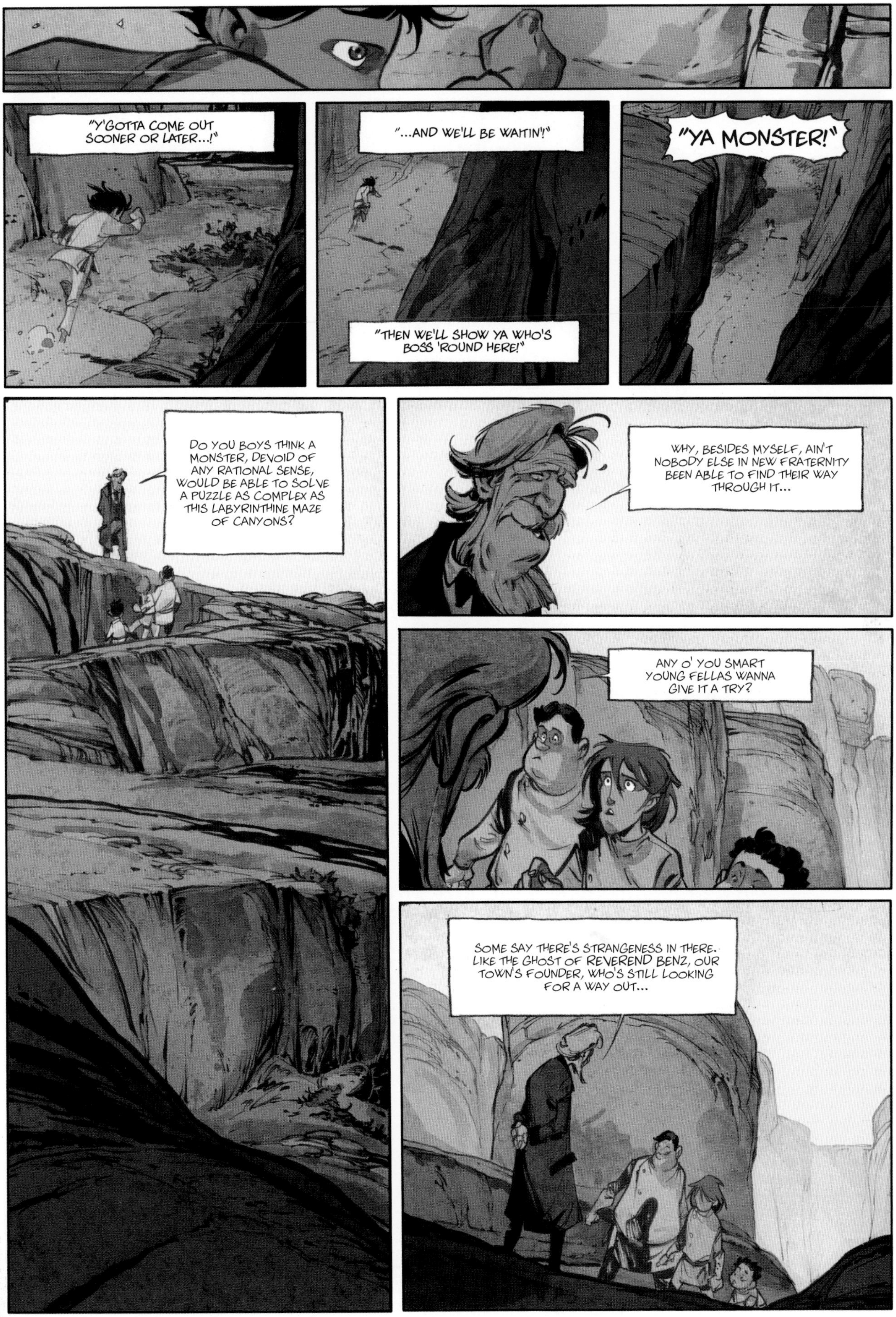

"Y'GOTTA COME OUT SOONER OR LATER...!"
"...AND WE'LL BE WAITIN'!"
"THEN WE'LL SHOW YA WHO'S BOSS 'ROUND HERE!"
"YA MONSTER!"
DO YOU BOYS THINK A MONSTER, DEVOID OF ANY RATIONAL SENSE, WOULD BE ABLE TO SOLVE A PUZZLE AS COMPLEX AS THIS LABYRINTHINE MAZE OF CANYONS?
WHY, BESIDES MYSELF, AIN'T NOBODY ELSE IN NEW FRATERNITY BEEN ABLE TO FIND THEIR WAY THROUGH IT...
ANY O' YOU SMART YOUNG FELLAS WANNA GIVE IT A TRY?
SOME SAY THERE'S STRANGENESS IN THERE. LIKE THE GHOST OF REVEREND BENZ, OUR TOWN'S FOUNDER, WHO'S STILL LOOKING FOR A WAY OUT...

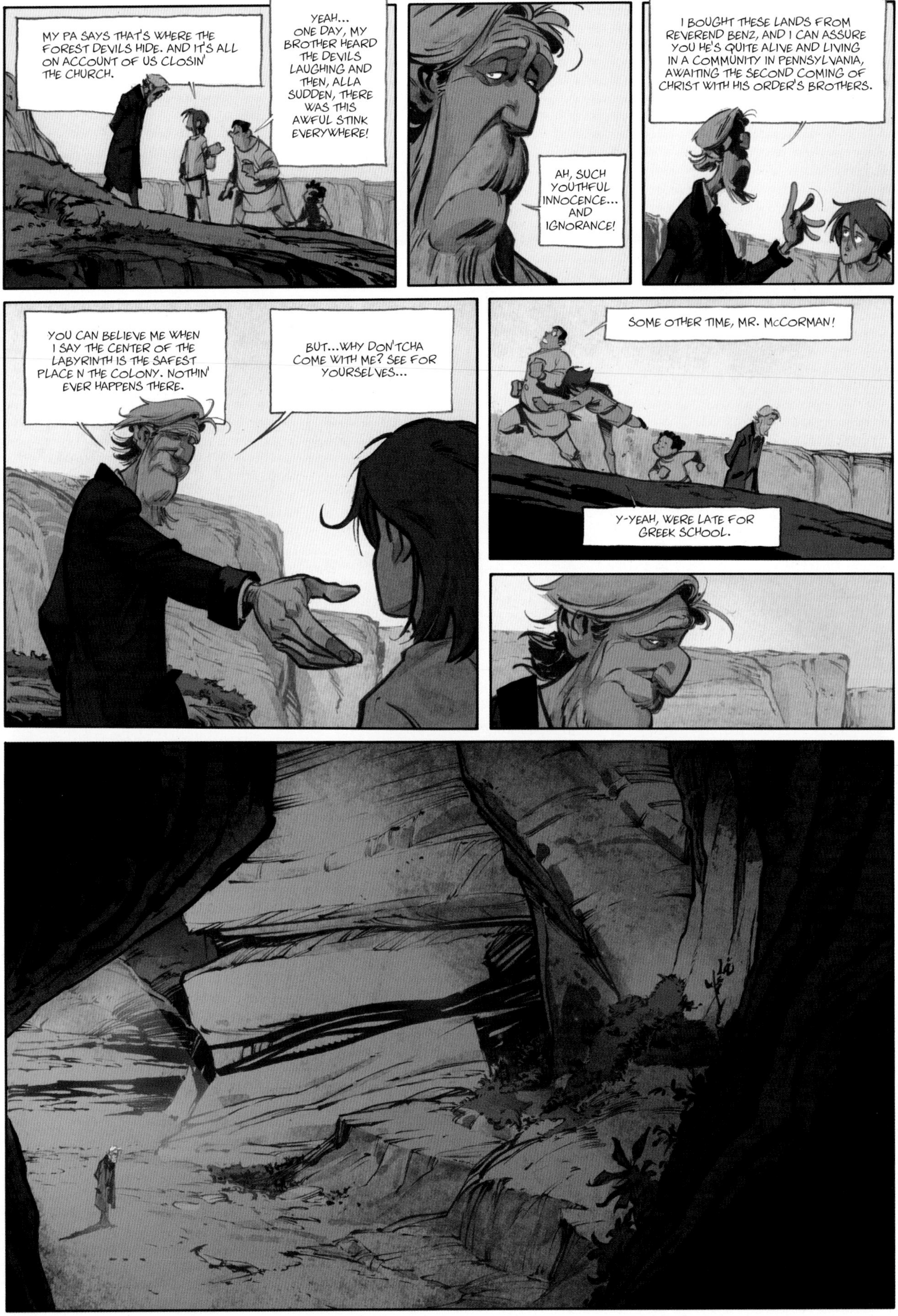
MY PA SAYS THAT'S WHERE THE FOREST DEVILS HIDE. AND IT'S ALL ON ACCOUNT OF US CLOSIN' THE CHURCH.
YEAH... ONE DAY, MY BROTHER HEARD THE DEVILS LAUGHING AND THEN, ALLA SUDDEN, THERE WAS THIS AWFUL STINK EVERYWHERE!
AH, SUCH YOUTHFUL INNOCENCE... AND IGNORANCE!
I BOUGHT THESE LANDS FROM REVEREND BENZ, AND I CAN ASSURE YOU HE'S QUITE ALIVE AND LIVING IN A COMMUNITY IN PENNSYLVANIA, AWAITING THE SECOND COMING OF CHRIST WITH HIS ORDER'S BROTHERS.
YOU CAN BELIEVE ME WHEN I SAY THE CENTER OF THE LABYRINTH IS THE SAFEST PLACE N THE COLONY. NOTHIN' EVER HAPPENS THERE.
BUT...WHY DON'TCHA COME WITH ME? SEE FOR YOURSELVES...
SOME OTHER TIME, MR. MCCORMAN!
Y-YEAH, WERE LATE FOR GREEK SCHOOL.

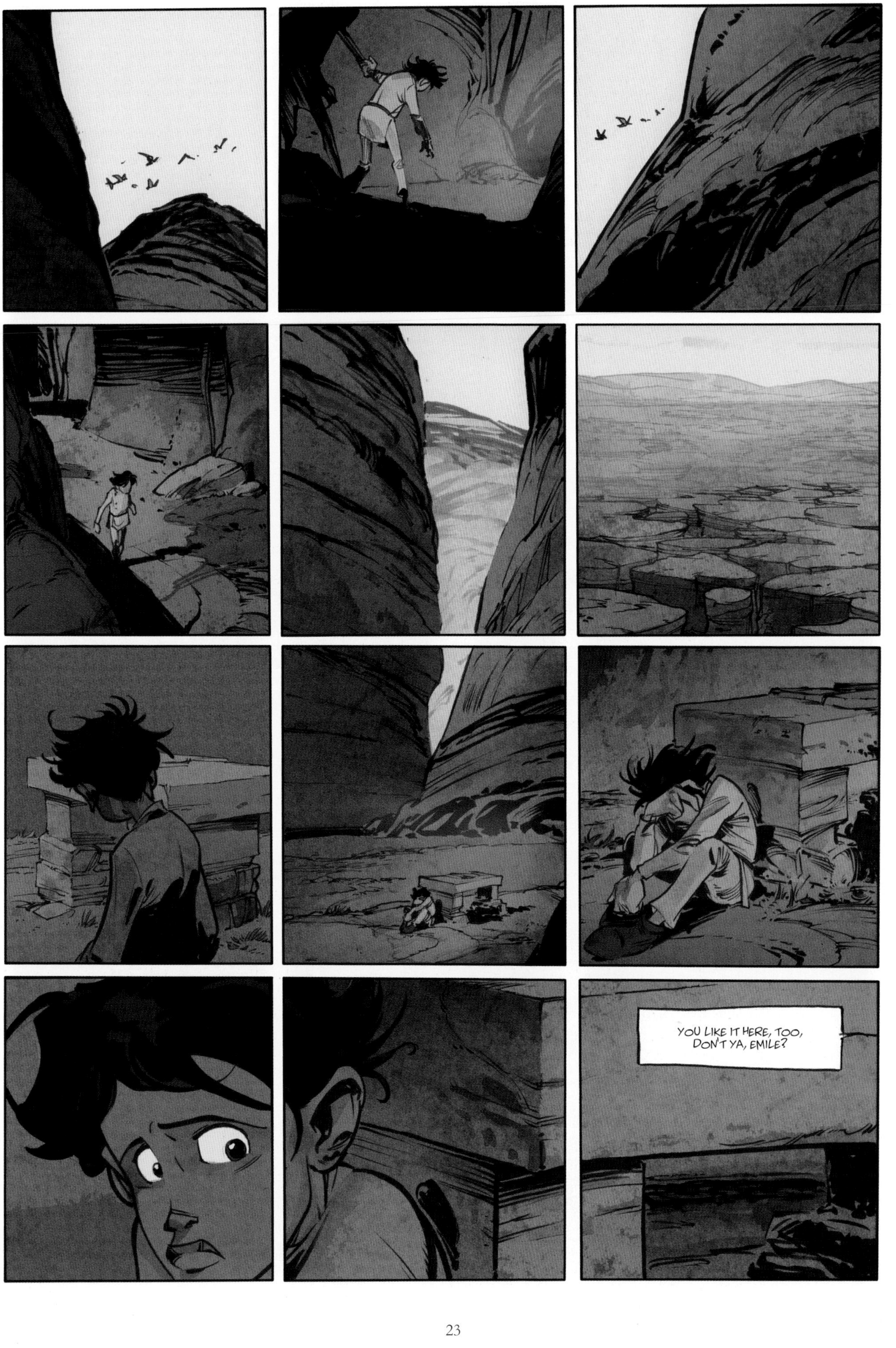
YOU LIKE IT HERE, TOO,
DON'T YA, EMILE?

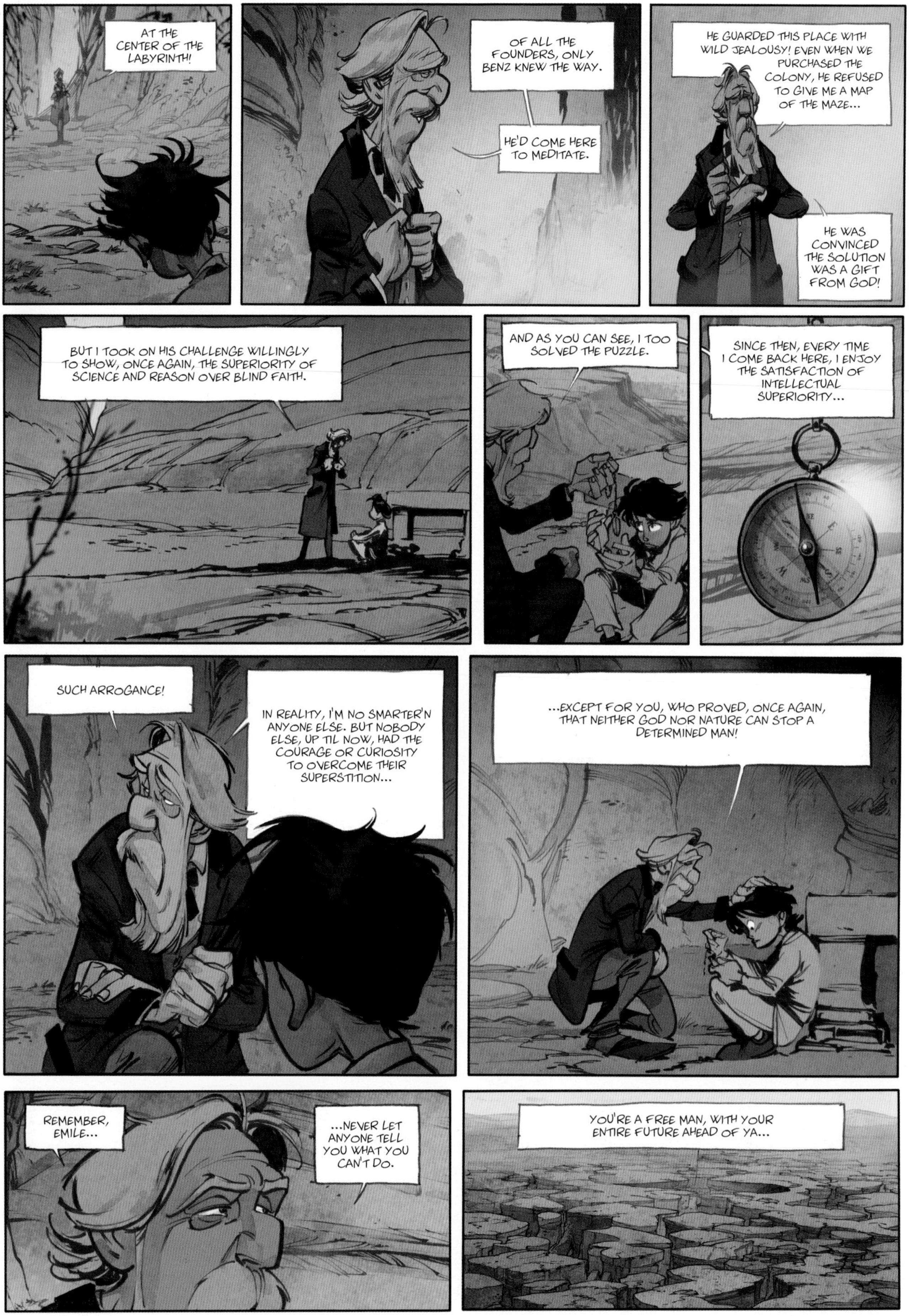
AT THE CENTER OF THE LABYRINTH!
OF ALL THE FOUNDERS, ONLY BENZ KNEW THE WAY.
HE'D COME HERE TO MEDITATE.
HE GUARDED THIS PLACE WITH WILD JEALOUSY! EVEN WHEN WE PURCHASED THE COLONY, HE REFUSED TO GIVE ME A MAP OF THE MAZE...
HE WAS CONVINCED THE SOLUTION WAS A GIFT FROM GOD!
BUT I TOOK ON HIS CHALLENGE WILLINGLY TO SHOW, ONCE AGAIN, THE SUPERIORITY OF SCIENCE AND REASON OVER BLIND FAITH.
AND AS YOU CAN SEE, I TOO SOLVED THE PUZZLE.
SINCE THEN, EVERY TIME I COME BACK HERE, I ENJOY THE SATISFACTION OF INTELLECTUAL SUPERIORITY...
SUCH ARROGANCE!
IN REALITY, I'M NO SMARTER'N ANYONE ELSE. BUT NOBODY ELSE, UP TIL NOW, HAD THE COURAGE OR CURIOSITY TO OVERCOME THEIR SUPERSTITION...
...EXCEPT FOR YOU, WHO PROVED, ONCE AGAIN, THAT NEITHER GOD NOR NATURE CAN STOP A DETERMINED MAN!
REMEMBER, EMILE...
...NEVER LET ANYONE TELL YOU WHAT YOU CAN'T DO.
YOU'RE A FREE MAN, WITH YOUR ENTIRE FUTURE AHEAD OF YA...

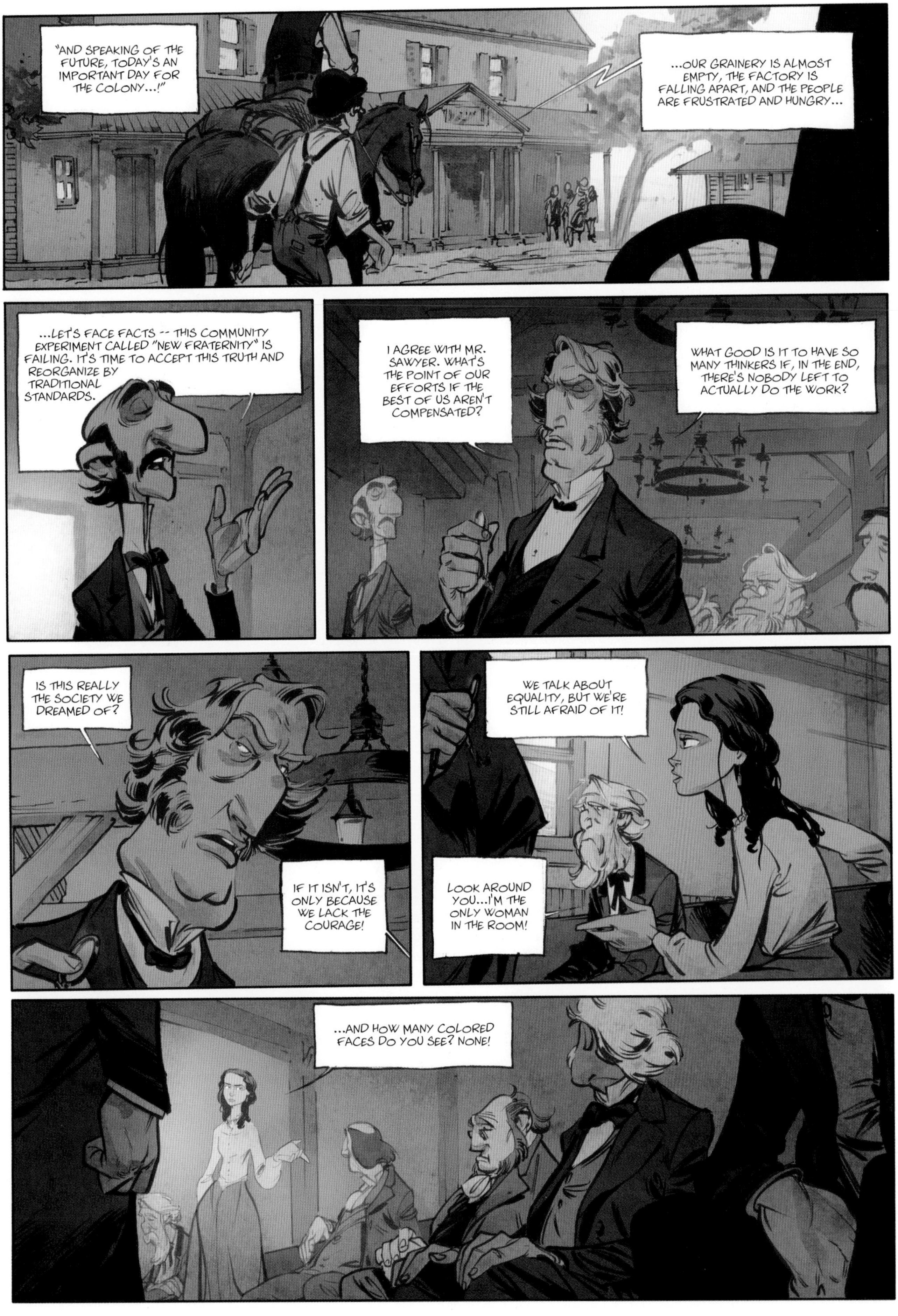
"AND SPEAKING OF THE FUTURE, TODAY'S AN IMPORTANT DAY FOR THE COLONY...!"
...OUR GRAINERY IS ALMOST EMPTY, THE FACTORY IS FALLING APART, AND THE PEOPLE ARE FRUSTRATED AND HUNGRY...
...LET'S FACE FACTS -- THIS COMMUNITY EXPERIMENT CALLED "NEW FRATERNITY" IS FAILING. IT'S TIME TO ACCEPT THIS TRUTH AND REORGANIZE BY TRADITIONAL STANDARDS.
I AGREE WITH MR. SAWYER. WHAT'S THE POINT OF OUR EFFORTS IF THE BEST OF US AREN'T COMPENSATED?
WHAT GOOD IS IT TO HAVE SO MANY THINKERS IF, IN THE END, THERE'S NOBODY LEFT TO ACTUALLY DO THE WORK?
IS THIS REALLY THE SOCIETY WE DREAMED OF?
IF IT ISN'T, IT'S ONLY BECAUSE WE LACK THE COURAGE!
WE TALK ABOUT EQUALITY, BUT WE'RE STILL AFRAID OF IT!
LOOK AROUND YOU...I'M THE ONLY WOMAN IN THE ROOM!
...AND HOW MANY COLORED FACES DO YOU SEE? NONE!

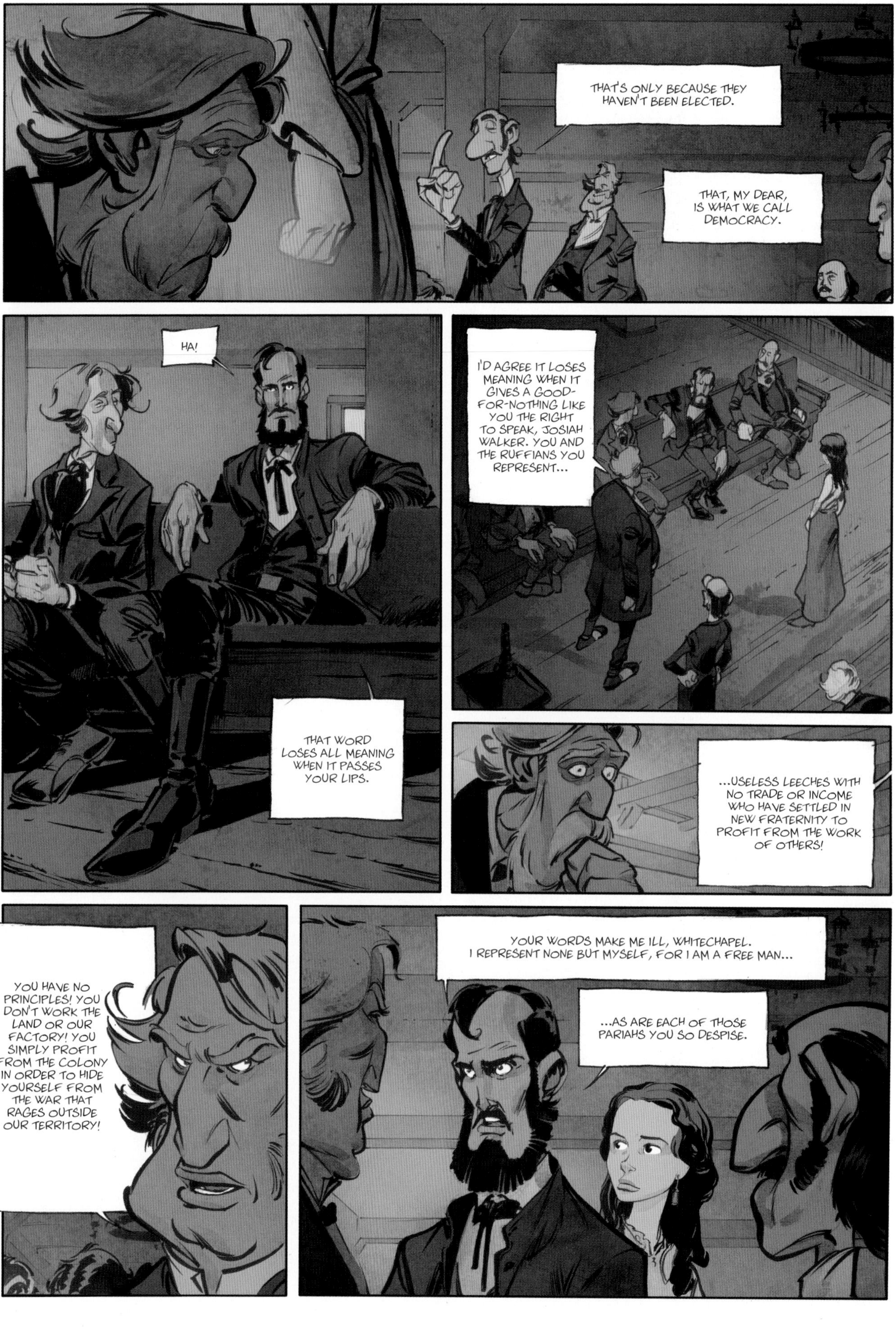
THAT'S ONLY BECAUSE THEY HAVEN'T BEEN ELECTED.
THAT, MY DEAR, IS WHAT WE CALL DEMOCRACY.
HA!
THAT WORD LOSES ALL MEANING WHEN IT PASSES YOUR LIPS.
I'D AGREE IT LOSES MEANING WHEN IT GIVES A GOOD-FOR-NOTHING LIKE YOU THE RIGHT TO SPEAK, JOSIAH WALKER. YOU AND THE RUFFIANS YOU REPRESENT...
...USELESS LEECHES WITH NO TRADE OR INCOME WHO HAVE SETTLED IN NEW FRATERNITY TO PROFIT FROM THE WORK OF OTHERS!
YOU HAVE NO PRINCIPLES! YOU DON'T WORK THE LAND OR OUR FACTORY! YOU SIMPLY PROFIT FROM THE COLONY IN ORDER TO HIDE YOURSELF FROM THE WAR THAT RAGES OUTSIDE OUR TERRITORY!
YOUR WORDS MAKE ME ILL, WHITECHAPEL. I REPRESENT NONE BUT MYSELF, FOR I AM A FREE MAN...
...AS ARE EACH OF THOSE PARIAHS YOU SO DESPISE.

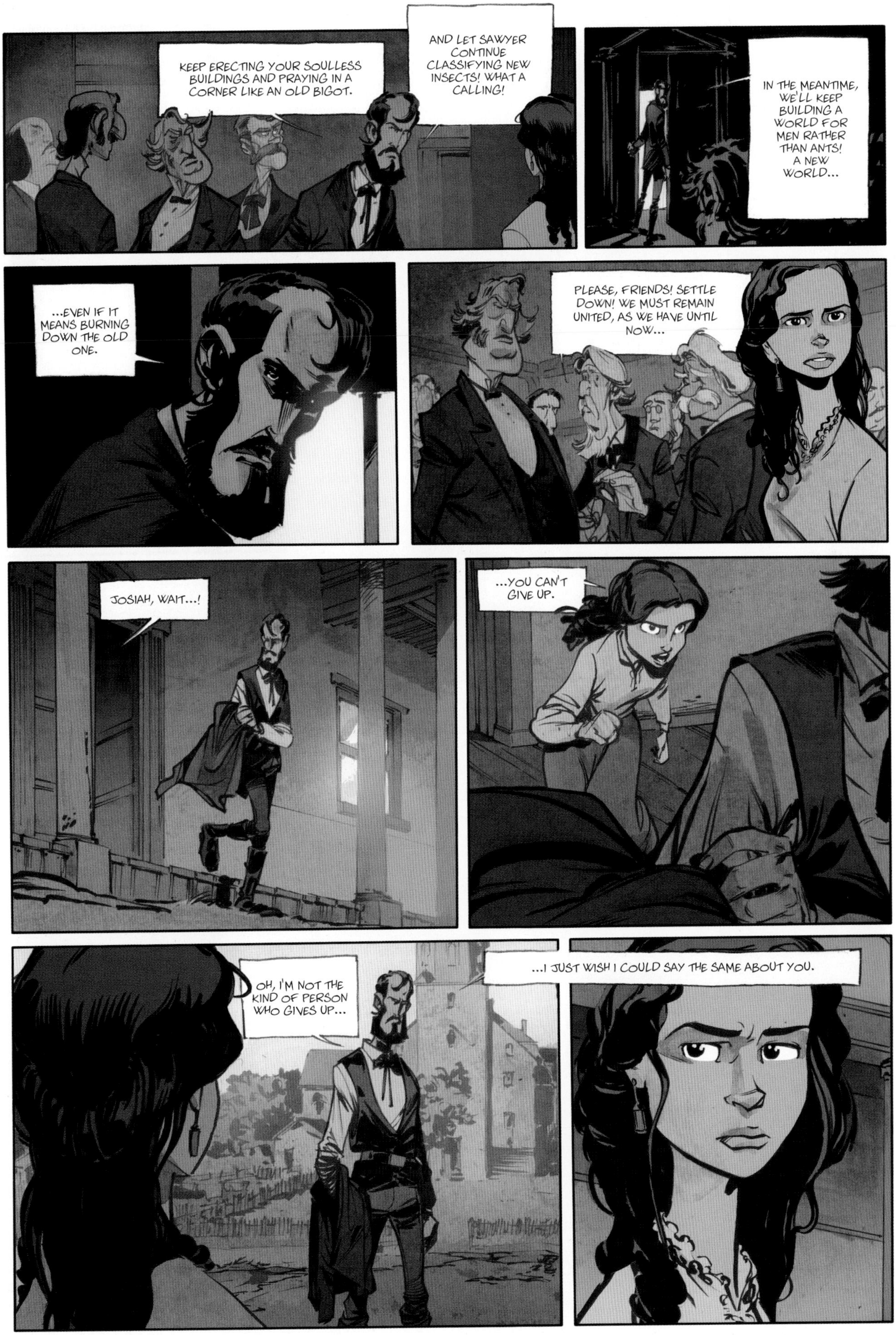
KEEP ERECTING YOUR SOULLESS BUILDINGS AND PRAYING IN A CORNER LIKE AN OLD BIGOT.
AND LET SAWYER CONTINUE CLASSIFYING NEW INSECTS! WHAT A CALLING!
IN THE MEANTIME, WE'LL KEEP BUILDING A WORLD FOR MEN RATHER THAN ANTS! A NEW WORLD...
...EVEN IF IT MEANS BURNING DOWN THE OLD ONE.
PLEASE, FRIENDS! SETTLE DOWN! WE MUST REMAIN UNITED, AS WE HAVE UNTIL NOW...
JOSIAH, WAIT...!
...YOU CAN'T GIVE UP.
OH, I'M NOT THE KIND OF PERSON WHO GIVES UP...
...I JUST WISH I COULD SAY THE SAME ABOUT YOU.

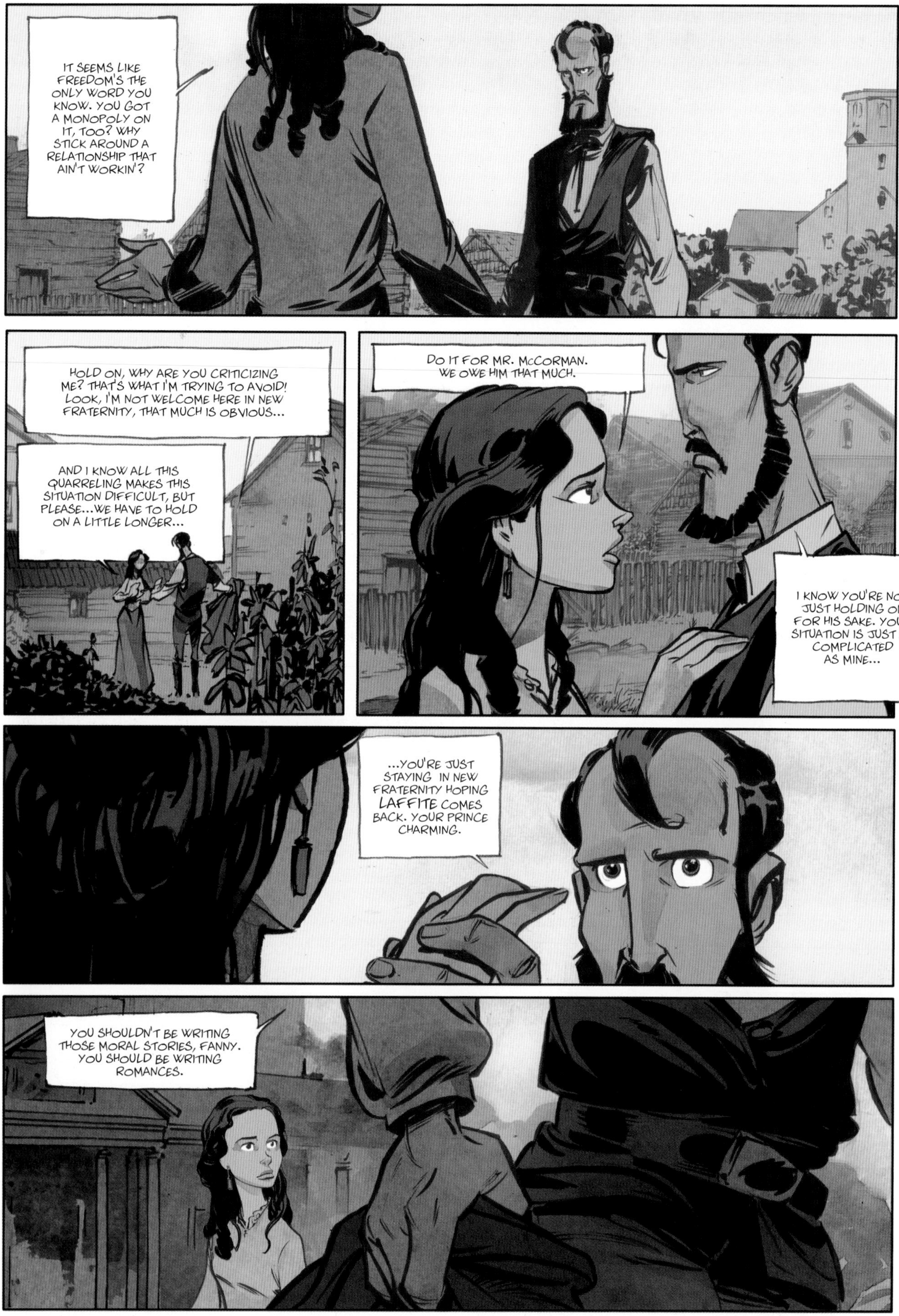
IT SEEMS LIKE FREEDOM'S THE ONLY WORD YOU KNOW. YOU GOT A MONOPOLY ON IT, TOO? WHY STICK AROUND A RELATIONSHIP THAT AIN'T WORKIN'?
HOLD ON, WHY ARE YOU CRITICIZING ME? THAT'S WHAT I'M TRYING TO AVOID! LOOK, I'M NOT WELCOME HERE IN NEW FRATERNITY, THAT MUCH IS OBVIOUS...
AND I KNOW ALL THIS QUARRELING MAKES THIS SITUATION DIFFICULT, BUT PLEASE...WE HAVE TO HOLD ON A LITTLE LONGER...
DO IT FOR MR. McCORMAN. WE OWE HIM THAT MUCH.
I KNOW YOU'RE NOT JUST HOLDING ON FOR HIS SAKE. YOUR SITUATION IS JUST AS COMPLICATED AS MINE...
...YOU'RE JUST STAYING IN NEW FRATERNITY HOPING LAFFITE COMES BACK. YOUR PRINCE CHARMING.
YOU SHOULDN'T BE WRITING THOSE MORAL STORIES, FANNY. YOU SHOULD BE WRITING ROMANCES.

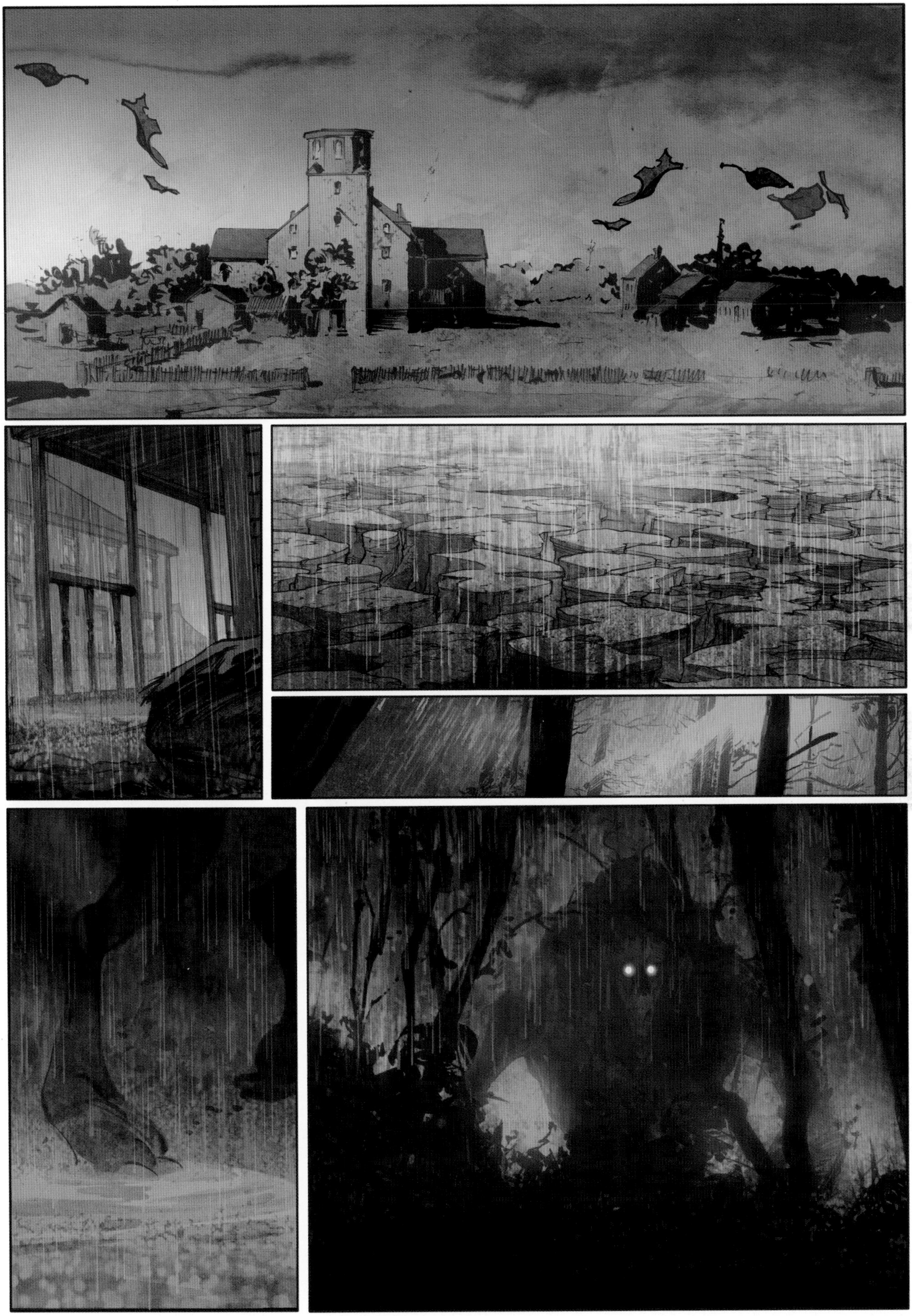

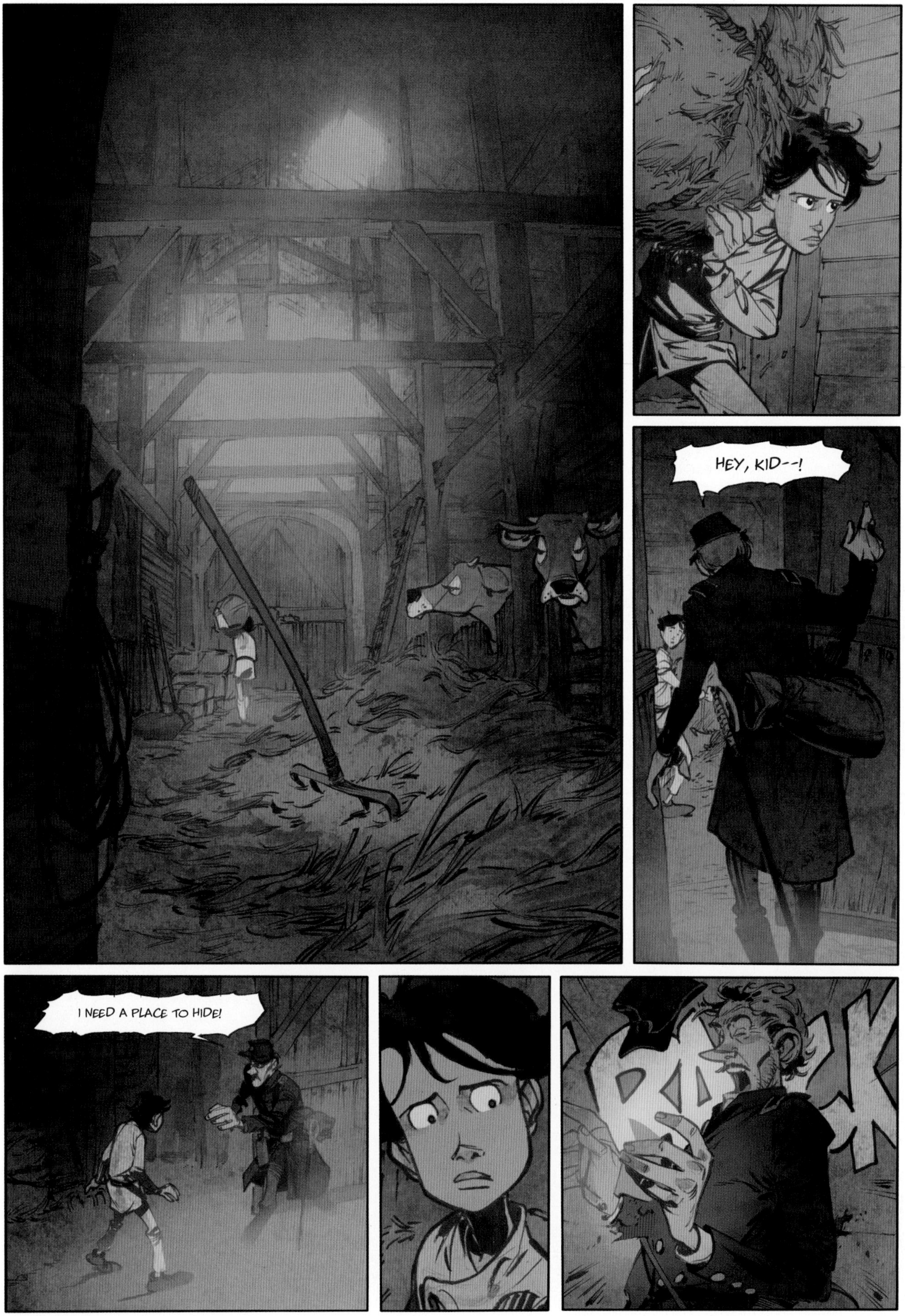
HEY, KID--!
I NEED A PLACE TO HIDE!

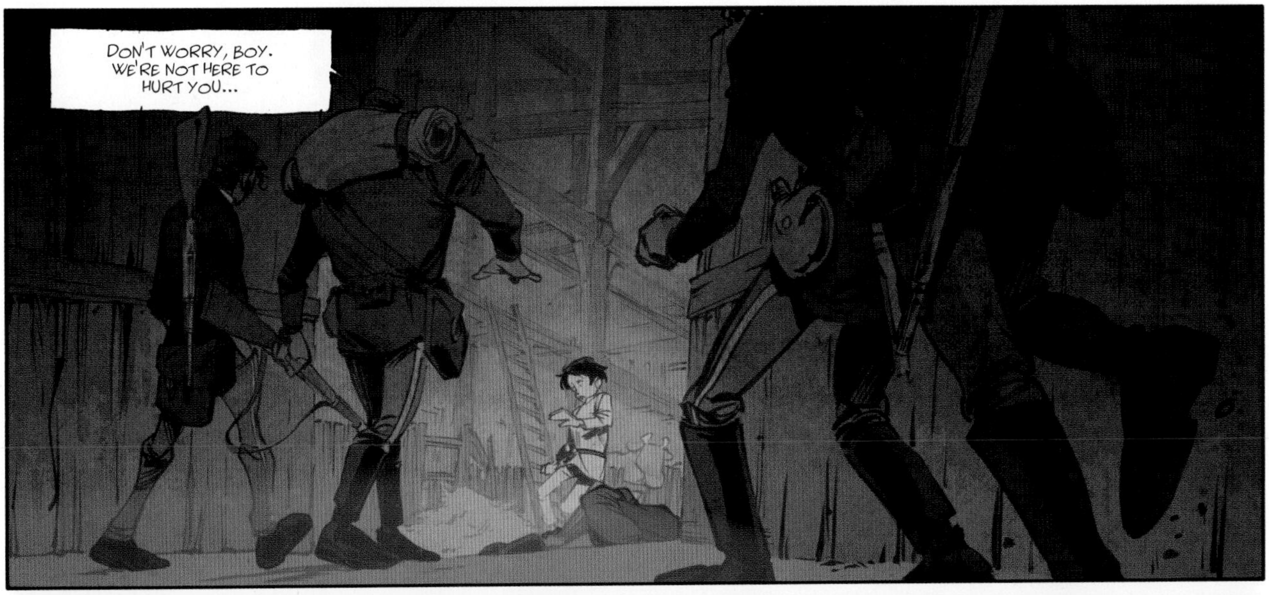
DON'T WORRY, BOY. WE'RE NOT HERE TO HURT YOU...

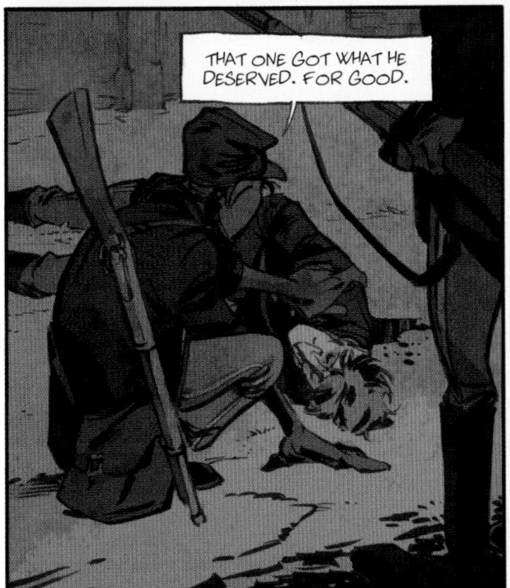
THAT ONE GOT WHAT HE DESERVED. FOR GOOD.

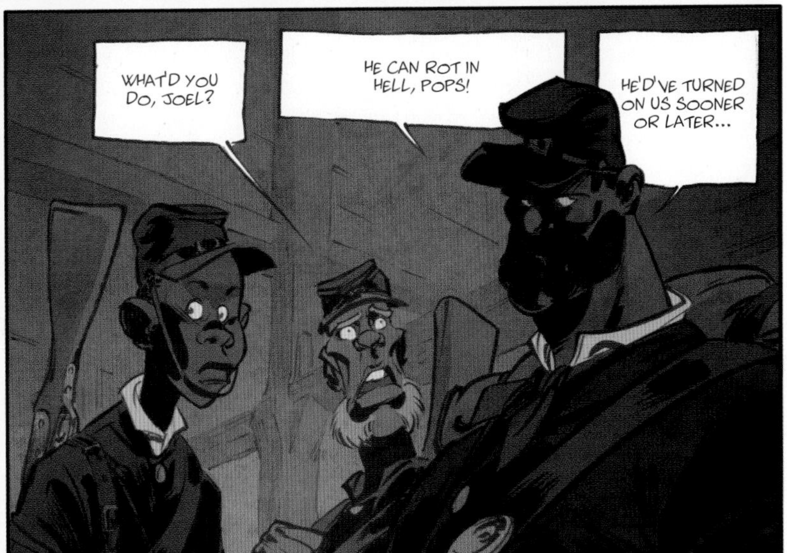
WHAT'D YOU DO, JOEL?
HE CAN ROT IN HELL, POPS!
HE'D'VE TURNED ON US SOONER OR LATER...

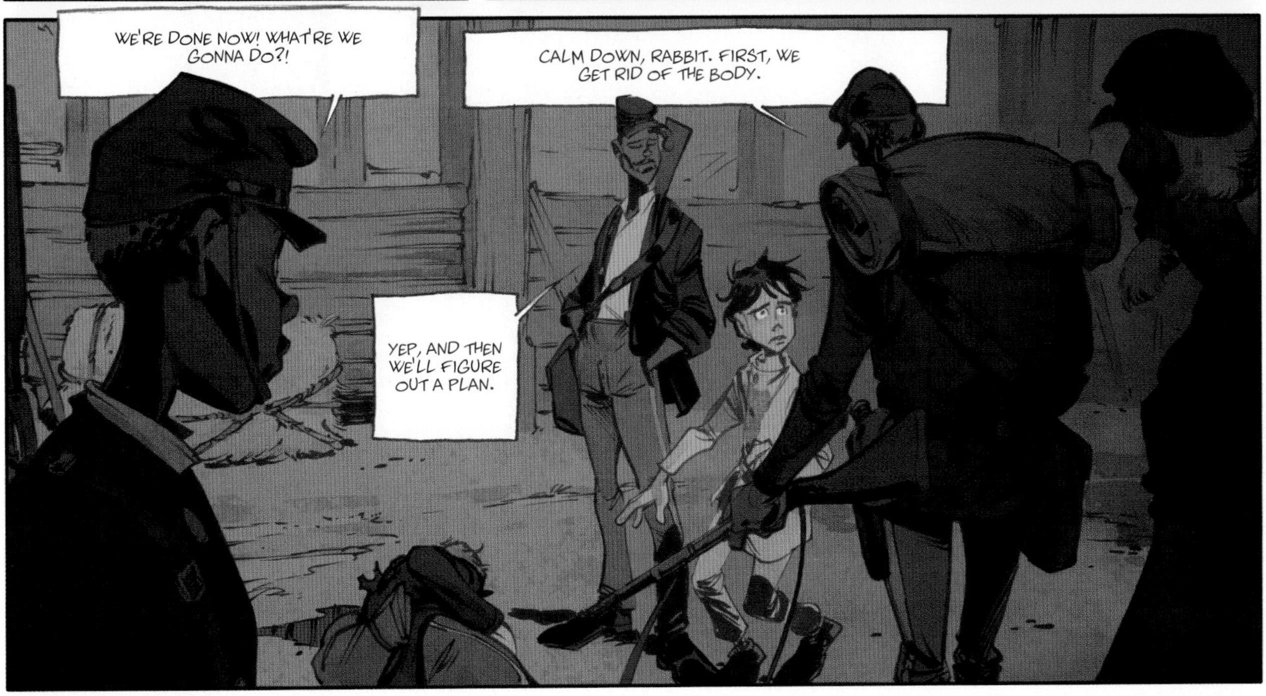
WE'RE DONE NOW! WHAT'RE WE GONNA DO?!
CALM DOWN, RABBIT. FIRST, WE GET RID OF THE BODY.
YEP, AND THEN WE'LL FIGURE OUT A PLAN.

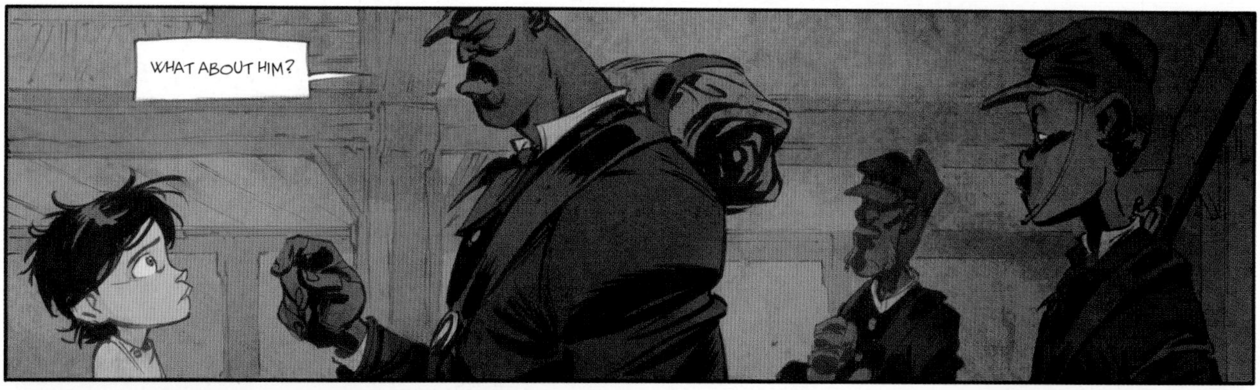
WHAT ABOUT HIM?

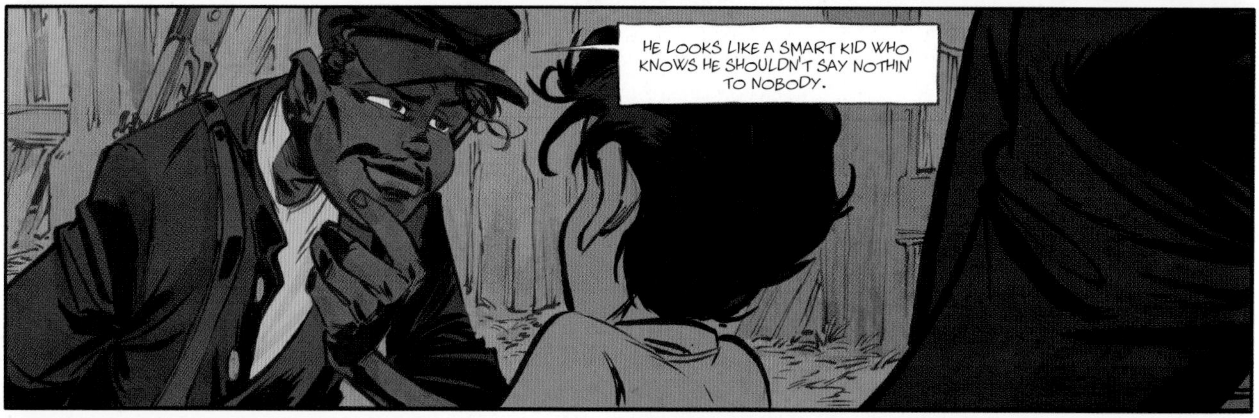
HE LOOKS LIKE A SMART KID WHO KNOWS HE SHOULDN'T SAY NOTHIN' TO NOBODY.

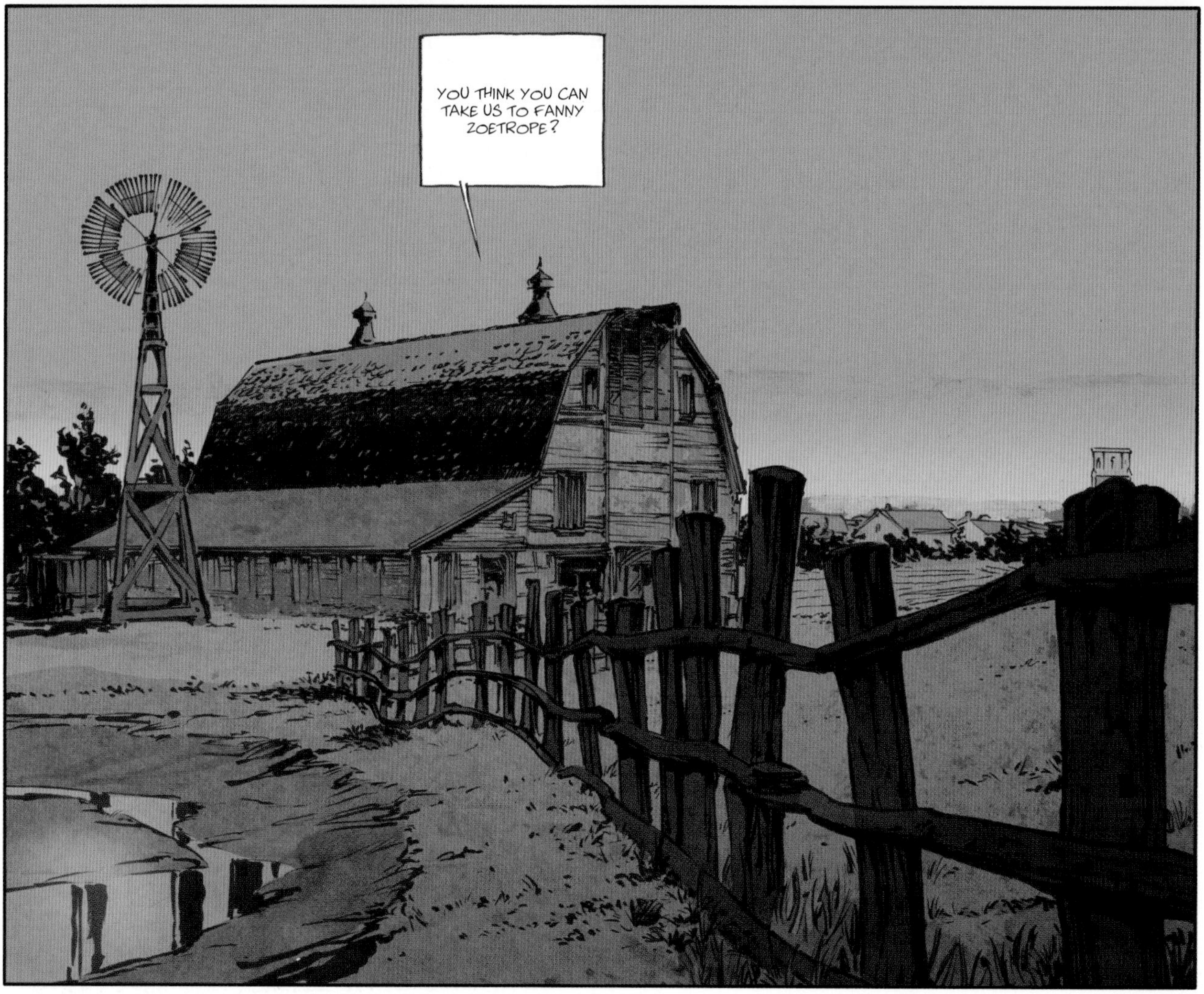
YOU THINK YOU CAN TAKE US TO FANNY ZOETROPE?

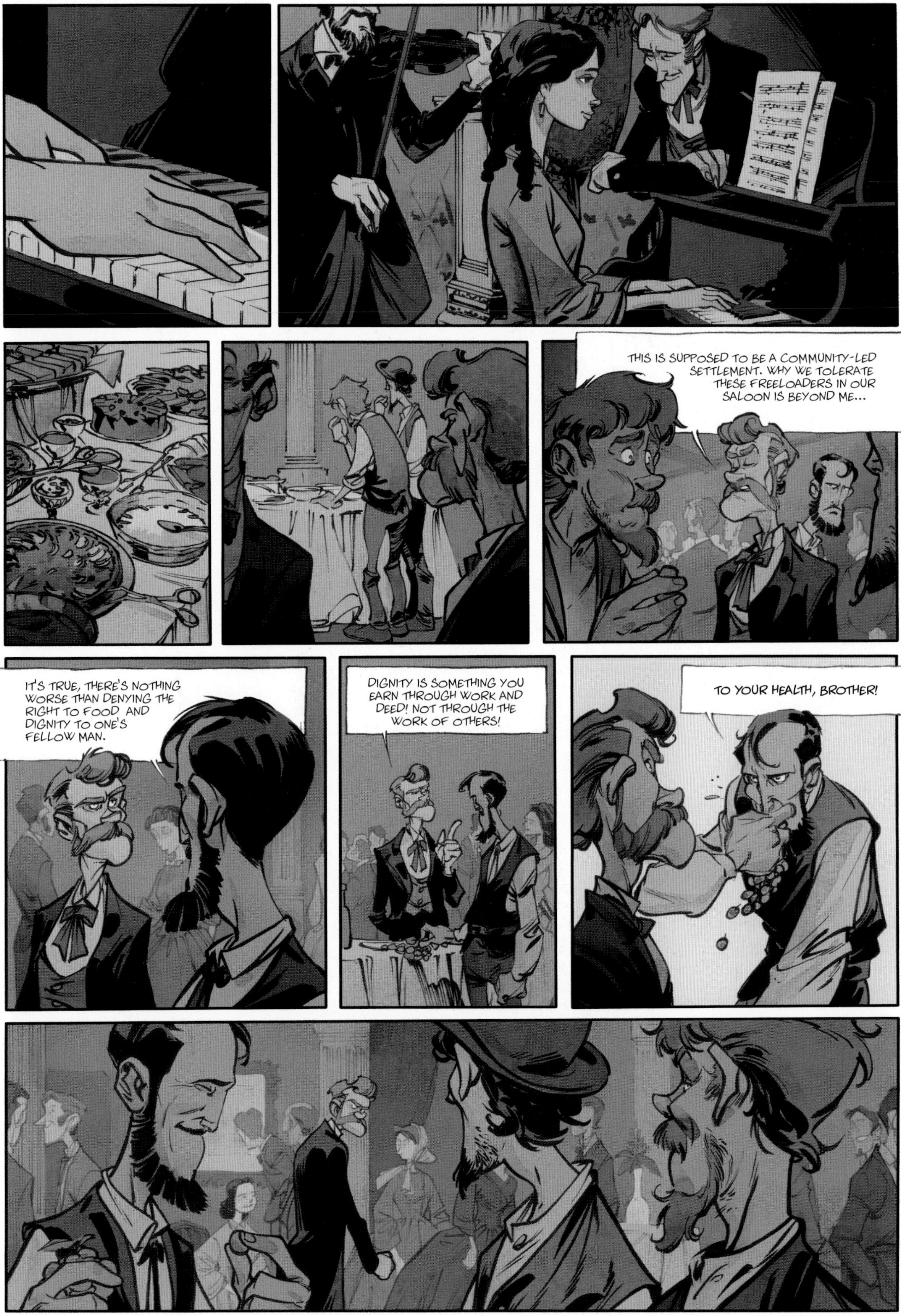
THIS IS SUPPOSED TO BE A COMMUNITY-LED SETTLEMENT. WHY WE TOLERATE THESE FREELOADERS IN OUR SALOON IS BEYOND ME...
IT'S TRUE, THERE'S NOTHING WORSE THAN DENYING THE RIGHT TO FOOD AND DIGNITY TO ONE'S FELLOW MAN.
DIGNITY IS SOMETHING YOU EARN THROUGH WORK AND DEED! NOT THROUGH THE WORK OF OTHERS!
TO YOUR HEALTH, BROTHER!

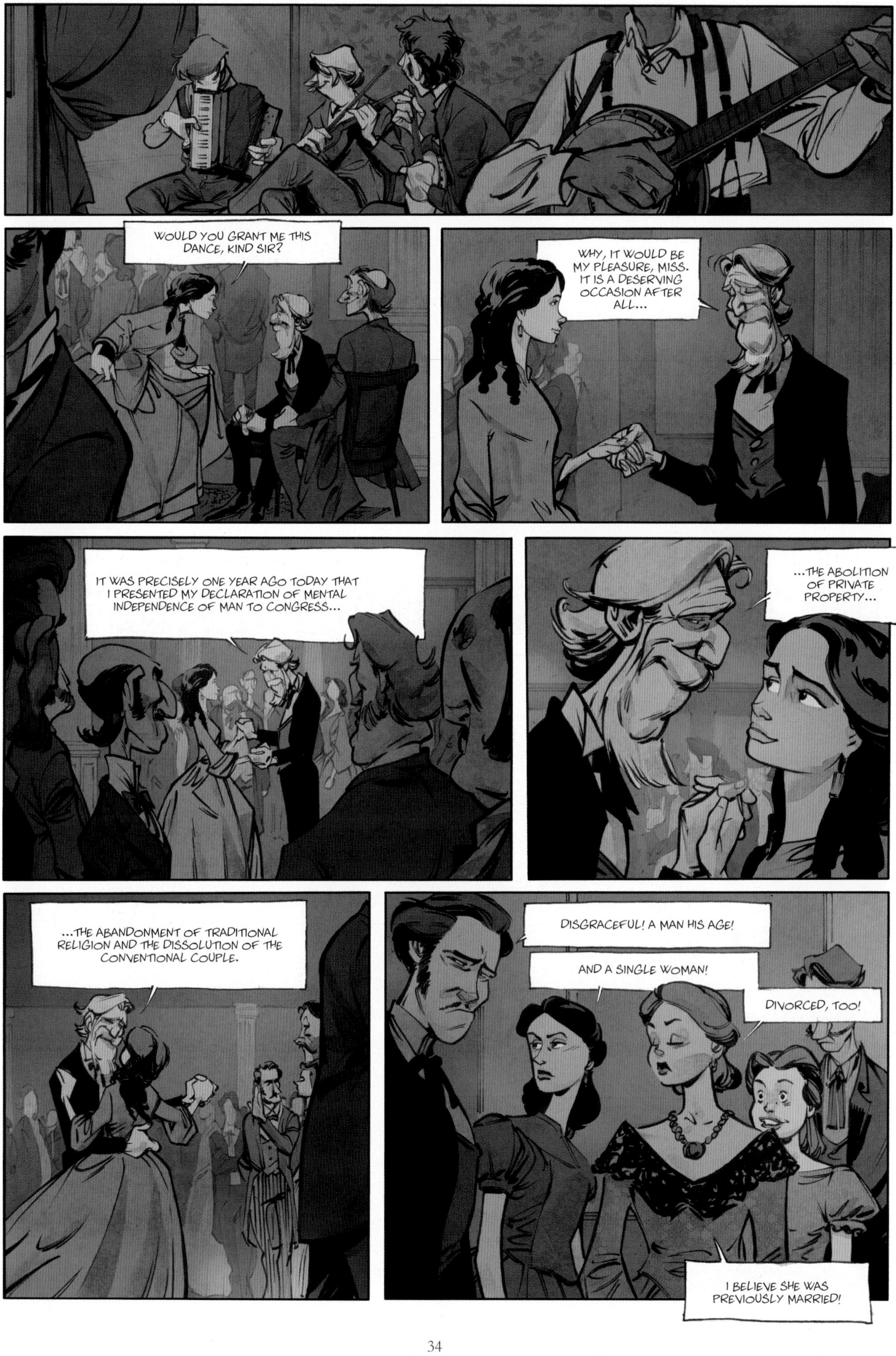
WOULD YOU GRANT ME THIS DANCE, KIND SIR?
WHY, IT WOULD BE MY PLEASURE, MISS. IT IS A DESERVING OCCASION AFTER ALL...
IT WAS PRECISELY ONE YEAR AGO TODAY THAT I PRESENTED MY DECLARATION OF MENTAL INDEPENDENCE OF MAN TO CONGRESS...
...THE ABOLITION OF PRIVATE PROPERTY...
...THE ABANDONMENT OF TRADITIONAL RELIGION AND THE DISSOLUTION OF THE CONVENTIONAL COUPLE.
DISGRACEFUL! A MAN HIS AGE!
AND A SINGLE WOMAN!
DIVORCED, TOO!
I BELIEVE SHE WAS PREVIOUSLY MARRIED!

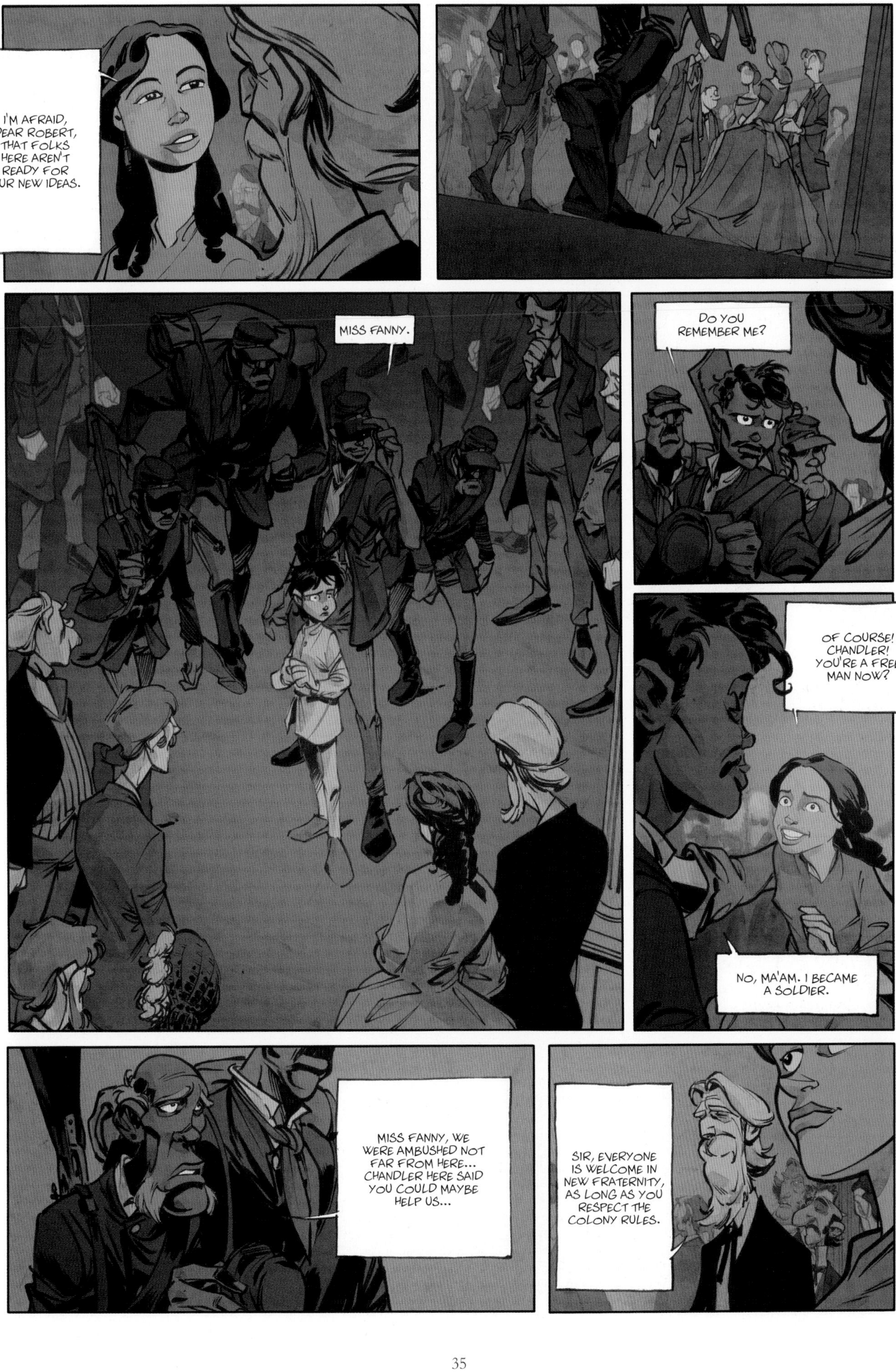
I'M AFRAID, DEAR ROBERT, THAT FOLKS HERE AREN'T READY FOR OUR NEW IDEAS.
MISS FANNY.
DO YOU REMEMBER ME?
OF COURSE! CHANDLER! YOU'RE A FREE MAN NOW?
NO, MA'AM. I BECAME A SOLDIER.
MISS FANNY, WE WERE AMBUSHED NOT FAR FROM HERE... CHANDLER HERE SAID YOU COULD MAYBE HELP US...
SIR, EVERYONE IS WELCOME IN NEW FRATERNITY, AS LONG AS YOU RESPECT THE COLONY RULES.

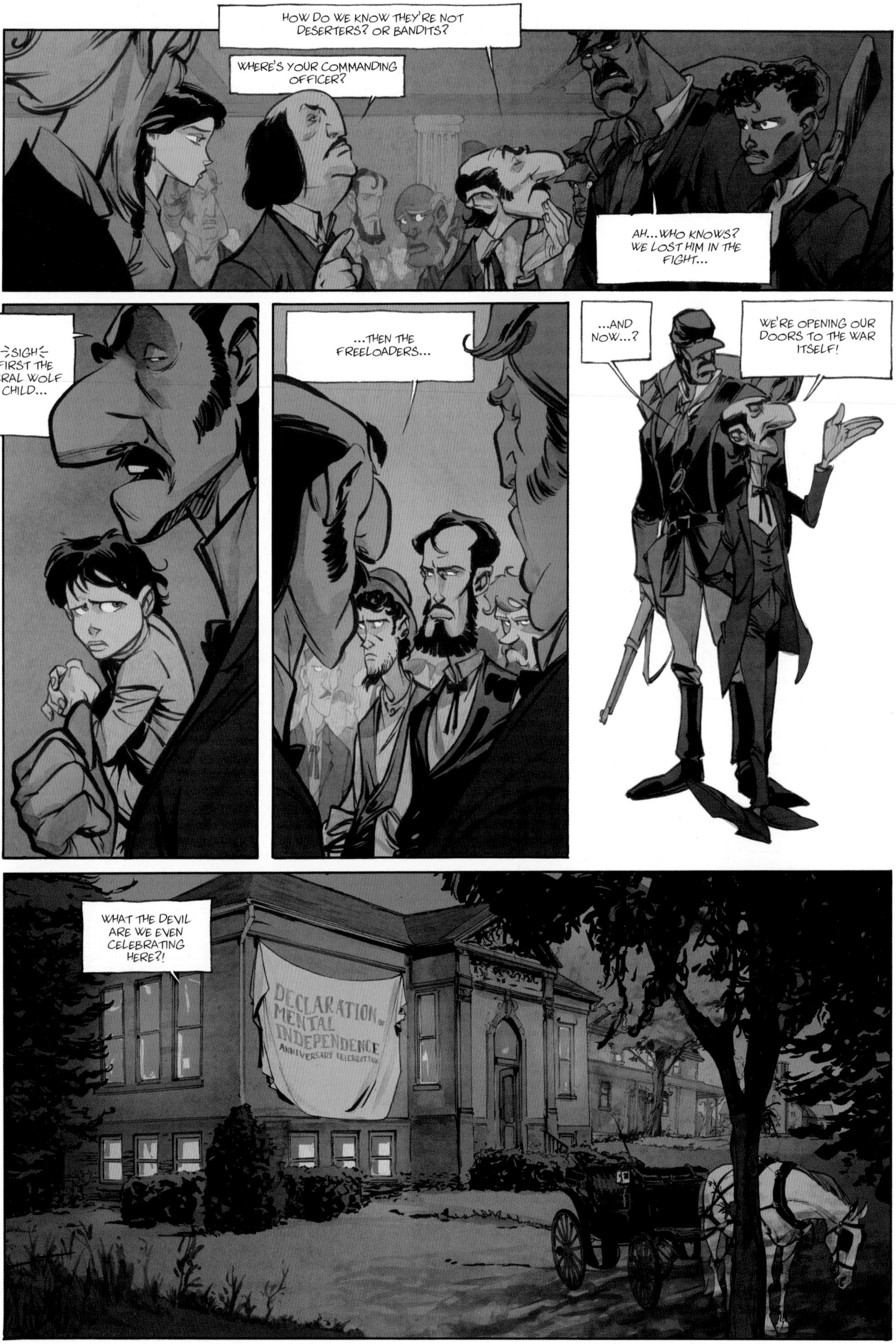
HOW DO WE KNOW THEY'RE NOT DESERTERS? OR BANDITS?
WHERE'S YOUR COMMANDING OFFICER?
AH...WHO KNOWS? WE LOST HIM IN THE FIGHT...
≈SIGH≈ FIRST THE FERAL WOLF CHILD...
...THEN THE FREELOADERS...
...AND NOW...?
WE'RE OPENING OUR DOORS TO THE WAR ITSELF!
WHAT THE DEVIL ARE WE EVEN CELEBRATING HERE?!
DECLARATION OF MENTAL INDEPENDENCE
ANNIVERSARY CELEBRATION

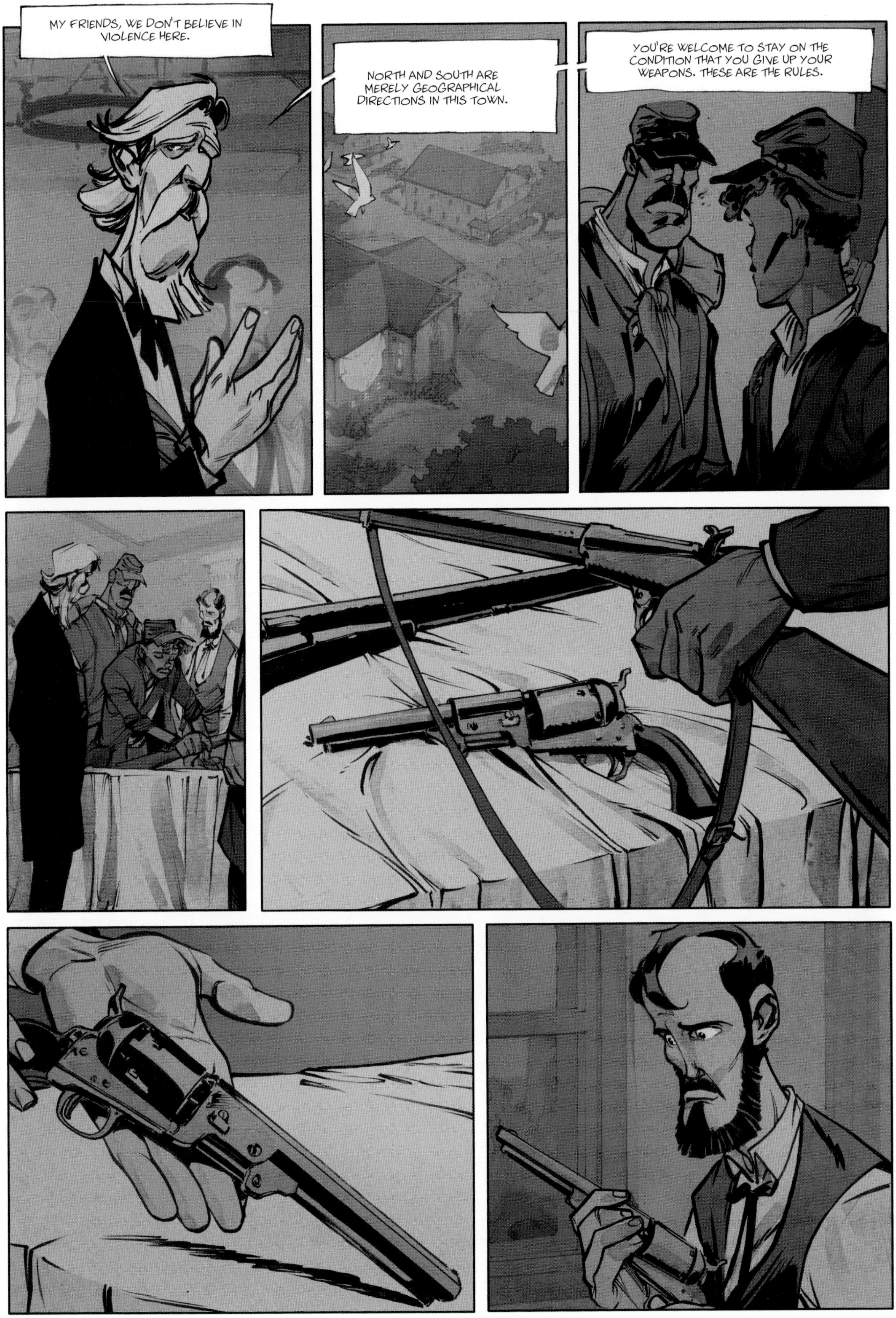
MY FRIENDS, WE DON'T BELIEVE IN VIOLENCE HERE.
NORTH AND SOUTH ARE MERELY GEOGRAPHICAL DIRECTIONS IN THIS TOWN.
YOU'RE WELCOME TO STAY ON THE CONDITION THAT YOU GIVE UP YOUR WEAPONS. THESE ARE THE RULES.

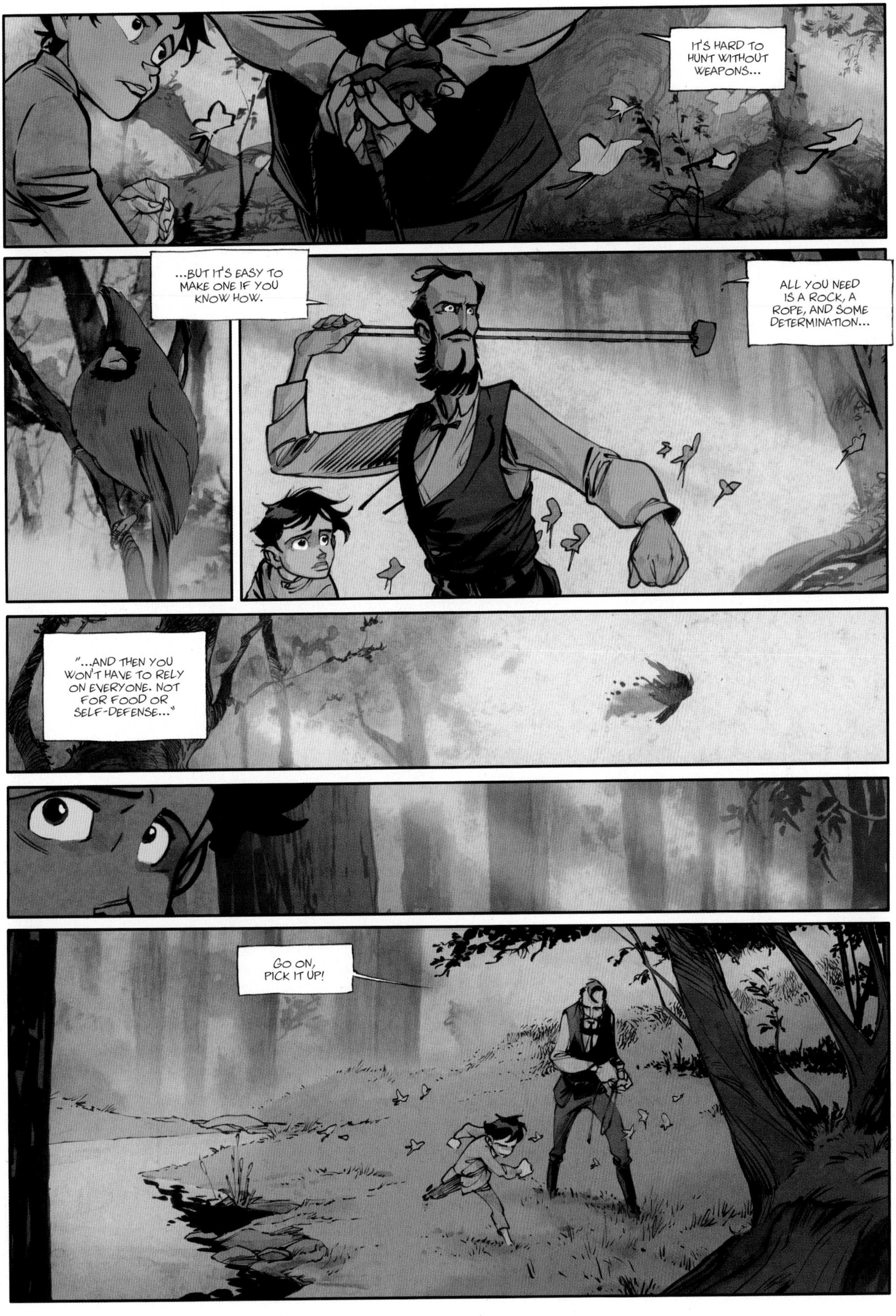
IT'S HARD TO HUNT WITHOUT WEAPONS...
...BUT IT'S EASY TO MAKE ONE IF YOU KNOW HOW.
ALL YOU NEED IS A ROCK, A ROPE, AND SOME DETERMINATION...
"...AND THEN YOU WON'T HAVE TO RELY ON EVERYONE. NOT FOR FOOD OR SELF-DEFENSE..."
GO ON, PICK IT UP!

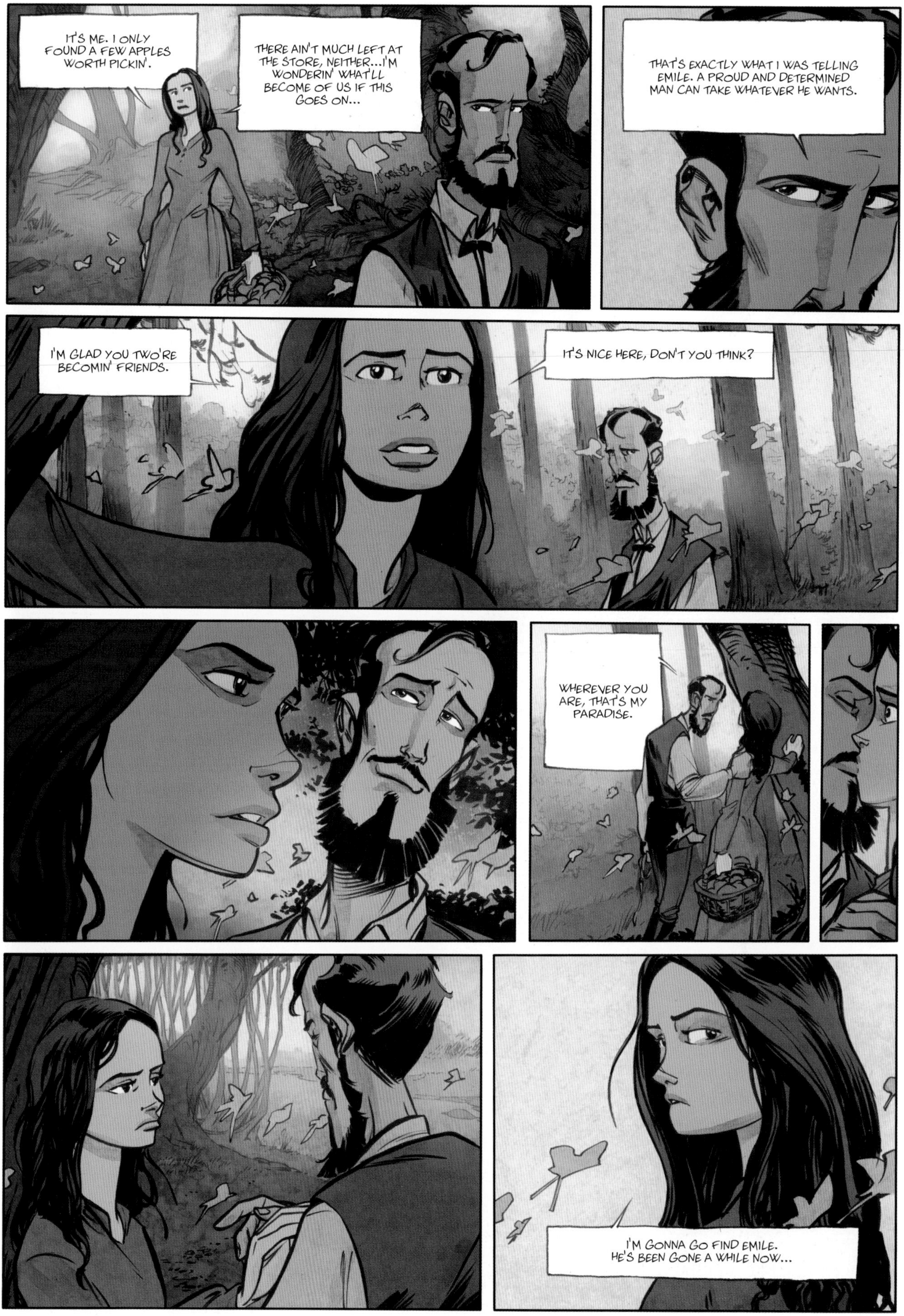
IT'S ME. I ONLY FOUND A FEW APPLES WORTH PICKIN'.
THERE AIN'T MUCH LEFT AT THE STORE, NEITHER...I'M WONDERIN' WHAT'LL BECOME OF US IF THIS GOES ON...
THAT'S EXACTLY WHAT I WAS TELLING EMILE. A PROUD AND DETERMINED MAN CAN TAKE WHATEVER HE WANTS.
I'M GLAD YOU TWO'RE BECOMIN' FRIENDS.
IT'S NICE HERE, DON'T YOU THINK?
WHEREVER YOU ARE, THAT'S MY PARADISE.
I'M GONNA GO FIND EMILE. HE'S BEEN GONE A WHILE NOW...

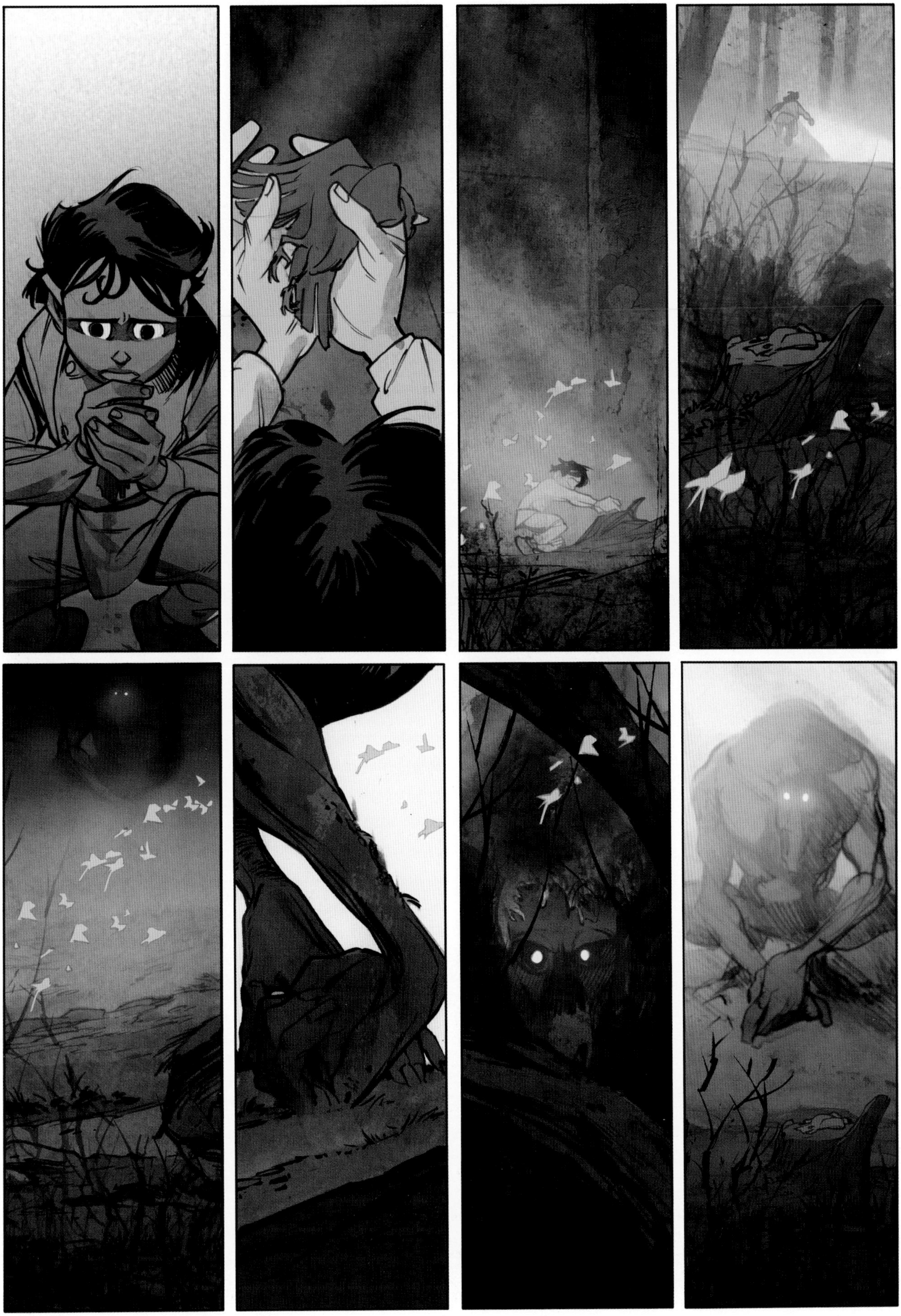

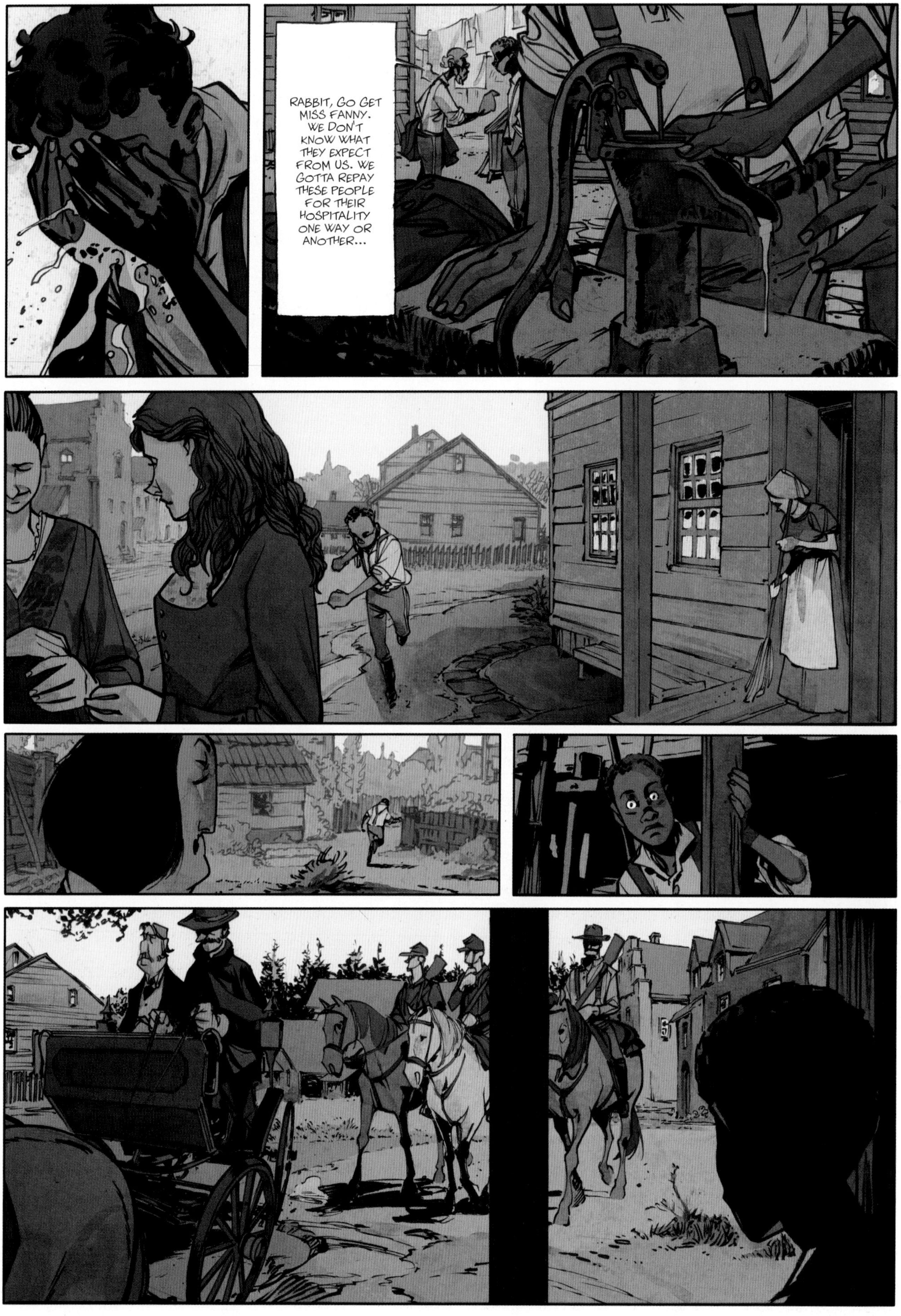
RABBIT, GO GET MISS FANNY. WE DON'T KNOW WHAT THEY EXPECT FROM US. WE GOTTA REPAY THESE PEOPLE FOR THEIR HOSPITALITY ONE WAY OR ANOTHER...

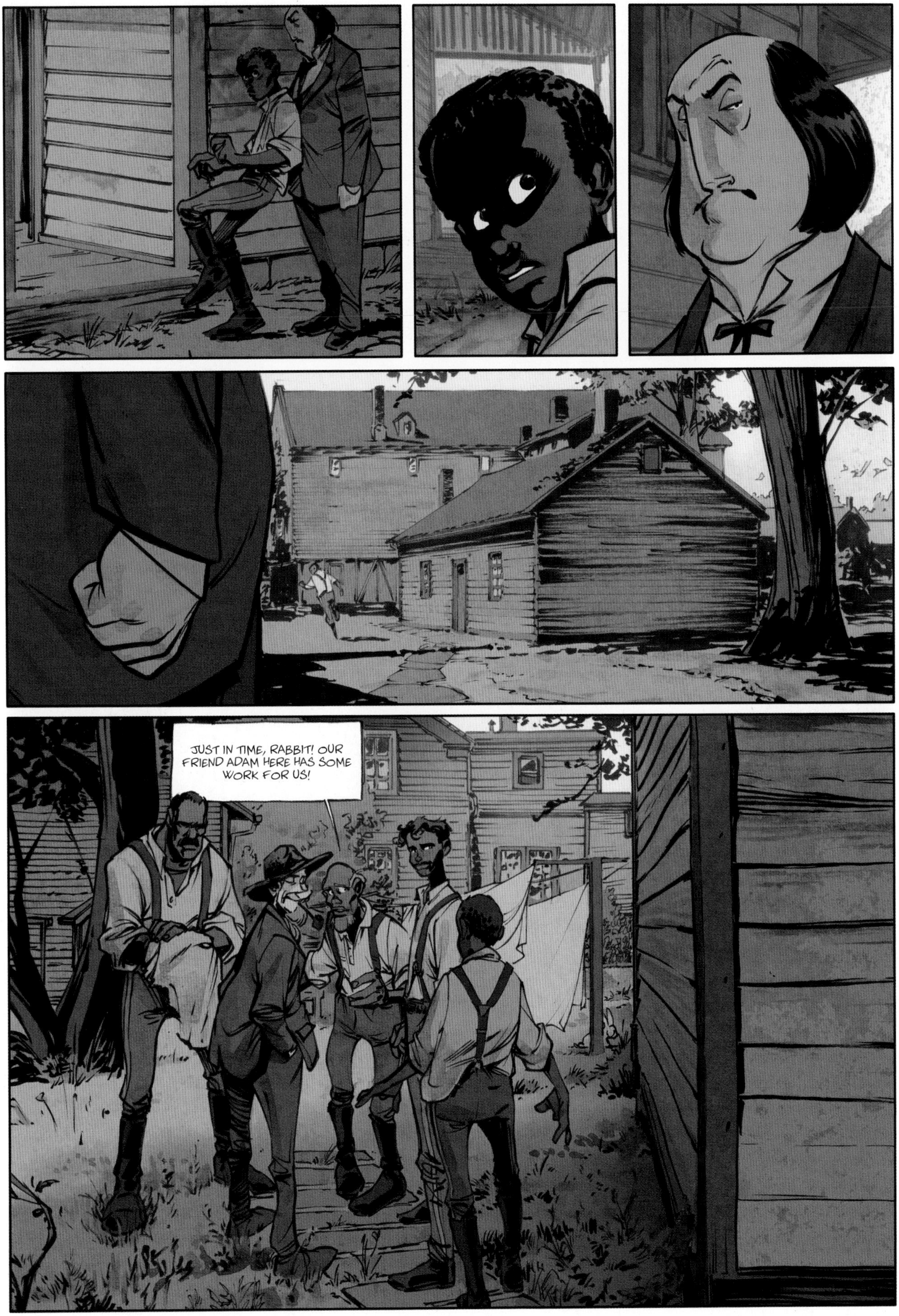
JUST IN TIME, RABBIT! OUR FRIEND ADAM HERE HAS SOME WORK FOR US!

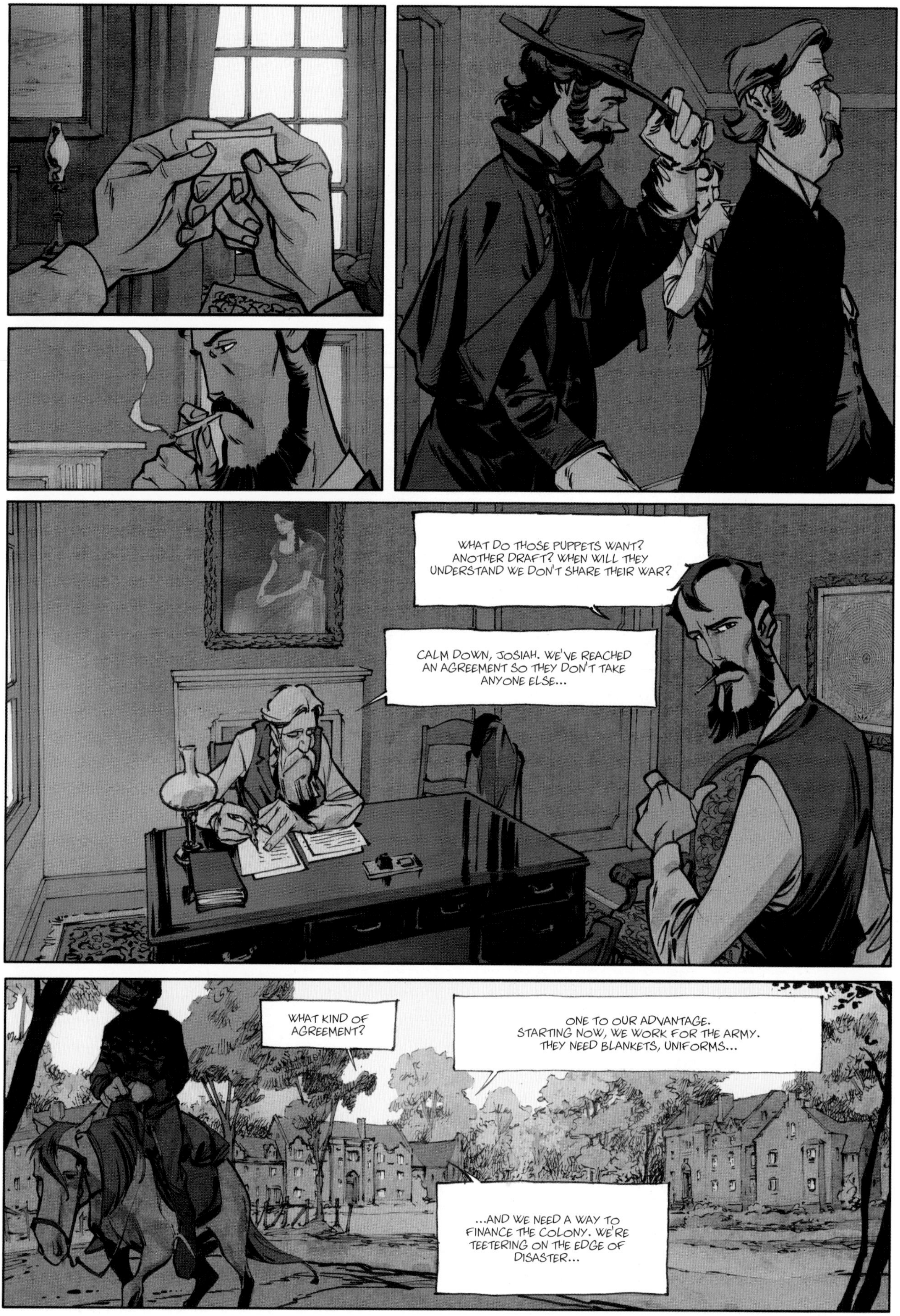
WHAT DO THOSE PUPPETS WANT? ANOTHER DRAFT? WHEN WILL THEY UNDERSTAND WE DON'T SHARE THEIR WAR?
CALM DOWN, JOSIAH. WE'VE REACHED AN AGREEMENT SO THEY DON'T TAKE ANYONE ELSE...
WHAT KIND OF AGREEMENT?
ONE TO OUR ADVANTAGE. STARTING NOW, WE WORK FOR THE ARMY. THEY NEED BLANKETS, UNIFORMS...
...AND WE NEED A WAY TO FINANCE THE COLONY. WE'RE TEETERING ON THE EDGE OF DISASTER...

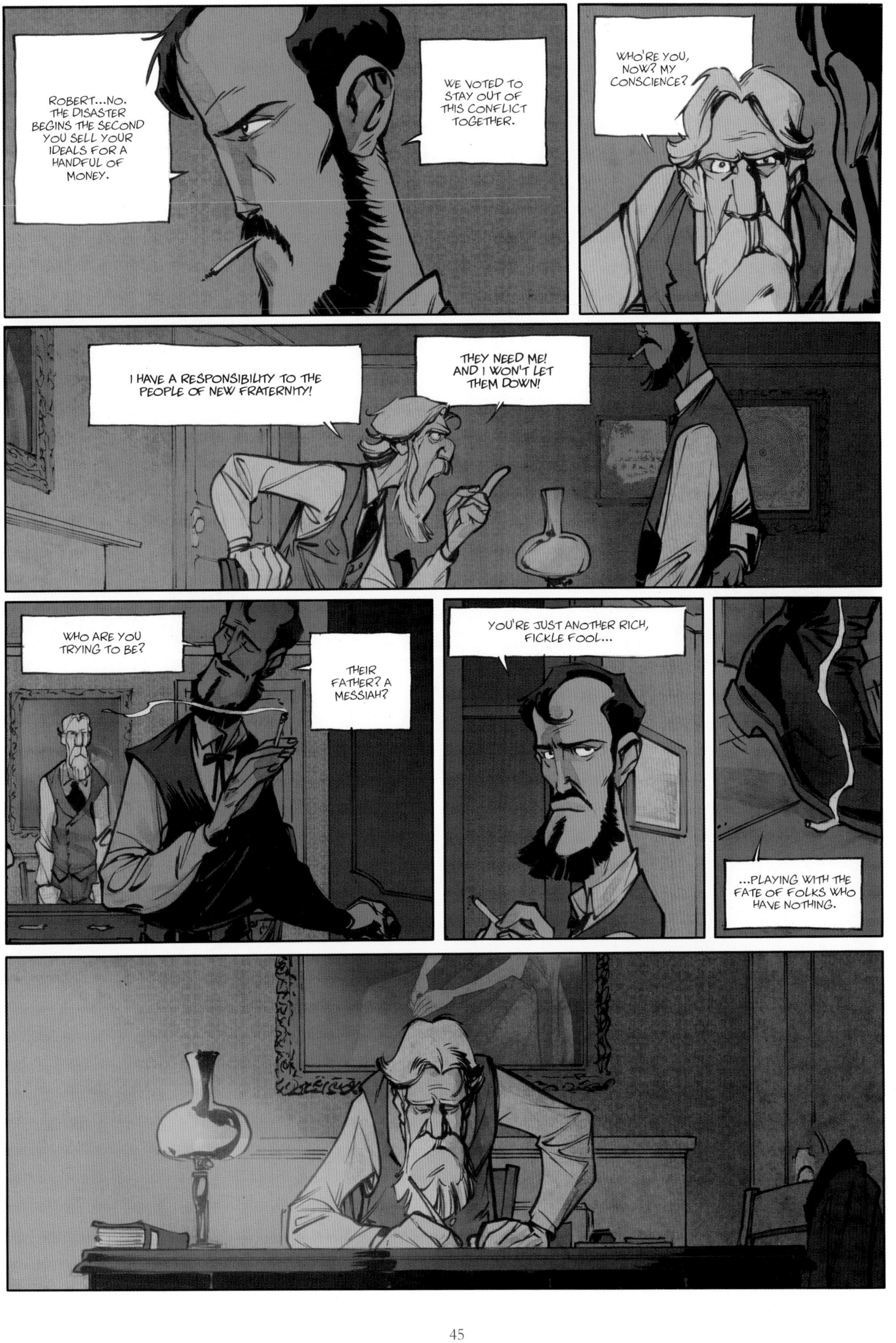

ROBERT...NO. THE DISASTER BEGINS THE SECOND YOU SELL YOUR IDEALS FOR A HANDFUL OF MONEY.
WE VOTED TO STAY OUT OF THIS CONFLICT TOGETHER.
WHO'RE YOU, NOW? MY CONSCIENCE?
I HAVE A RESPONSIBILITY TO THE PEOPLE OF NEW FRATERNITY!
THEY NEED ME! AND I WON'T LET THEM DOWN!
WHO ARE YOU TRYING TO BE?
THEIR FATHER? A MESSIAH?
YOU'RE JUST ANOTHER RICH, FICKLE FOOL...
...PLAYING WITH THE FATE OF FOLKS WHO HAVE NOTHING.

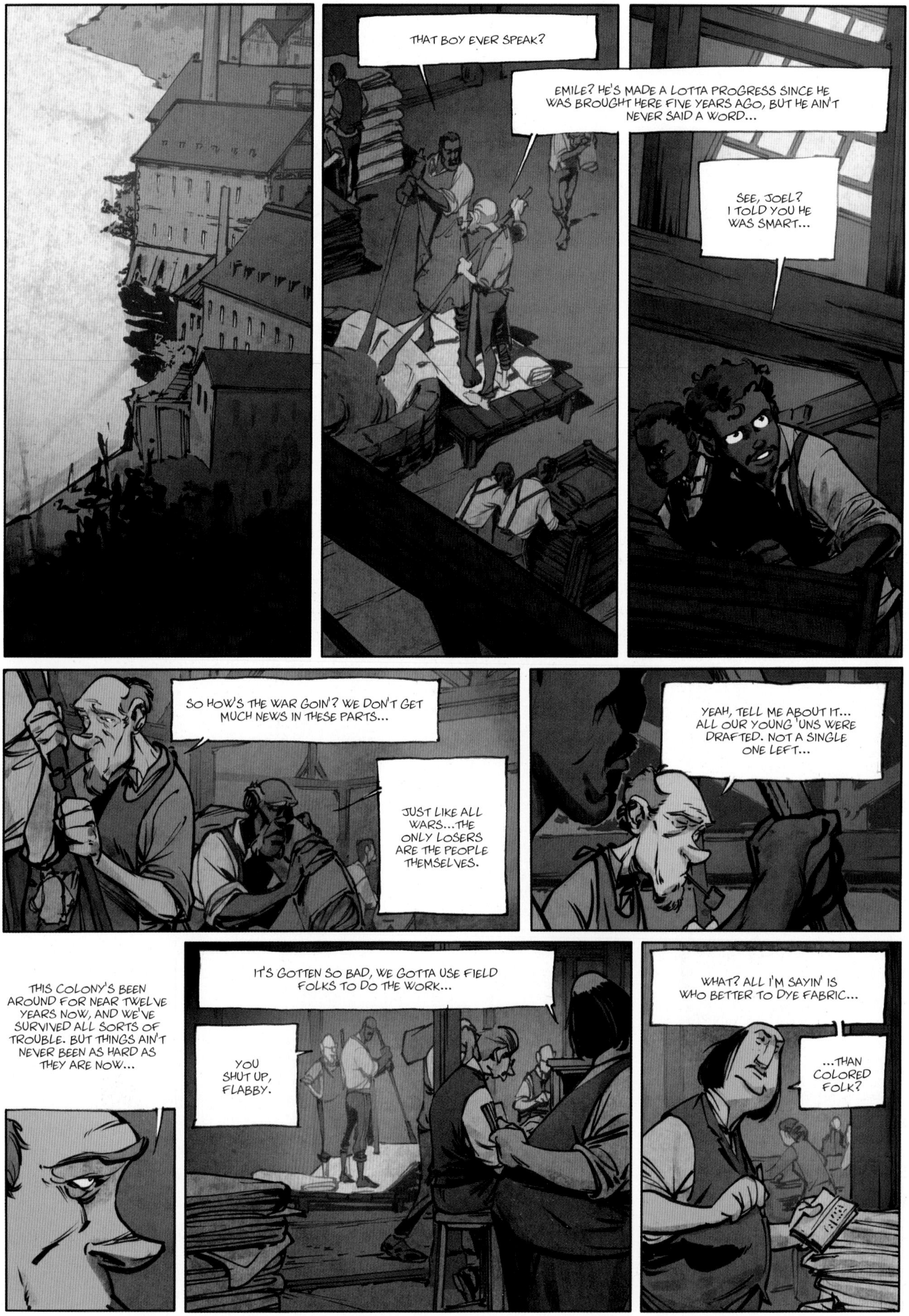
THAT BOY EVER SPEAK?
EMILE? HE'S MADE A LOTTA PROGRESS SINCE HE WAS BROUGHT HERE FIVE YEARS AGO, BUT HE AIN'T NEVER SAID A WORD...
SEE, JOEL? I TOLD YOU HE WAS SMART...
SO HOW'S THE WAR GOIN'? WE DON'T GET MUCH NEWS IN THESE PARTS...
JUST LIKE ALL WARS...THE ONLY LOSERS ARE THE PEOPLE THEMSELVES.
YEAH, TELL ME ABOUT IT... ALL OUR YOUNG 'UNS WERE DRAFTED. NOT A SINGLE ONE LEFT...
THIS COLONY'S BEEN AROUND FOR NEAR TWELVE YEARS NOW, AND WE'VE SURVIVED ALL SORTS OF TROUBLE. BUT THINGS AIN'T NEVER BEEN AS HARD AS THEY ARE NOW...
IT'S GOTTEN SO BAD, WE GOTTA USE FIELD FOLKS TO DO THE WORK...
YOU SHUT UP, FLABBY.
WHAT? ALL I'M SAYIN' IS WHO BETTER TO DYE FABRIC...
...THAN COLORED FOLK?

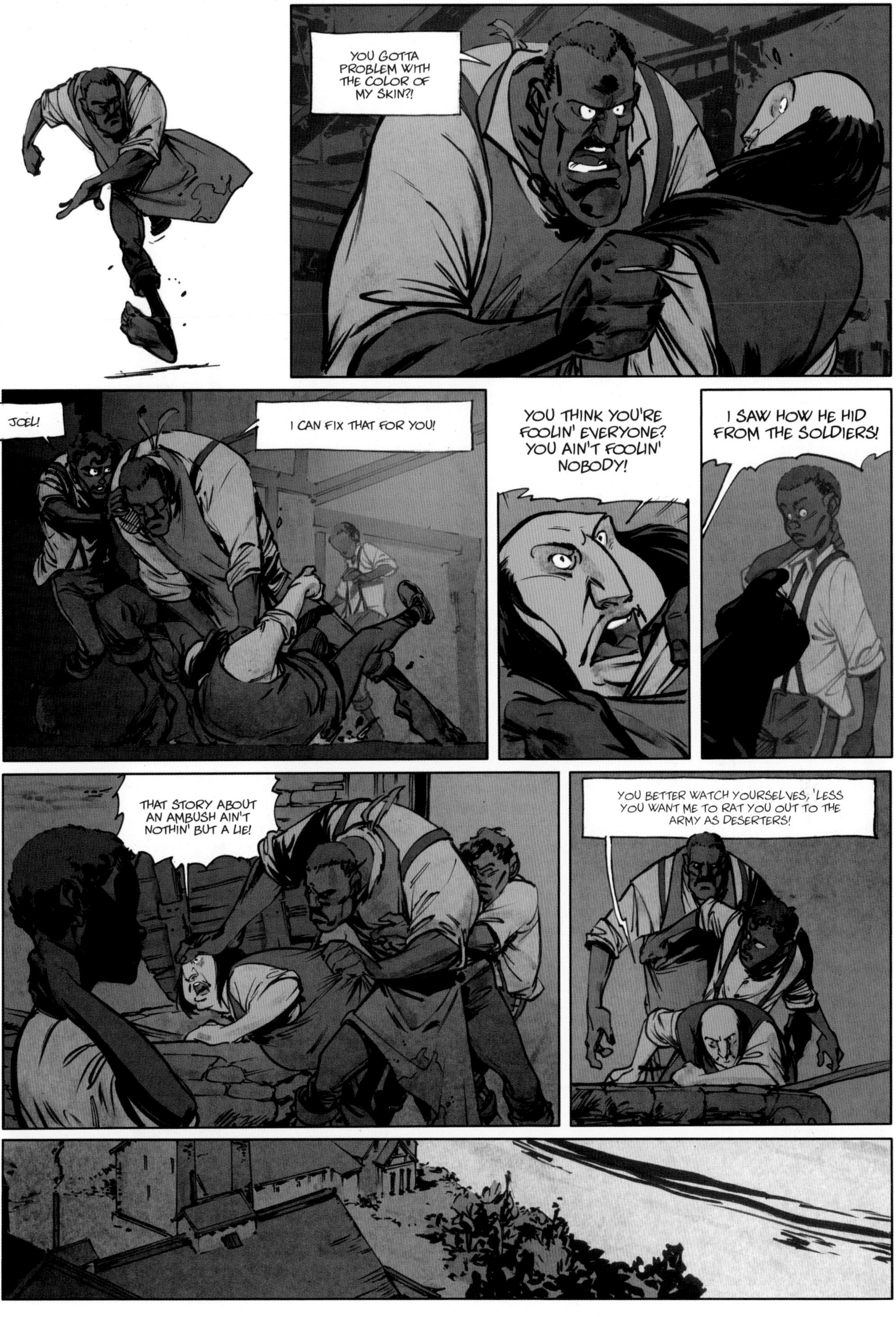
YOU GOTTA PROBLEM WITH THE COLOR OF MY SKIN?!
JOEL!
I CAN FIX THAT FOR YOU!
YOU THINK YOU'RE FOOLIN' EVERYONE? YOU AIN'T FOOLIN' NOBODY!
I SAW HOW HE HID FROM THE SOLDIERS!
THAT STORY ABOUT AN AMBUSH AIN'T NOTHIN' BUT A LIE!
YOU BETTER WATCH YOURSELVES, 'LESS YOU WANT ME TO RAT YOU OUT TO THE ARMY AS DESERTERS!

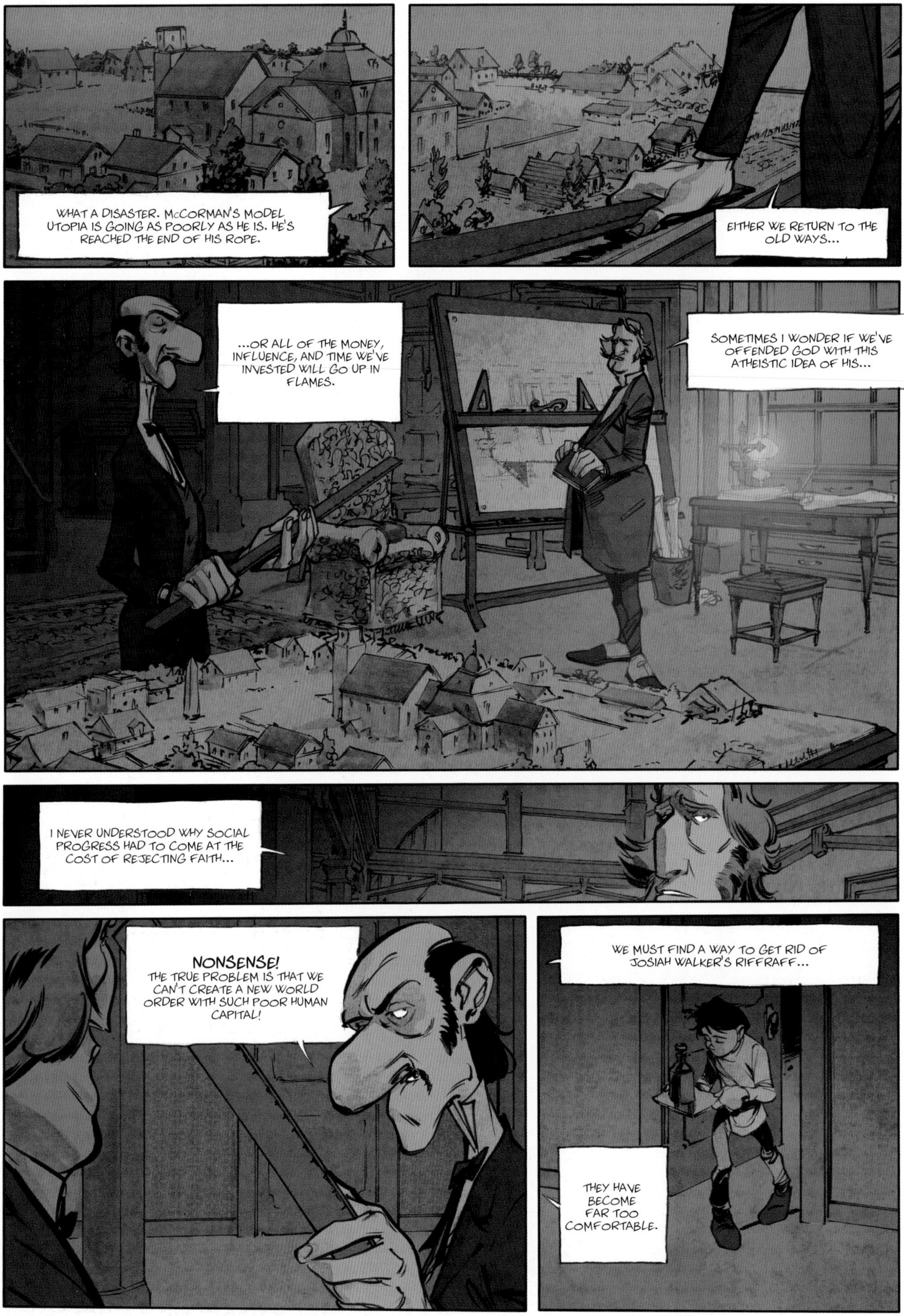

WHAT A DISASTER. McCORMAN'S MODEL UTOPIA IS GOING AS POORLY AS HE IS. HE'S REACHED THE END OF HIS ROPE.
EITHER WE RETURN TO THE OLD WAYS...
...OR ALL OF THE MONEY, INFLUENCE, AND TIME WE'VE INVESTED WILL GO UP IN FLAMES.
SOMETIMES I WONDER IF WE'VE OFFENDED GOD WITH THIS ATHEISTIC IDEA OF HIS...
I NEVER UNDERSTOOD WHY SOCIAL PROGRESS HAD TO COME AT THE COST OF REJECTING FAITH...
NONSENSE! THE TRUE PROBLEM IS THAT WE CAN'T CREATE A NEW WORLD ORDER WITH SUCH POOR HUMAN CAPITAL!
WE MUST FIND A WAY TO GET RID OF JOSIAH WALKER'S RIFFRAFF...
THEY HAVE BECOME FAR TOO COMFORTABLE.

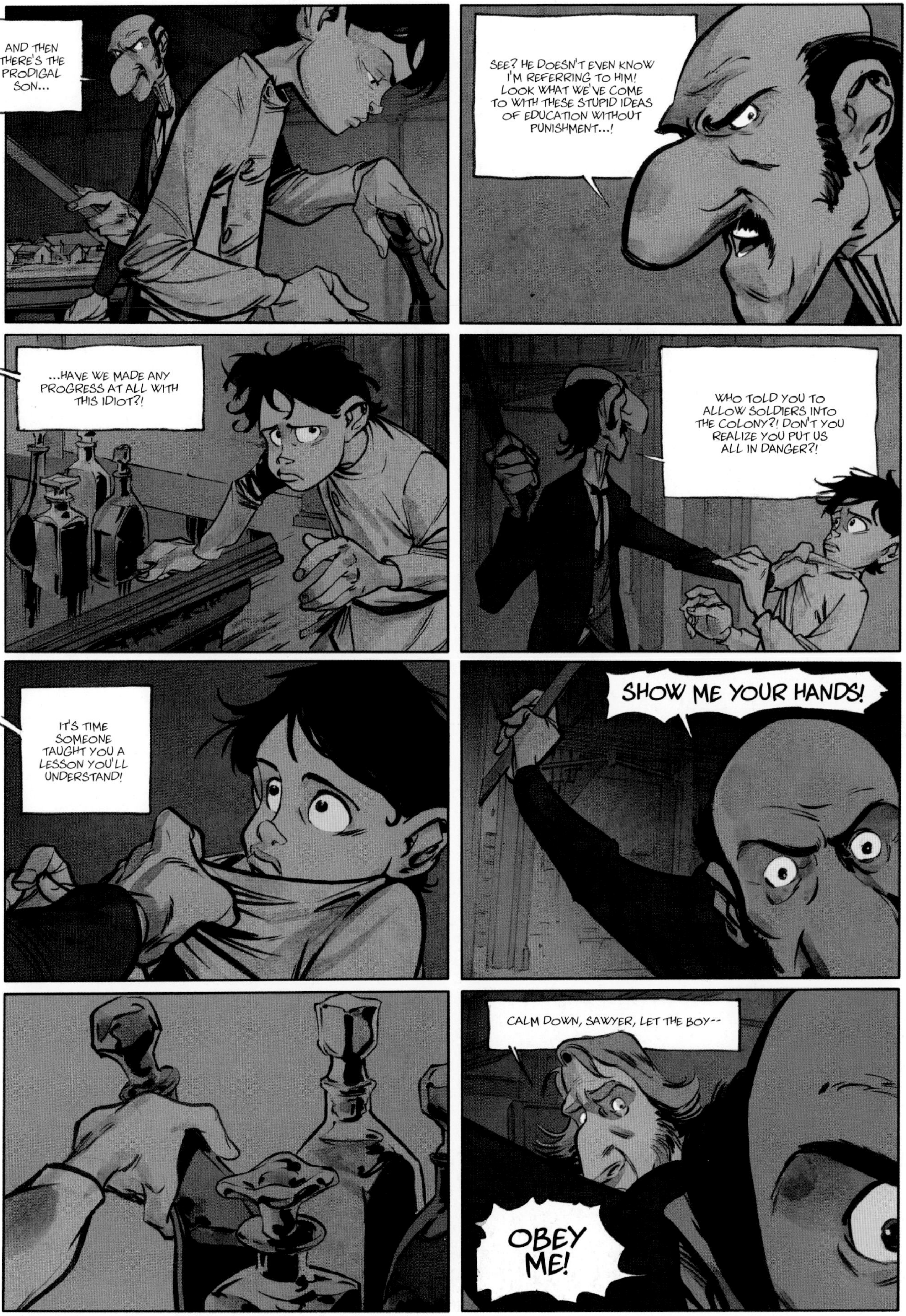
AND THEN THERE'S THE PRODIGAL SON...
SEE? HE DOESN'T EVEN KNOW I'M REFERRING TO HIM! LOOK WHAT WE'VE COME TO WITH THESE STUPID IDEAS OF EDUCATION WITHOUT PUNISHMENT...!
...HAVE WE MADE ANY PROGRESS AT ALL WITH THIS IDIOT?!
WHO TOLD YOU TO ALLOW SOLDIERS INTO THE COLONY?! DON'T YOU REALIZE YOU PUT US ALL IN DANGER?!
IT'S TIME SOMEONE TAUGHT YOU A LESSON YOU'LL UNDERSTAND!
SHOW ME YOUR HANDS!
CALM DOWN, SAWYER, LET THE BOY--
OBEY ME!

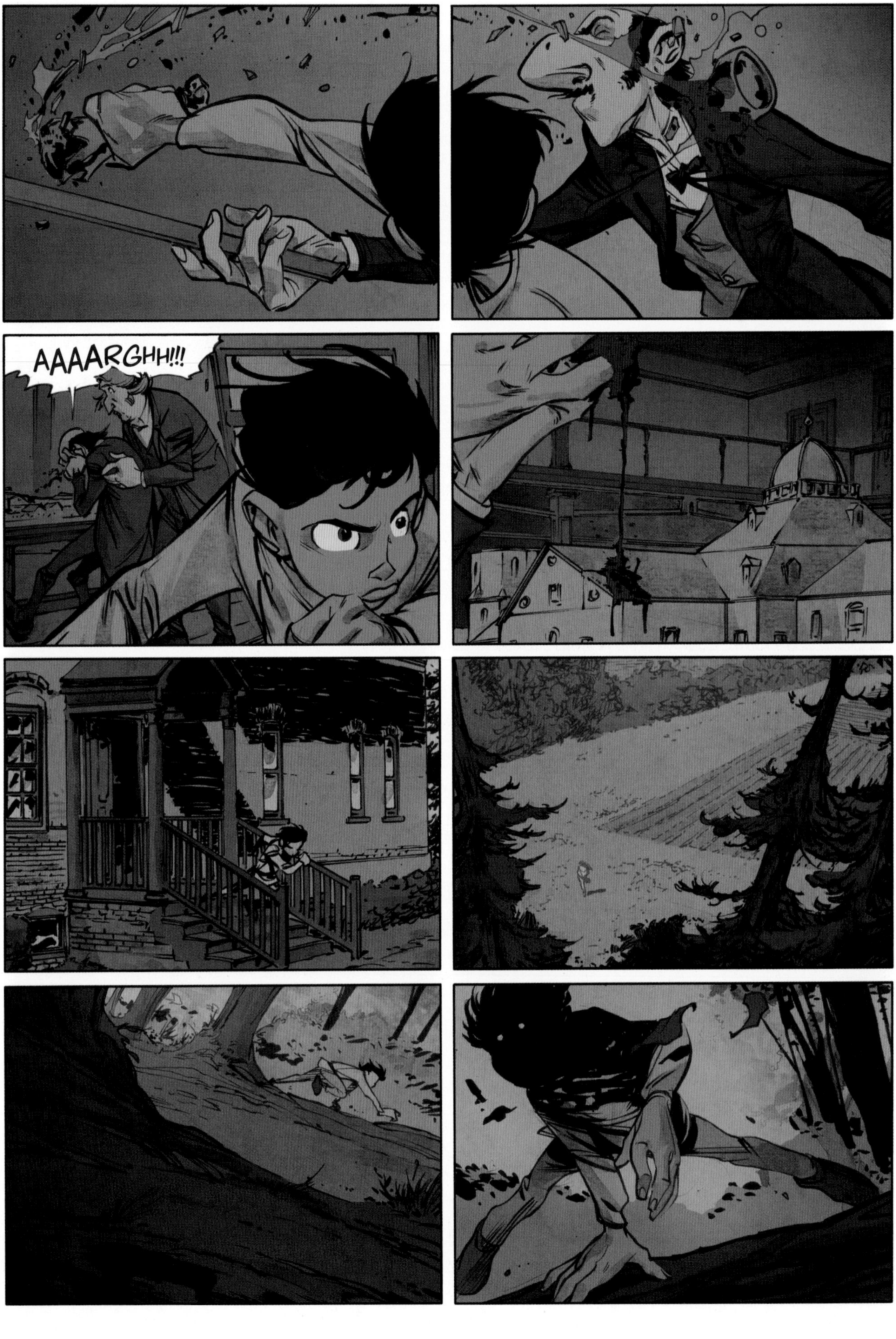
AAAARGHH!!!

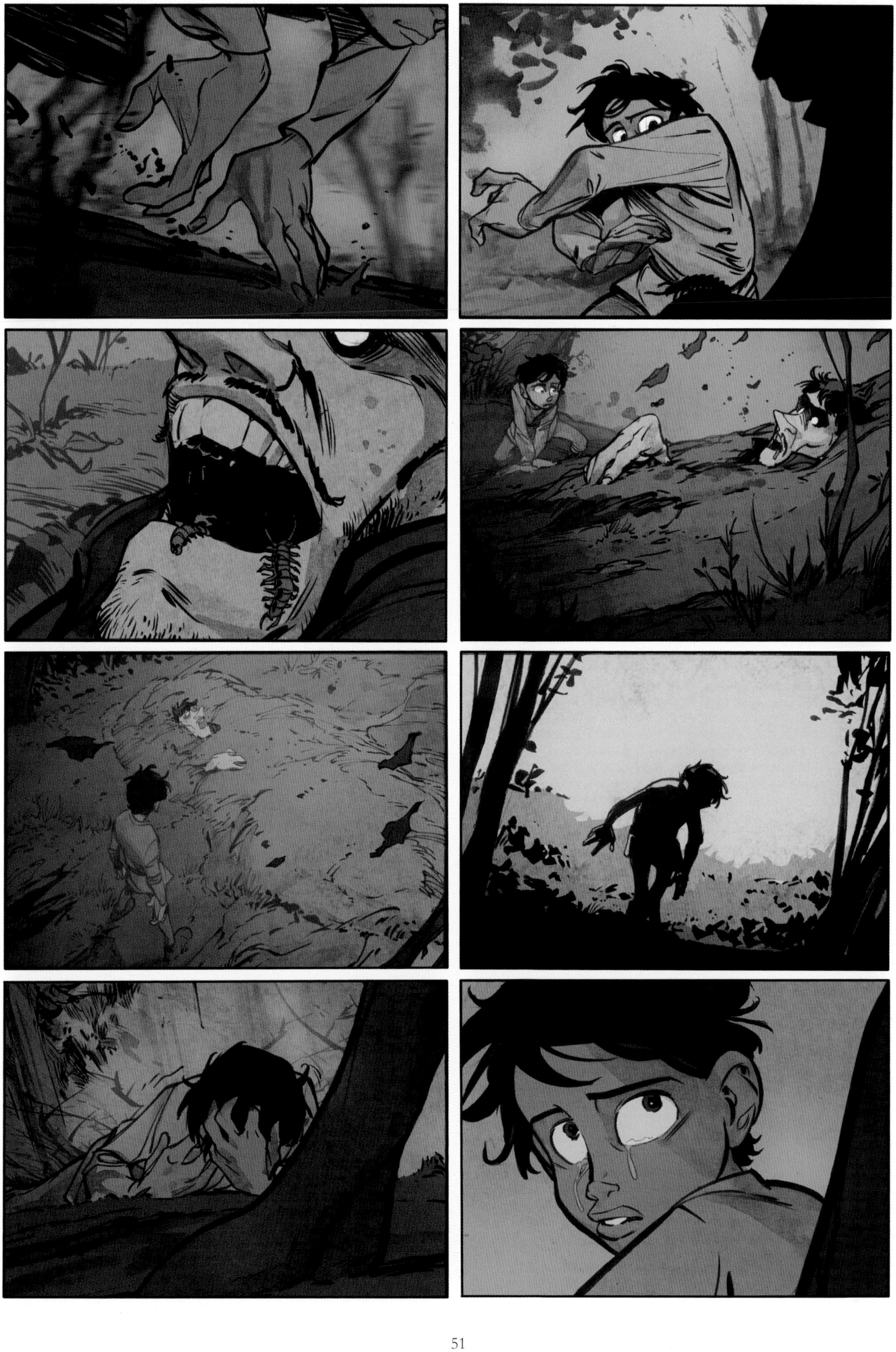

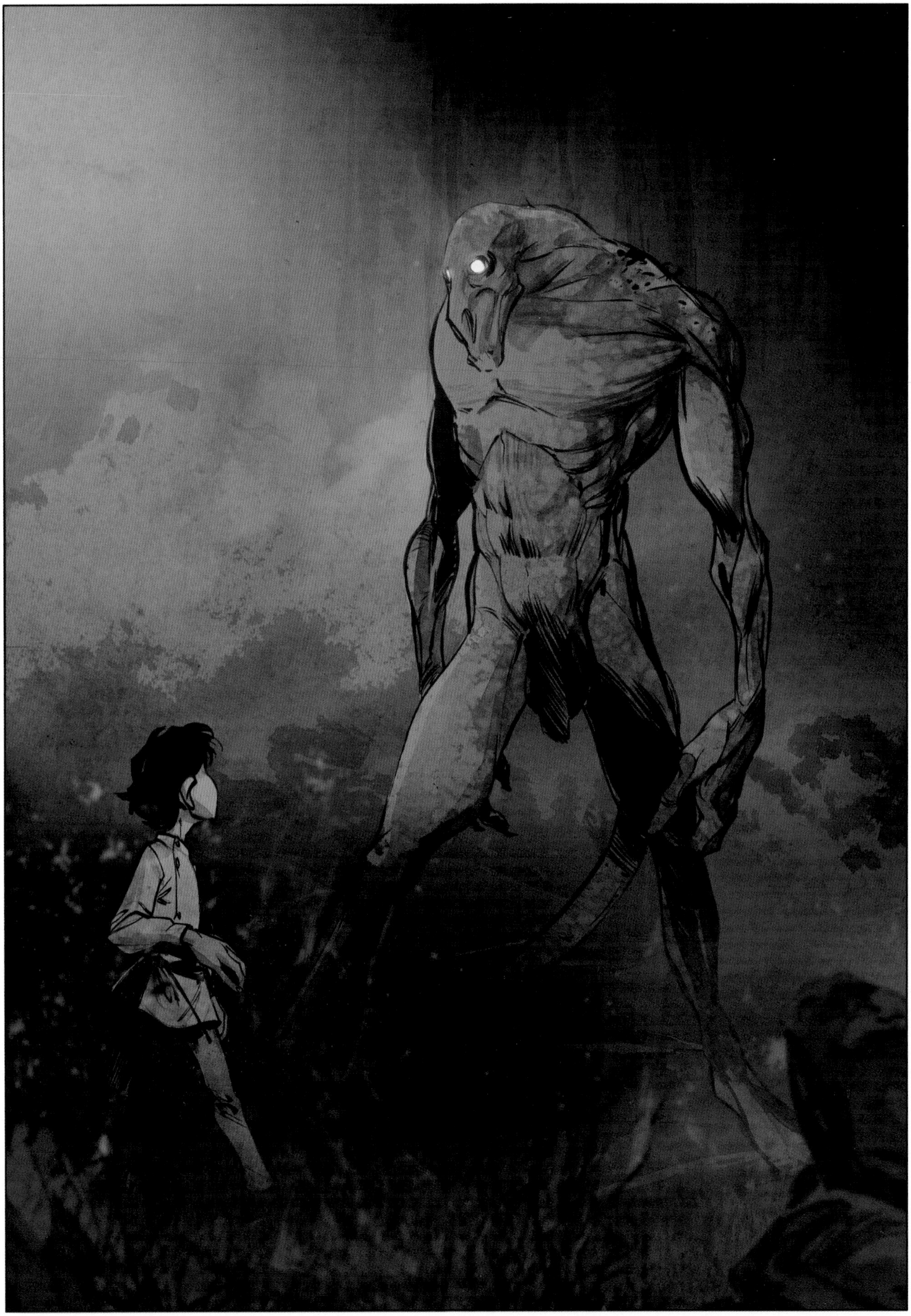

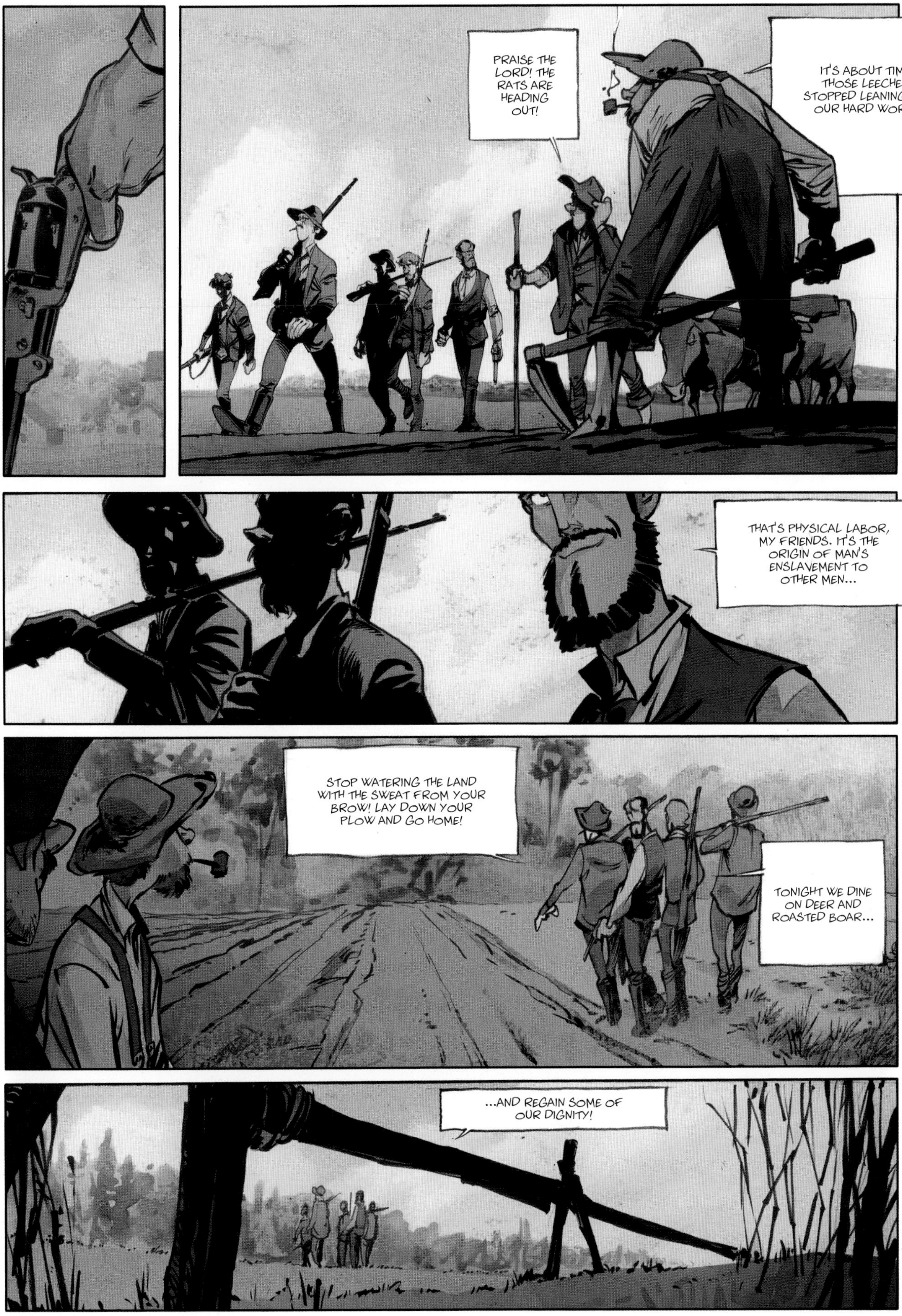
PRAISE THE LORD! THE RATS ARE HEADING OUT!
IT'S ABOUT TIME THOSE LEECHES STOPPED LEANING ON OUR HARD WORK!
THAT'S PHYSICAL LABOR, MY FRIENDS. IT'S THE ORIGIN OF MAN'S ENSLAVEMENT TO OTHER MEN...
STOP WATERING THE LAND WITH THE SWEAT FROM YOUR BROW! LAY DOWN YOUR PLOW AND GO HOME!
TONIGHT WE DINE ON DEER AND ROASTED BOAR...
...AND REGAIN SOME OF OUR DIGNITY!

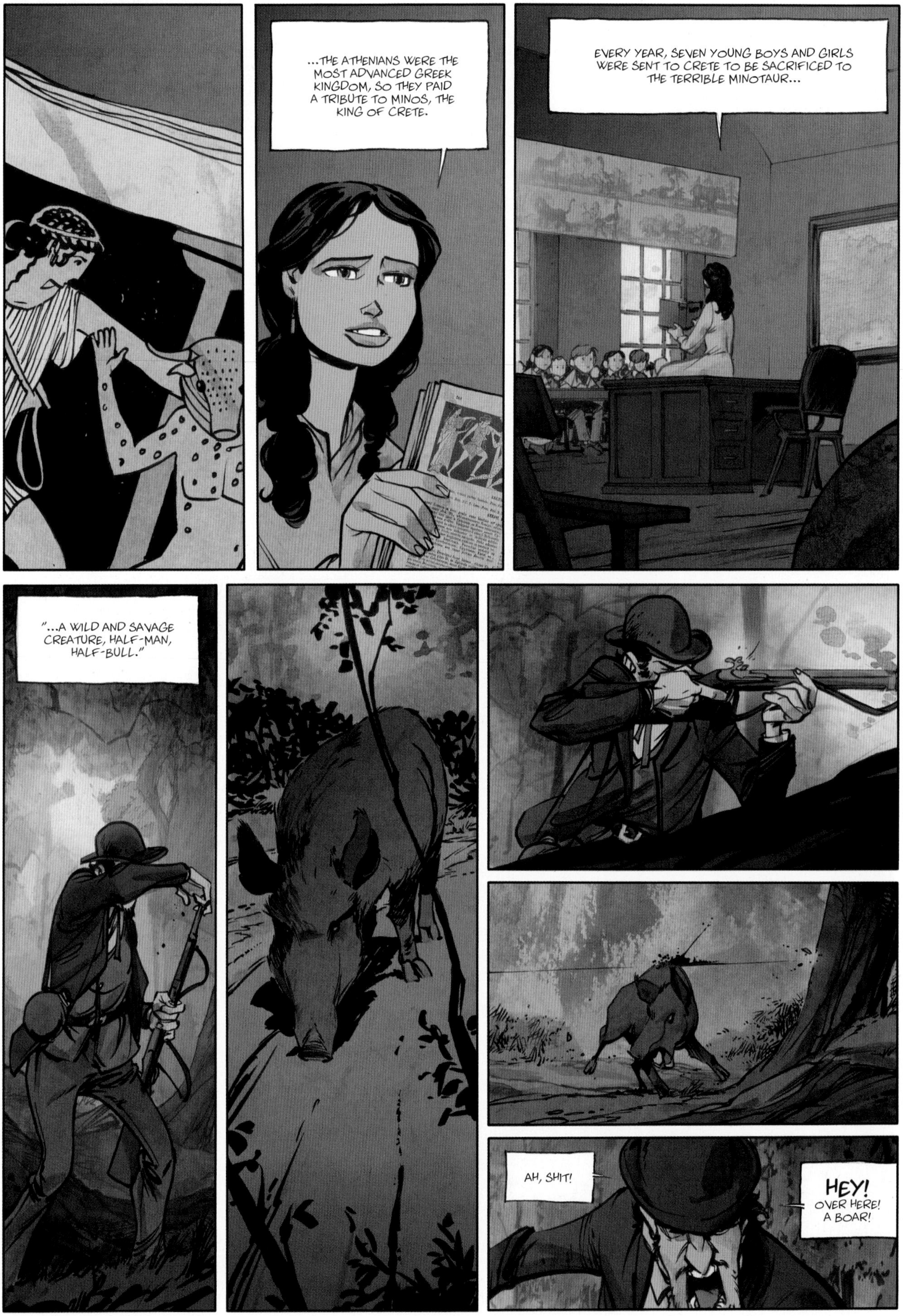
...THE ATHENIANS WERE THE MOST ADVANCED GREEK KINGDOM, SO THEY PAID A TRIBUTE TO MINOS, THE KING OF CRETE.
EVERY YEAR, SEVEN YOUNG BOYS AND GIRLS WERE SENT TO CRETE TO BE SACRIFICED TO THE TERRIBLE MINOTAUR...
"...A WILD AND SAVAGE CREATURE, HALF-MAN, HALF-BULL."
AH, SHIT!
HEY! OVER HERE! A BOAR!

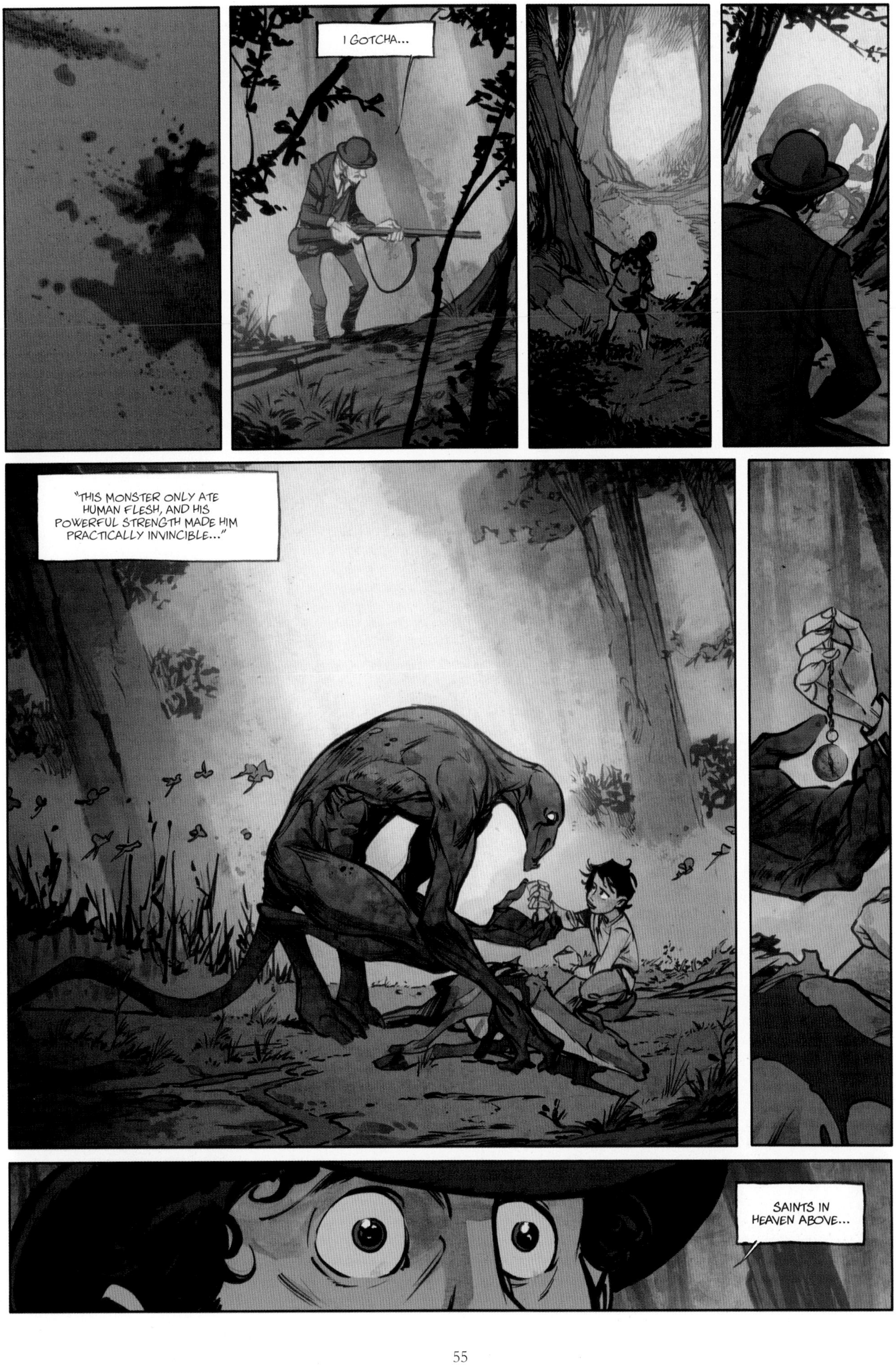
I GOTCHA...
"THIS MONSTER ONLY ATE HUMAN FLESH, AND HIS POWERFUL STRENGTH MADE HIM PRACTICALLY INVINCIBLE..."
SAINTS IN HEAVEN ABOVE...

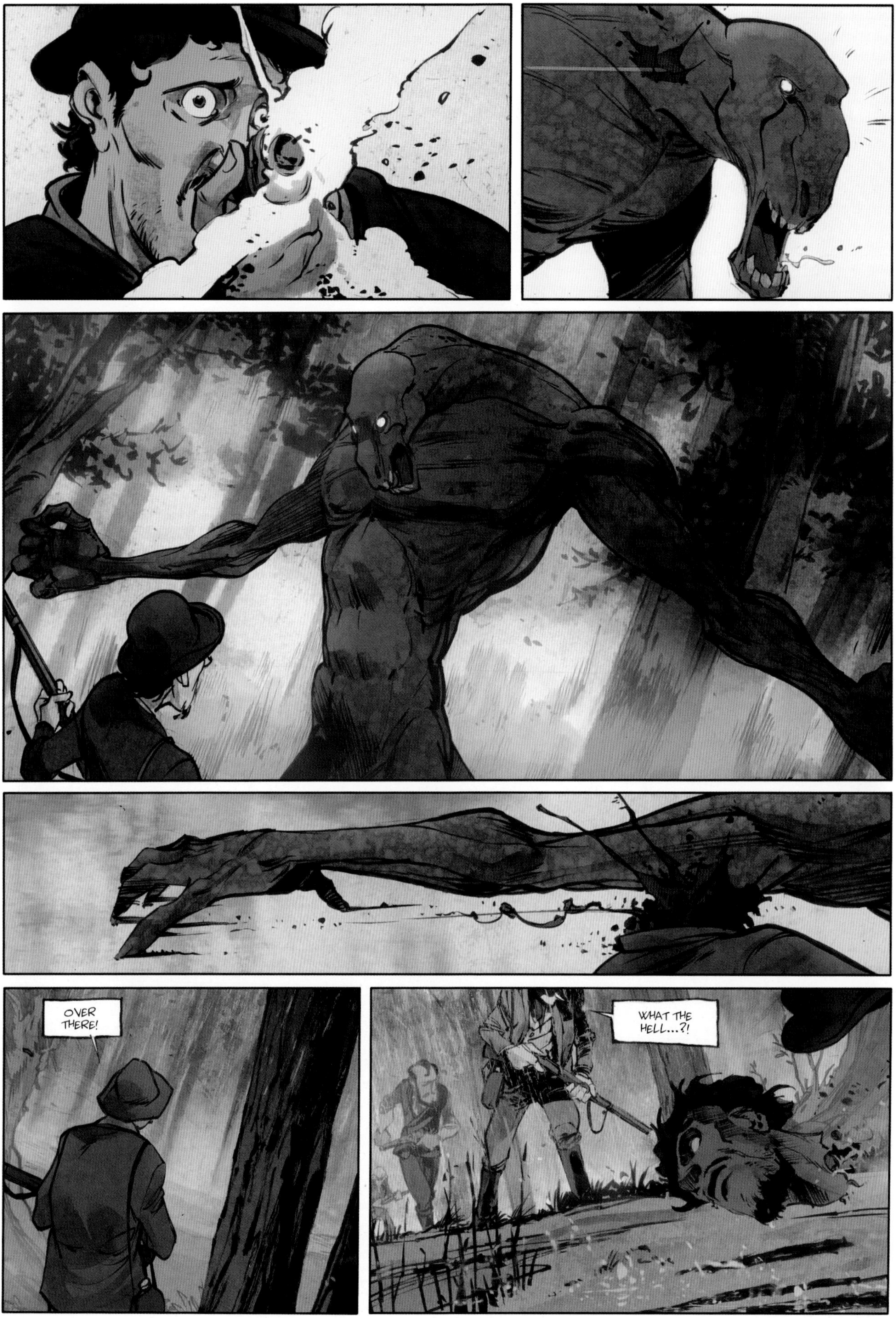
OVER THERE!
WHAT THE HELL...?!

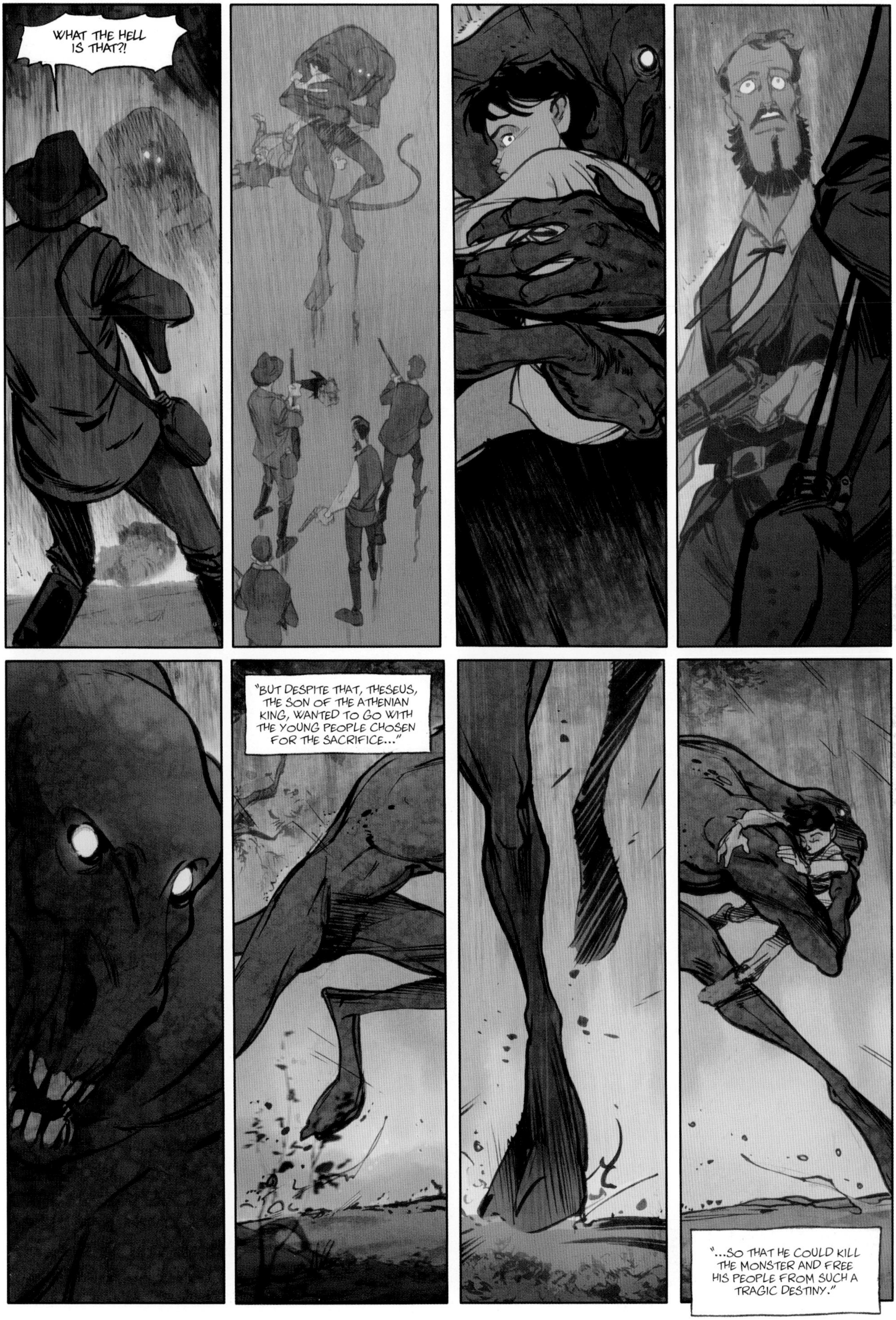
WHAT THE HELL IS THAT?!
"BUT DESPITE THAT, THESEUS, THE SON OF THE ATHENIAN KING, WANTED TO GO WITH THE YOUNG PEOPLE CHOSEN FOR THE SACRIFICE..."
"...SO THAT HE COULD KILL THE MONSTER AND FREE HIS PEOPLE FROM SUCH A TRAGIC DESTINY."

DON'T LET IT GET AWAY!

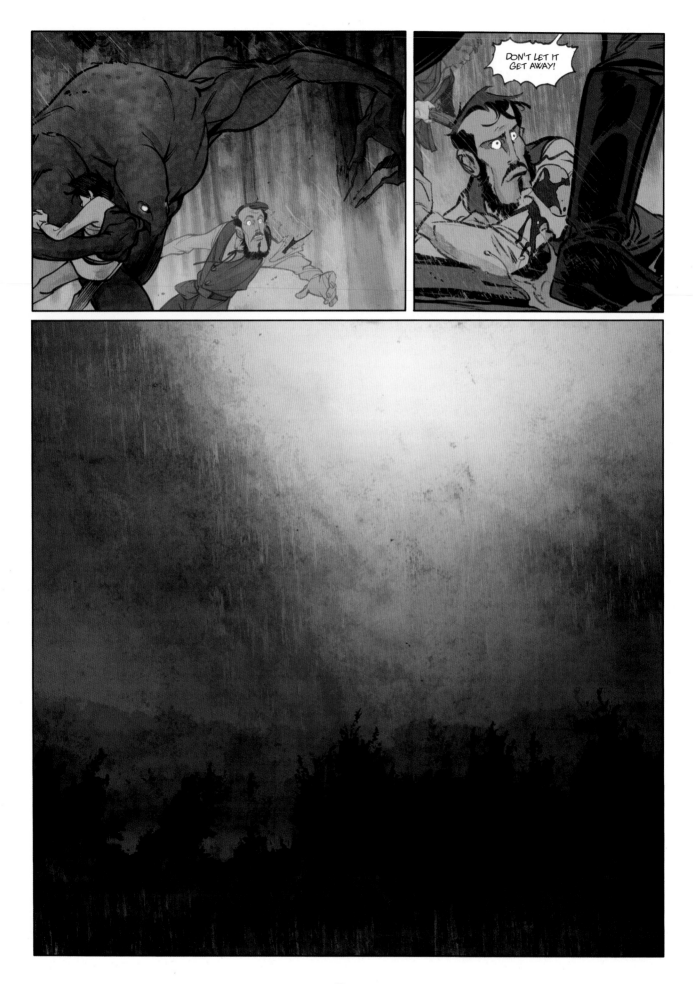

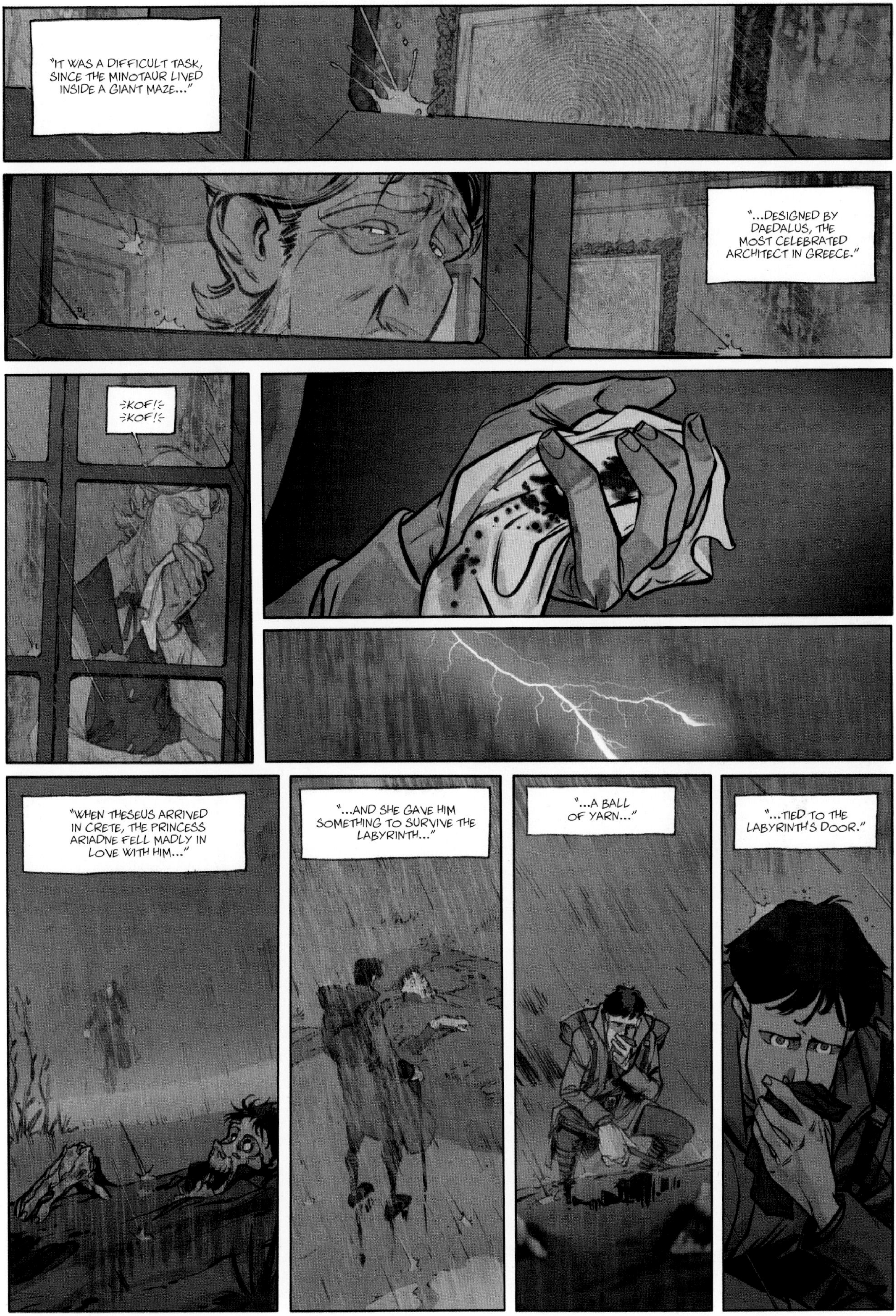
"IT WAS A DIFFICULT TASK, SINCE THE MINOTAUR LIVED INSIDE A GIANT MAZE..."
"...DESIGNED BY DAEDALUS, THE MOST CELEBRATED ARCHITECT IN GREECE."
KOF! KOF!
"WHEN THESEUS ARRIVED IN CRETE, THE PRINCESS ARIADNE FELL MADLY IN LOVE WITH HIM..."
"...AND SHE GAVE HIM SOMETHING TO SURVIVE THE LABYRINTH..."
"...A BALL OF YARN..."
"...TIED TO THE LABYRINTH'S DOOR."

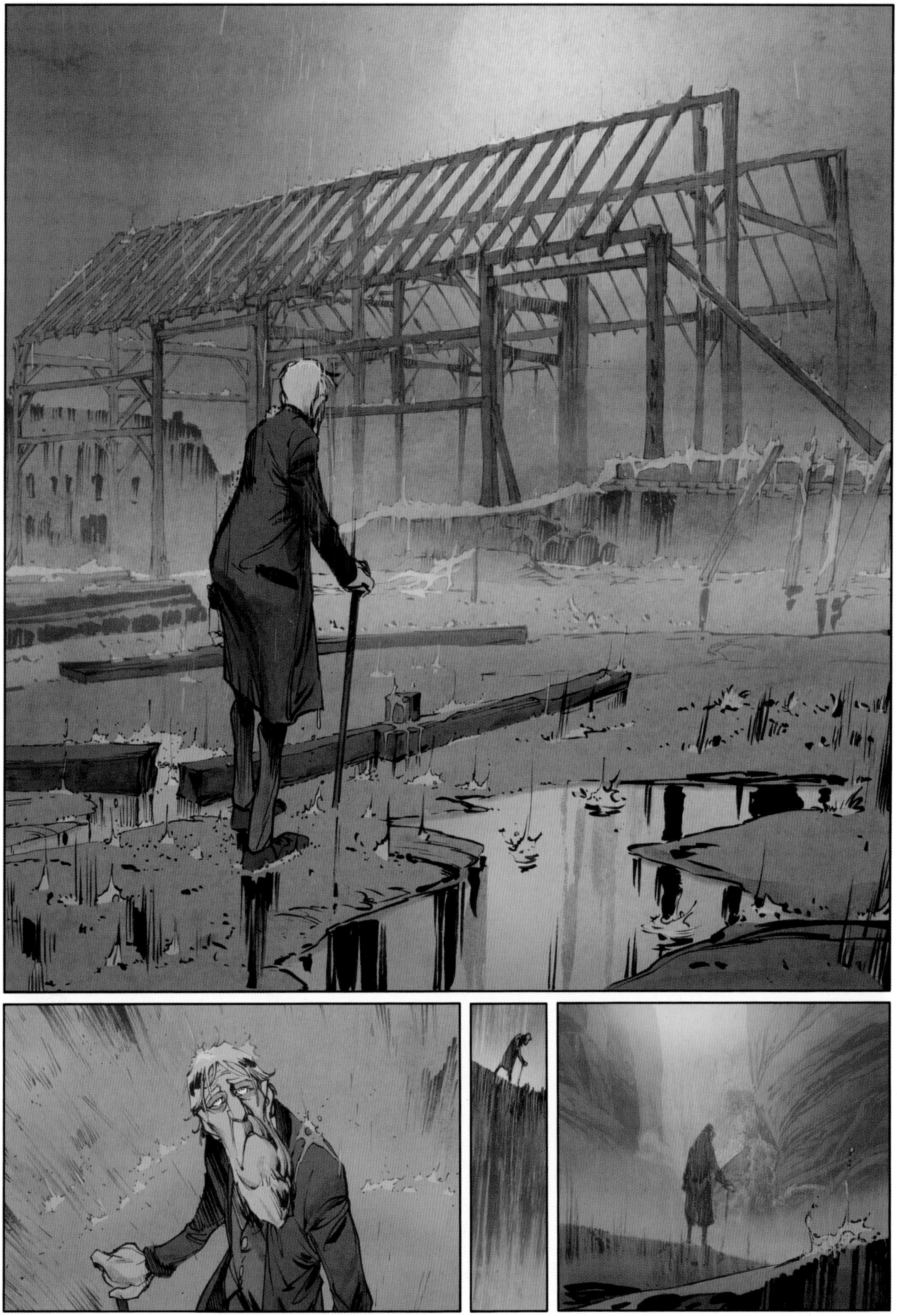

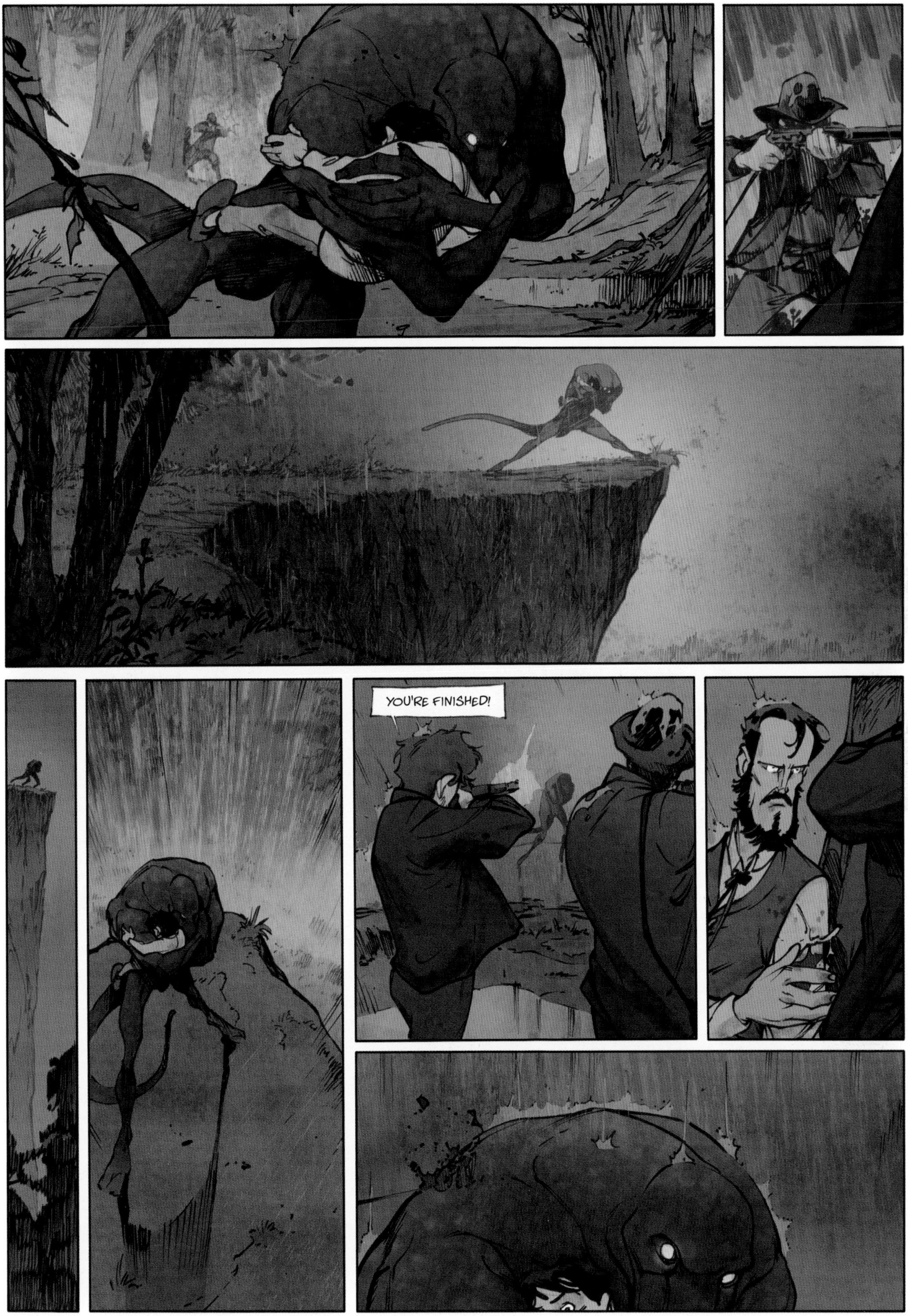
YOU'RE FINISHED!

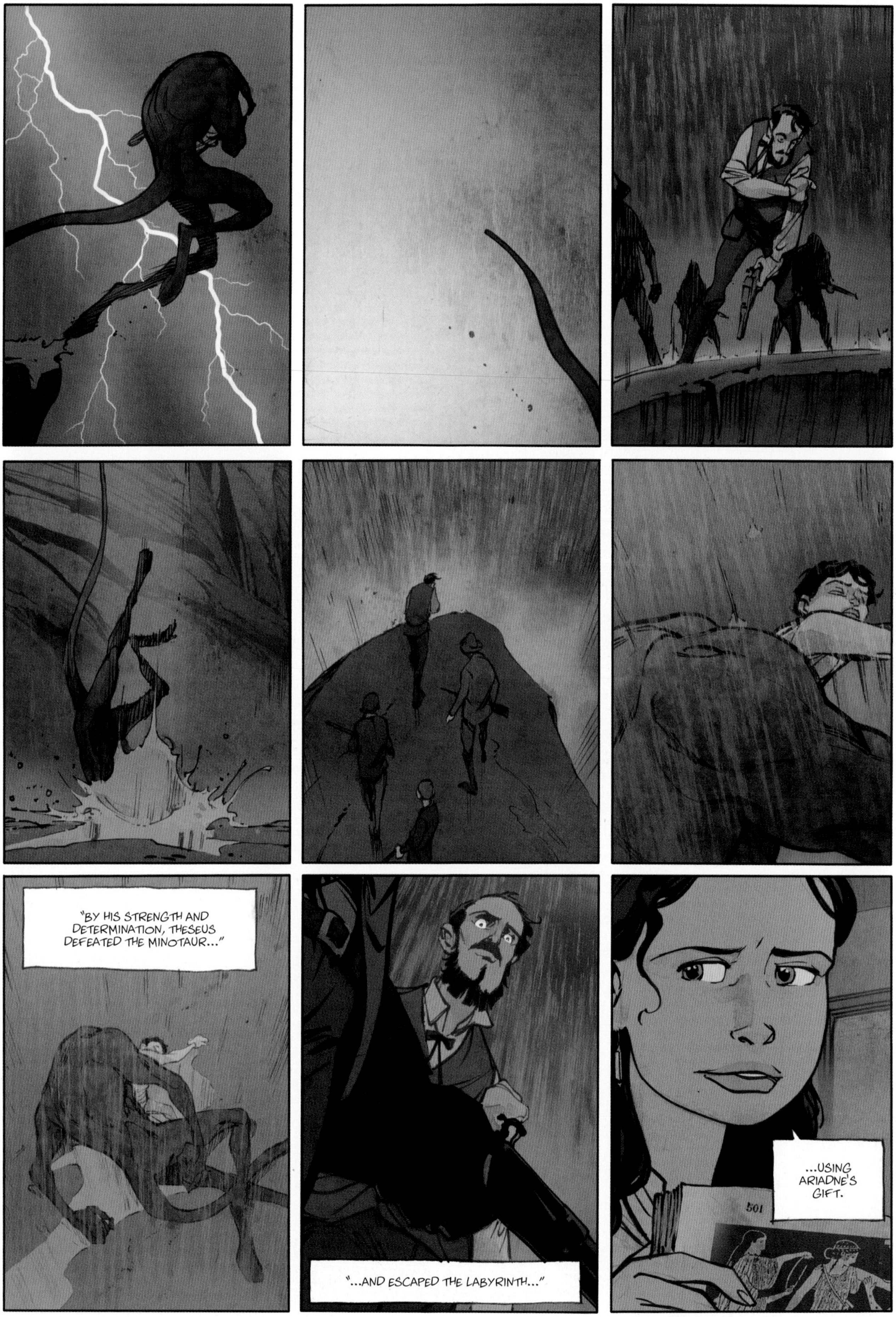
"BY HIS STRENGTH AND DETERMINATION, THESEUS DEFEATED THE MINOTAUR..."
"...AND ESCAPED THE LABYRINTH..."
...USING ARIADNE'S GIFT.
501

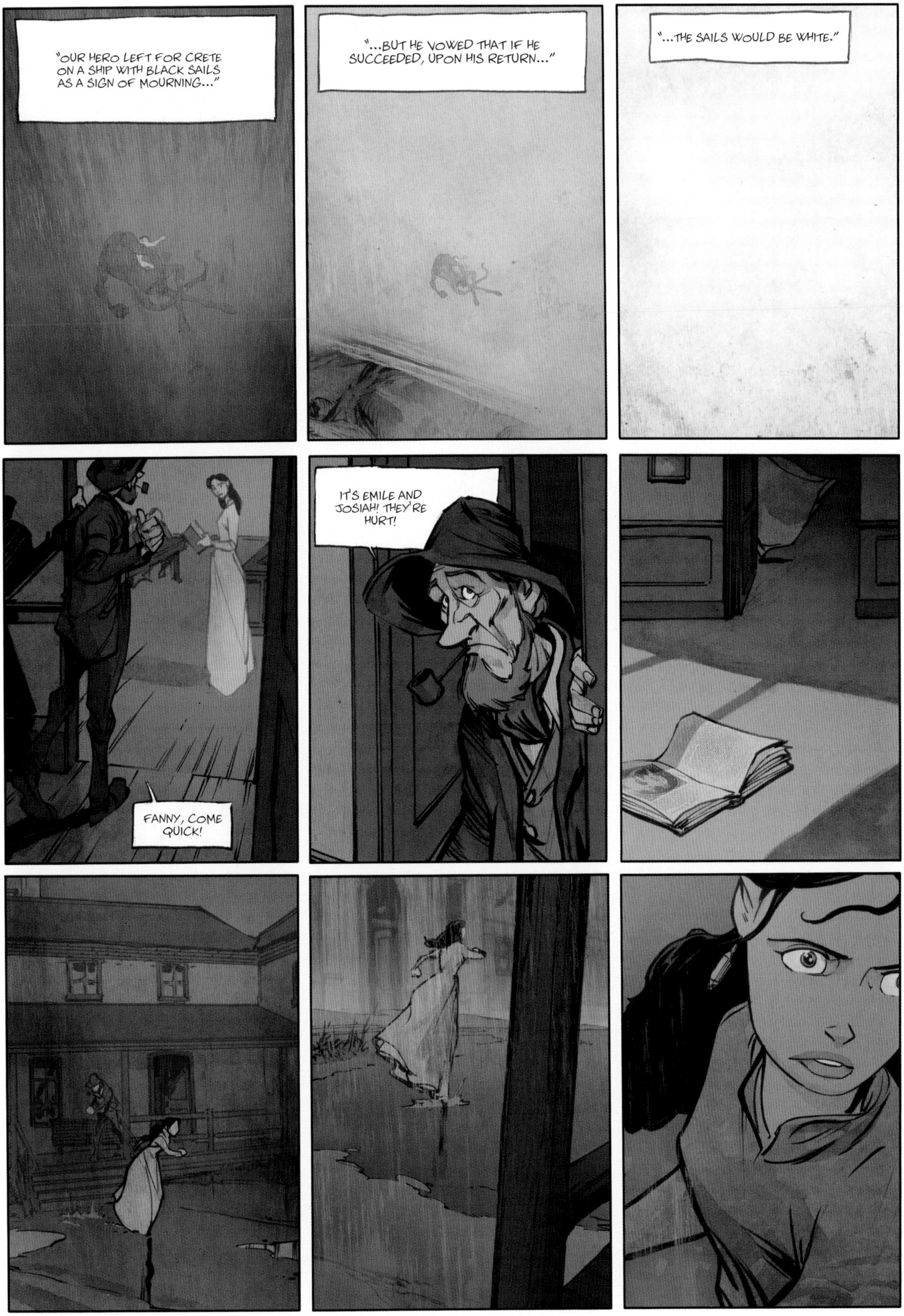
"OUR HERO LEFT FOR CRETE ON A SHIP WITH BLACK SAILS AS A SIGN OF MOURNING..."
"...BUT HE VOWED THAT IF HE SUCCEEDED, UPON HIS RETURN..."
"...THE SAILS WOULD BE WHITE."
FANNY, COME QUICK!
IT'S EMILE AND JOSIAH! THEY'RE HURT!

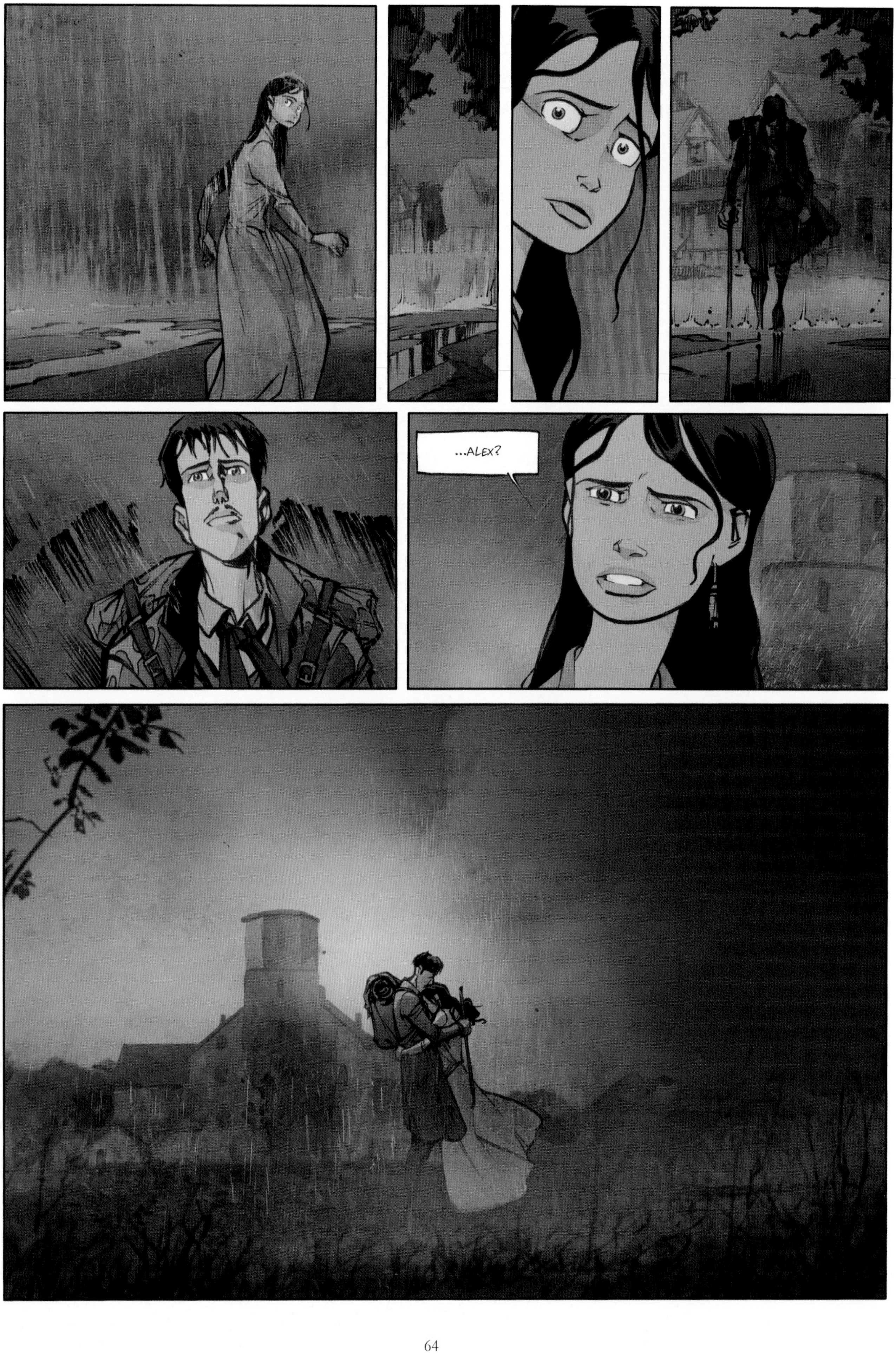
...ALEX?

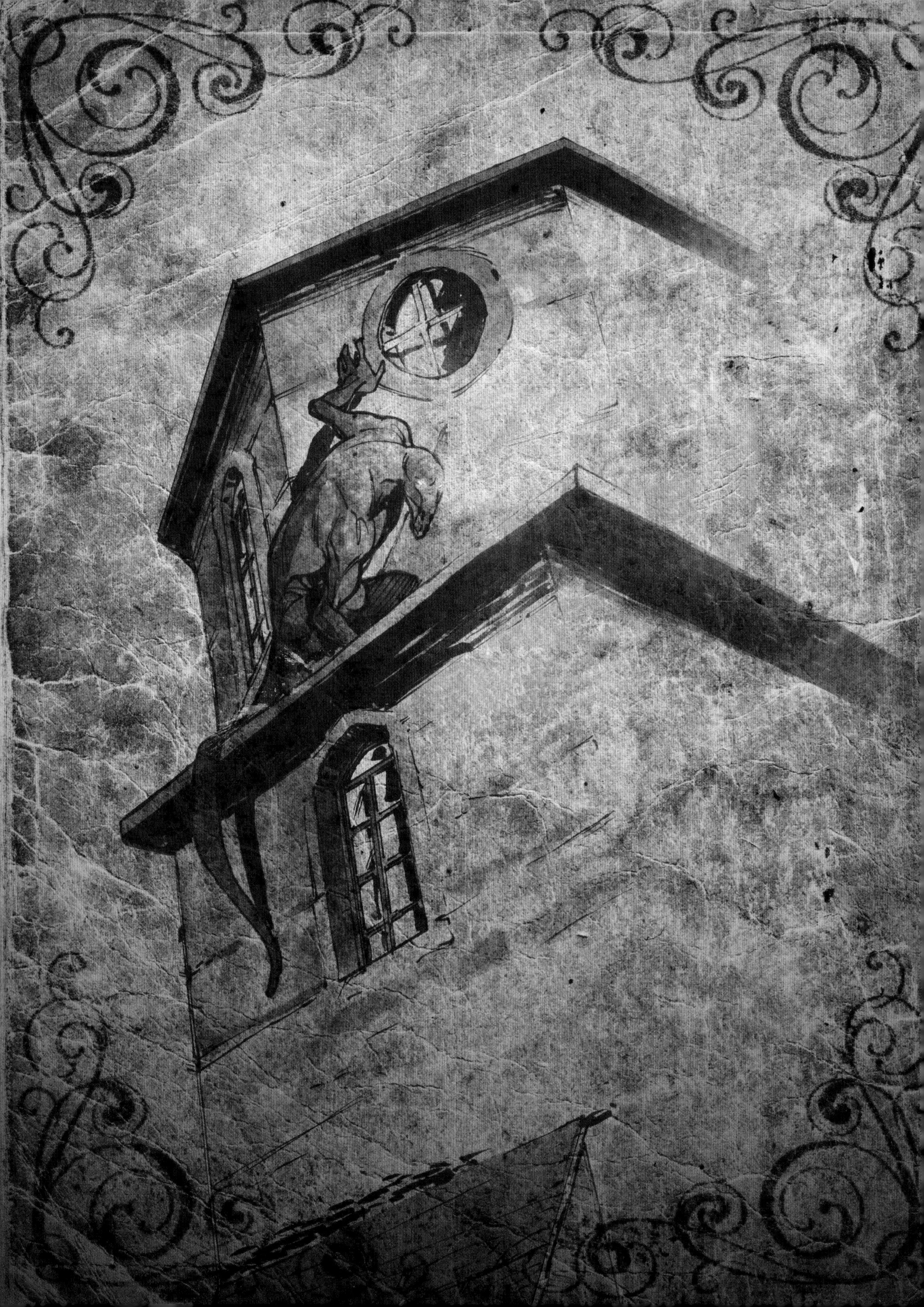

FRATERNITY

PART II

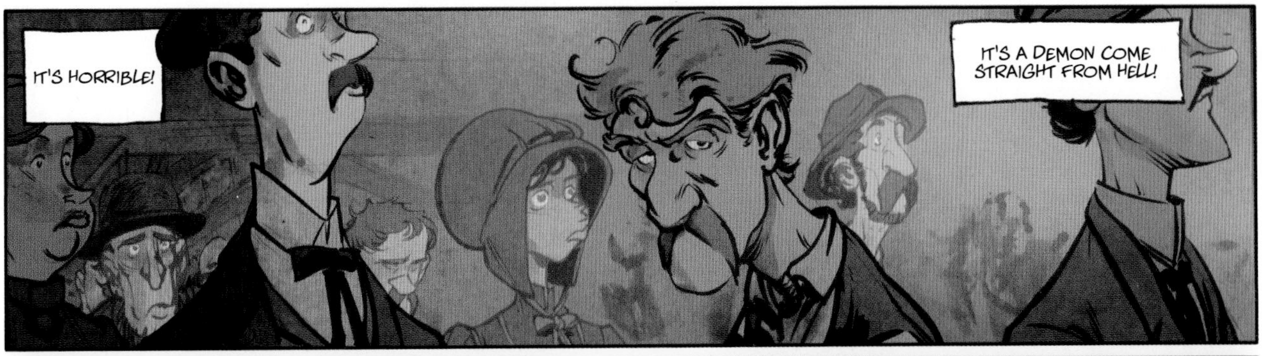
IT'S HORRIBLE!
IT'S A DEMON COME STRAIGHT FROM HELL!

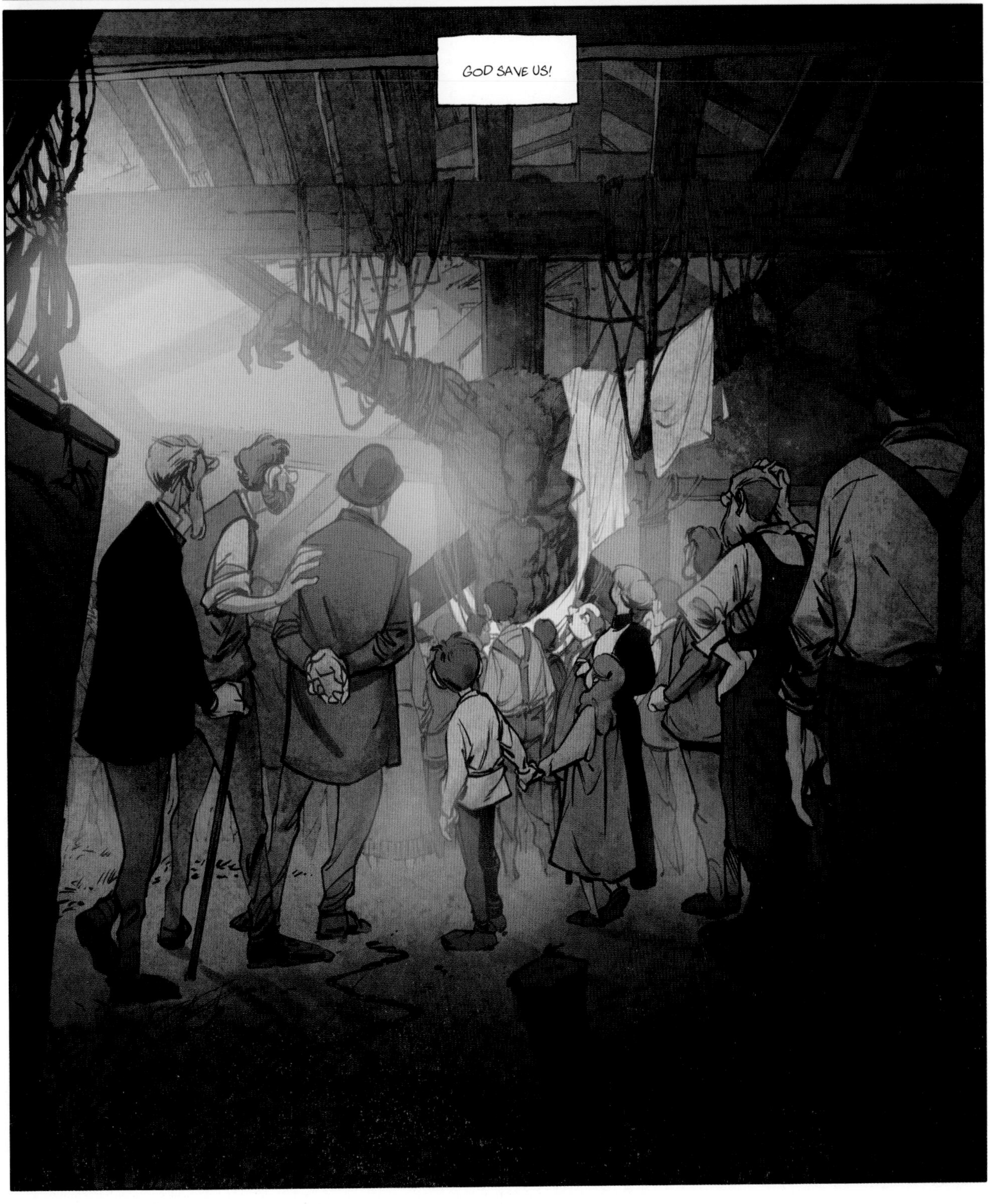
GOD SAVE US!

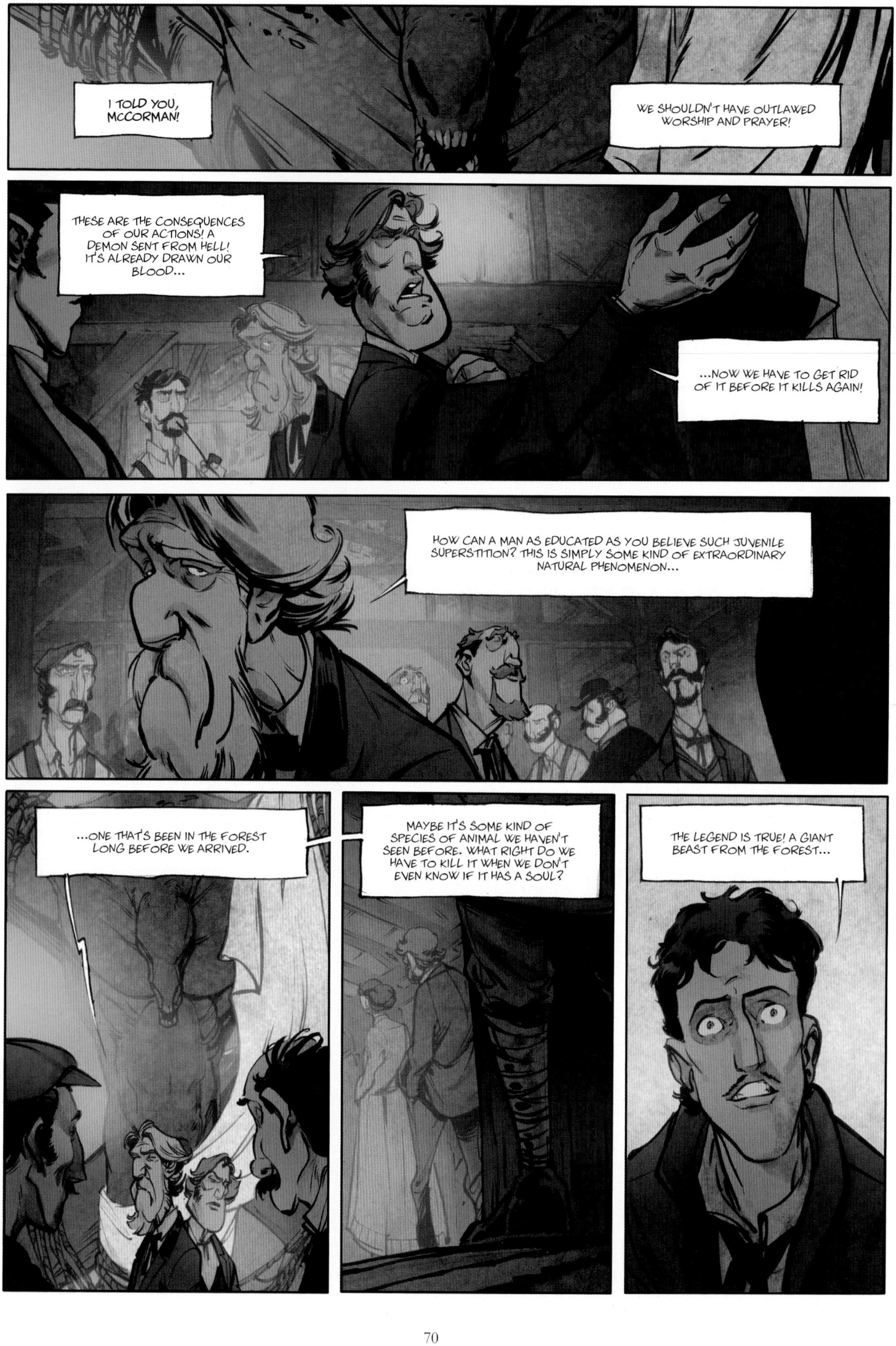

I TOLD YOU, MCCORMAN!
WE SHOULDN'T HAVE OUTLAWED WORSHIP AND PRAYER!
THESE ARE THE CONSEQUENCES OF OUR ACTIONS! A DEMON SENT FROM HELL! IT'S ALREADY DRAWN OUR BLOOD...
...NOW WE HAVE TO GET RID OF IT BEFORE IT KILLS AGAIN!
HOW CAN A MAN AS EDUCATED AS YOU BELIEVE SUCH JUVENILE SUPERSTITION? THIS IS SIMPLY SOME KIND OF EXTRAORDINARY NATURAL PHENOMENON...
...ONE THAT'S BEEN IN THE FOREST LONG BEFORE WE ARRIVED.
MAYBE IT'S SOME KIND OF SPECIES OF ANIMAL WE HAVEN'T SEEN BEFORE. WHAT RIGHT DO WE HAVE TO KILL IT WHEN WE DON'T EVEN KNOW IF IT HAS A SOUL?
THE LEGEND IS TRUE! A GIANT BEAST FROM THE FOREST...

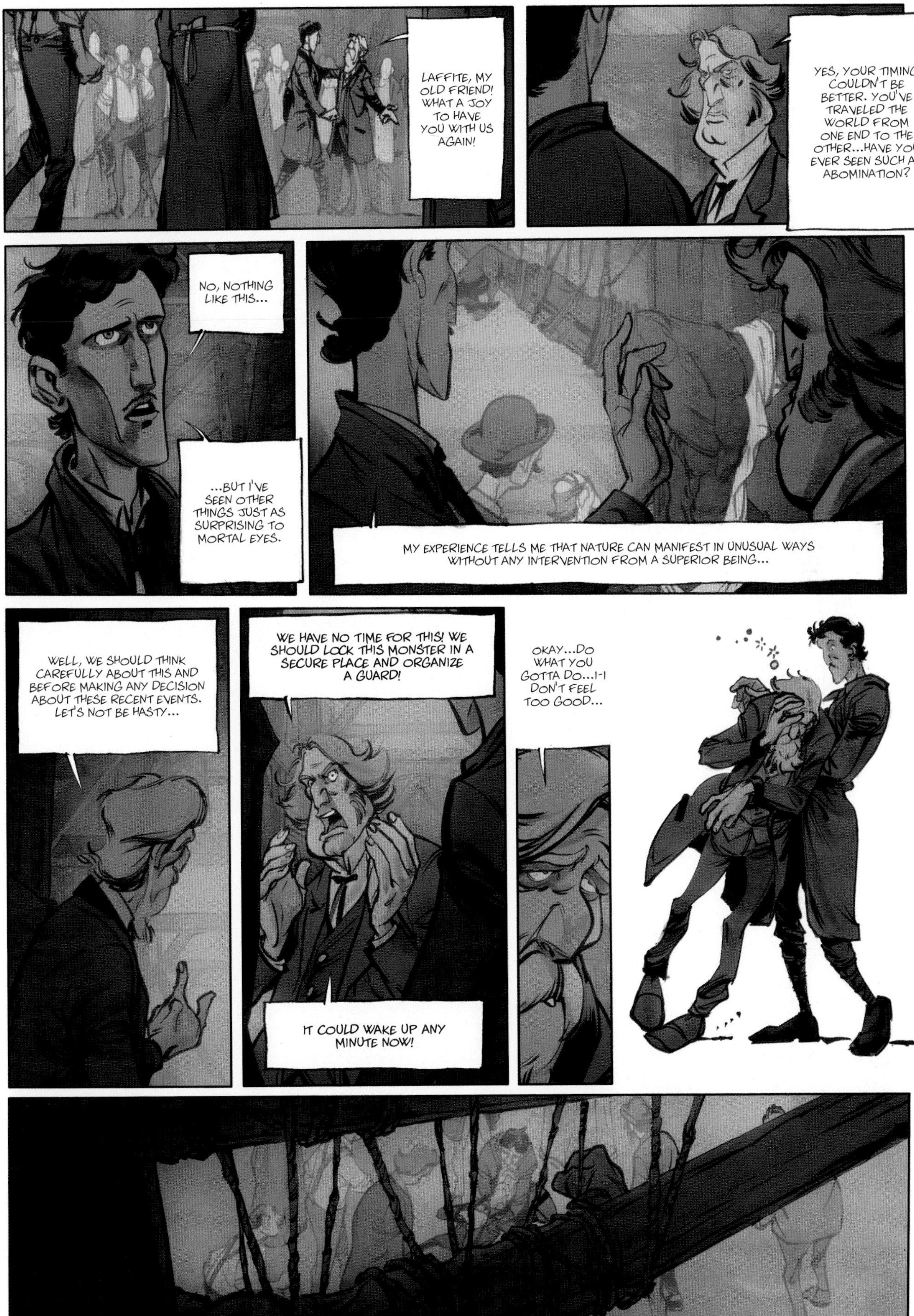
LAFFITE, MY OLD FRIEND! WHAT A JOY TO HAVE YOU WITH US AGAIN!
YES, YOUR TIMING COULDN'T BE BETTER. YOU'VE TRAVELED THE WORLD FROM ONE END TO THE OTHER...HAVE YOU EVER SEEN SUCH AN ABOMINATION?
NO, NOTHING LIKE THIS...
...BUT I'VE SEEN OTHER THINGS JUST AS SURPRISING TO MORTAL EYES.
MY EXPERIENCE TELLS ME THAT NATURE CAN MANIFEST IN UNUSUAL WAYS WITHOUT ANY INTERVENTION FROM A SUPERIOR BEING...
WELL, WE SHOULD THINK CAREFULLY ABOUT THIS AND BEFORE MAKING ANY DECISION ABOUT THESE RECENT EVENTS. LET'S NOT BE HASTY...
WE HAVE NO TIME FOR THIS! WE SHOULD LOCK THIS MONSTER IN A SECURE PLACE AND ORGANIZE A GUARD!
IT COULD WAKE UP ANY MINUTE NOW!
OKAY...DO WHAT YOU GOTTA DO...I-I DON'T FEEL TOO GOOD...

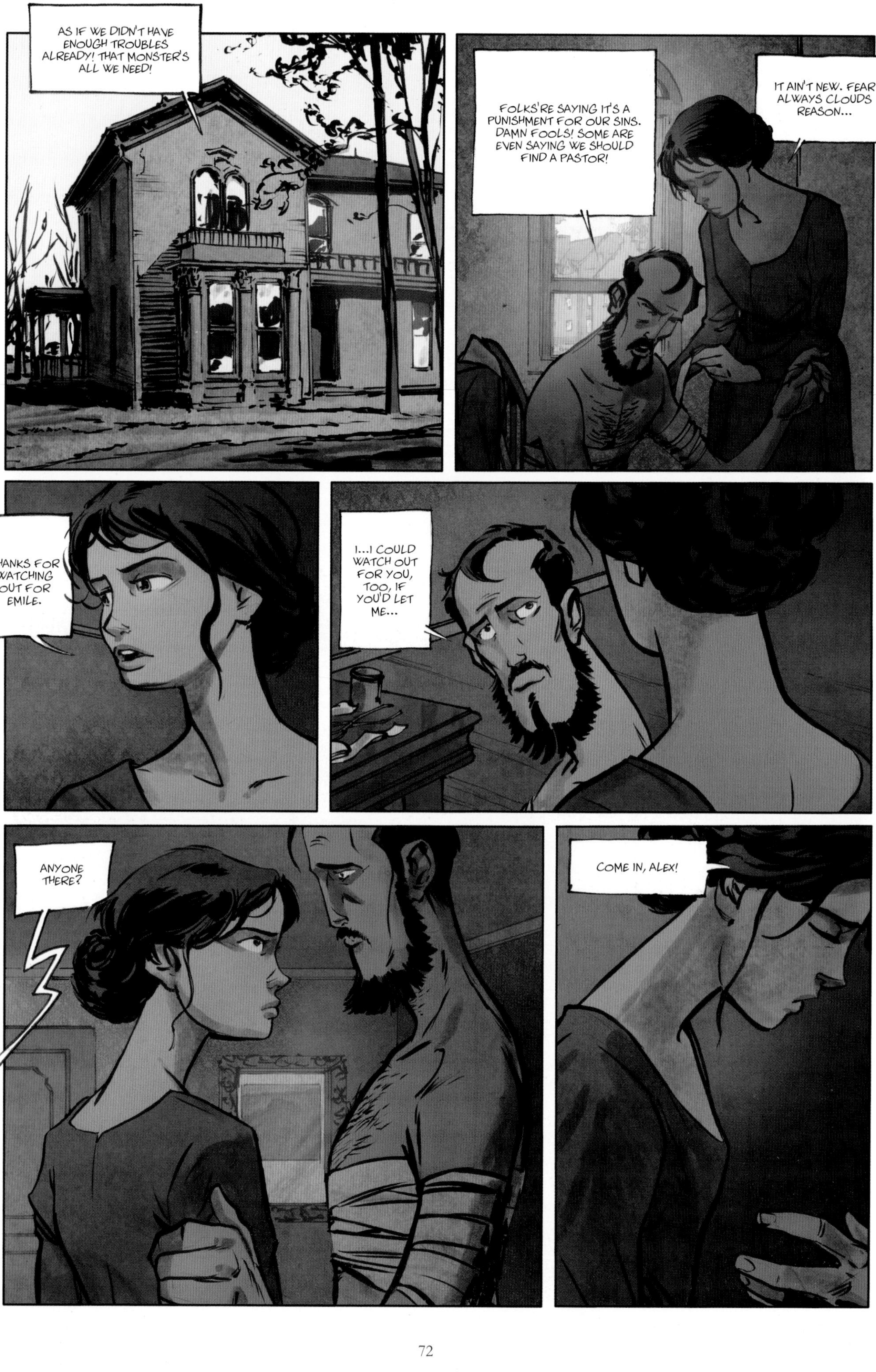
AS IF WE DIDN'T HAVE ENOUGH TROUBLES ALREADY! THAT MONSTER'S ALL WE NEED!
FOLKS'RE SAYING IT'S A PUNISHMENT FOR OUR SINS. DAMN FOOLS! SOME ARE EVEN SAYING WE SHOULD FIND A PASTOR!
IT AIN'T NEW. FEAR ALWAYS CLOUDS REASON...
THANKS FOR WATCHING OUT FOR EMILE.
I...I COULD WATCH OUT FOR YOU, TOO, IF YOU'D LET ME...
ANYONE THERE?
COME IN, ALEX!

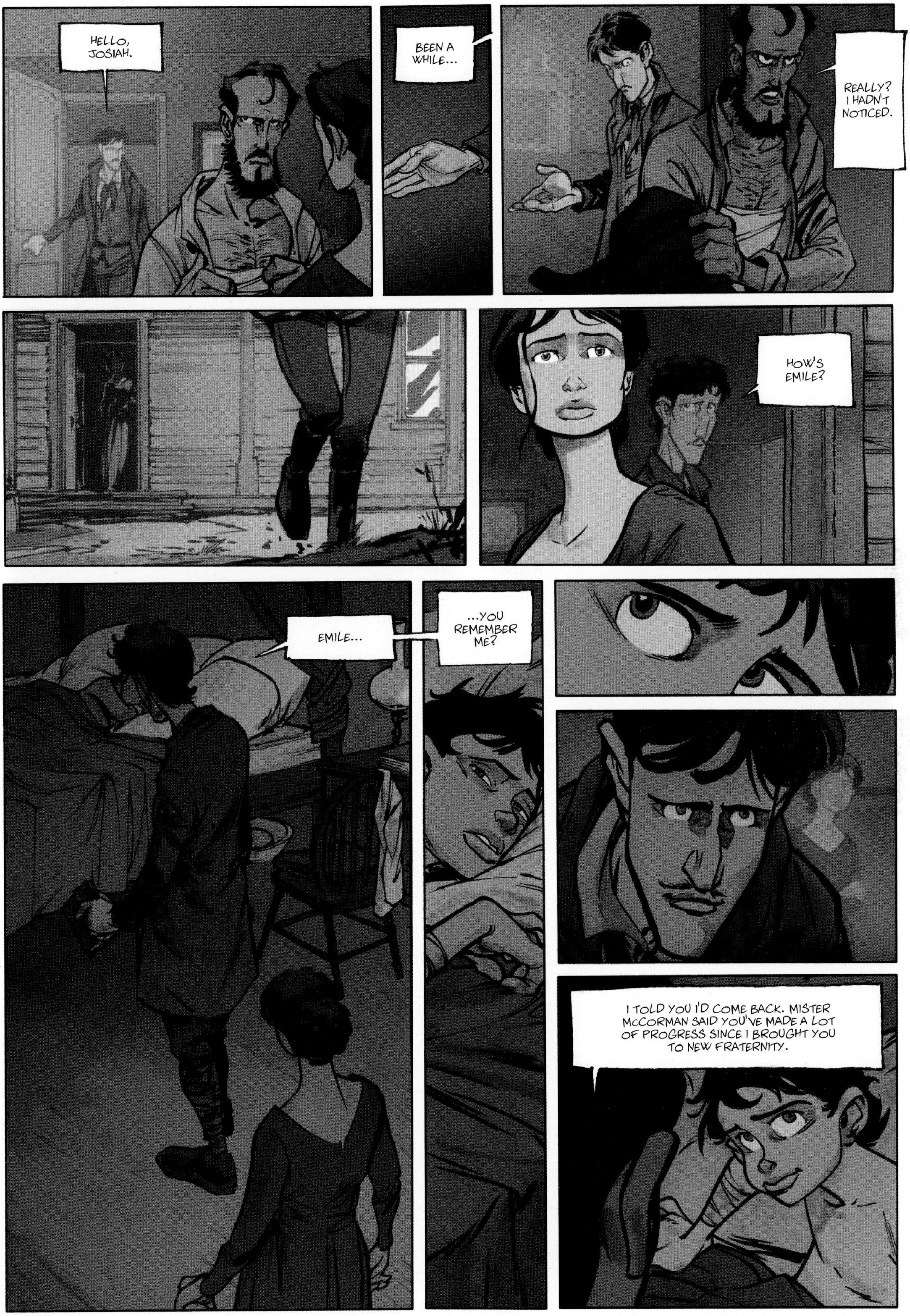
HELLO, JOSIAH.
BEEN A WHILE...
REALLY? I HADN'T NOTICED.
HOW'S EMILE?
EMILE...
...YOU REMEMBER ME?
I TOLD YOU I'D COME BACK. MISTER McCORMAN SAID YOU'VE MADE A LOT OF PROGRESS SINCE I BROUGHT YOU TO NEW FRATERNITY.

HERE. FOR YOU.

Troglodytes Gorilla

IT'S FULL OF PICTURES AND DESCRIPTIONS OF ALL THE PLACES I VISITED SINCE I WENT AWAY...

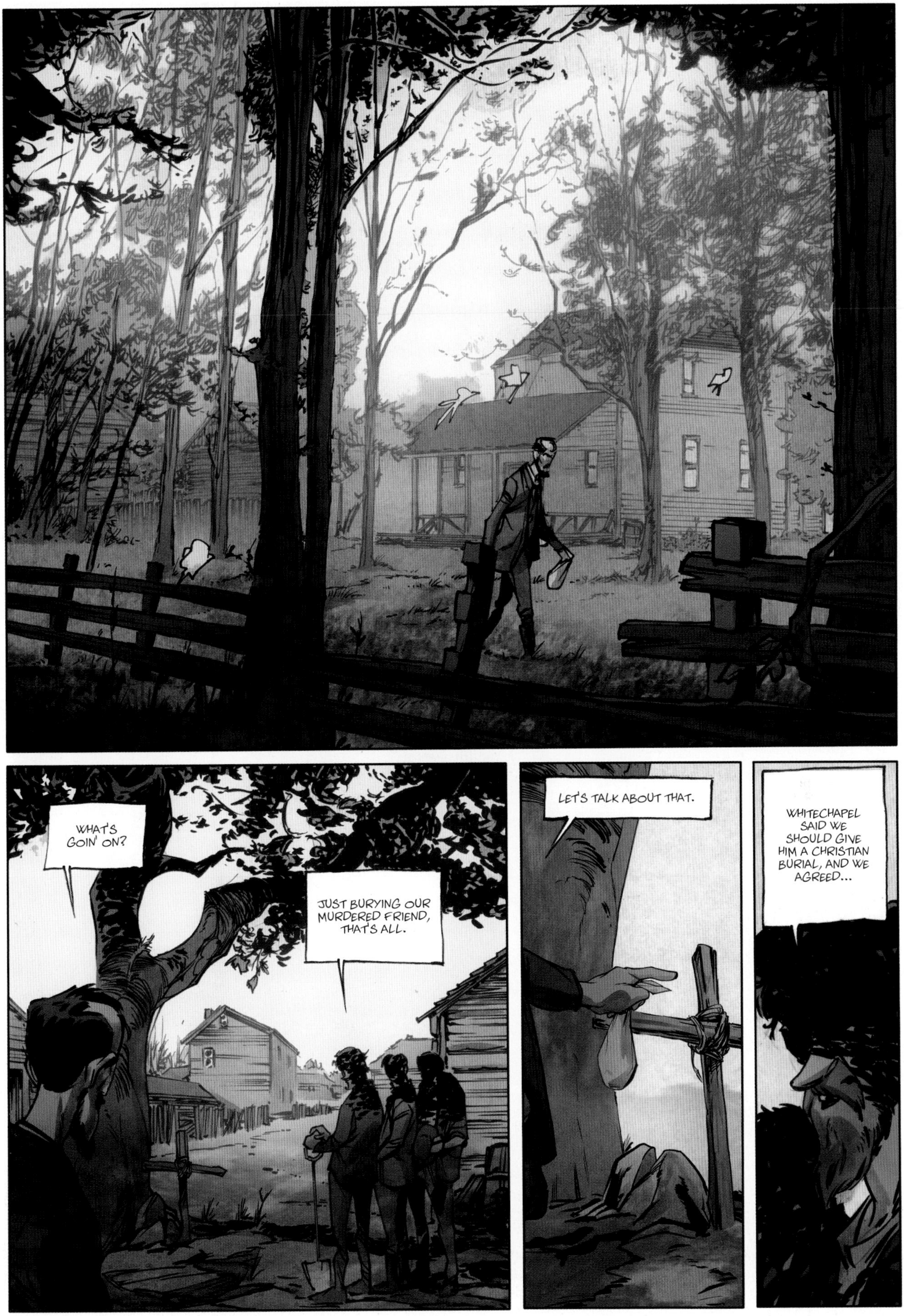
WHAT'S GOIN' ON?
JUST BURYING OUR MURDERED FRIEND, THAT'S ALL.
LET'S TALK ABOUT THAT.
WHITECHAPEL SAID WE SHOULD GIVE HIM A CHRISTIAN BURIAL, AND WE AGREED...

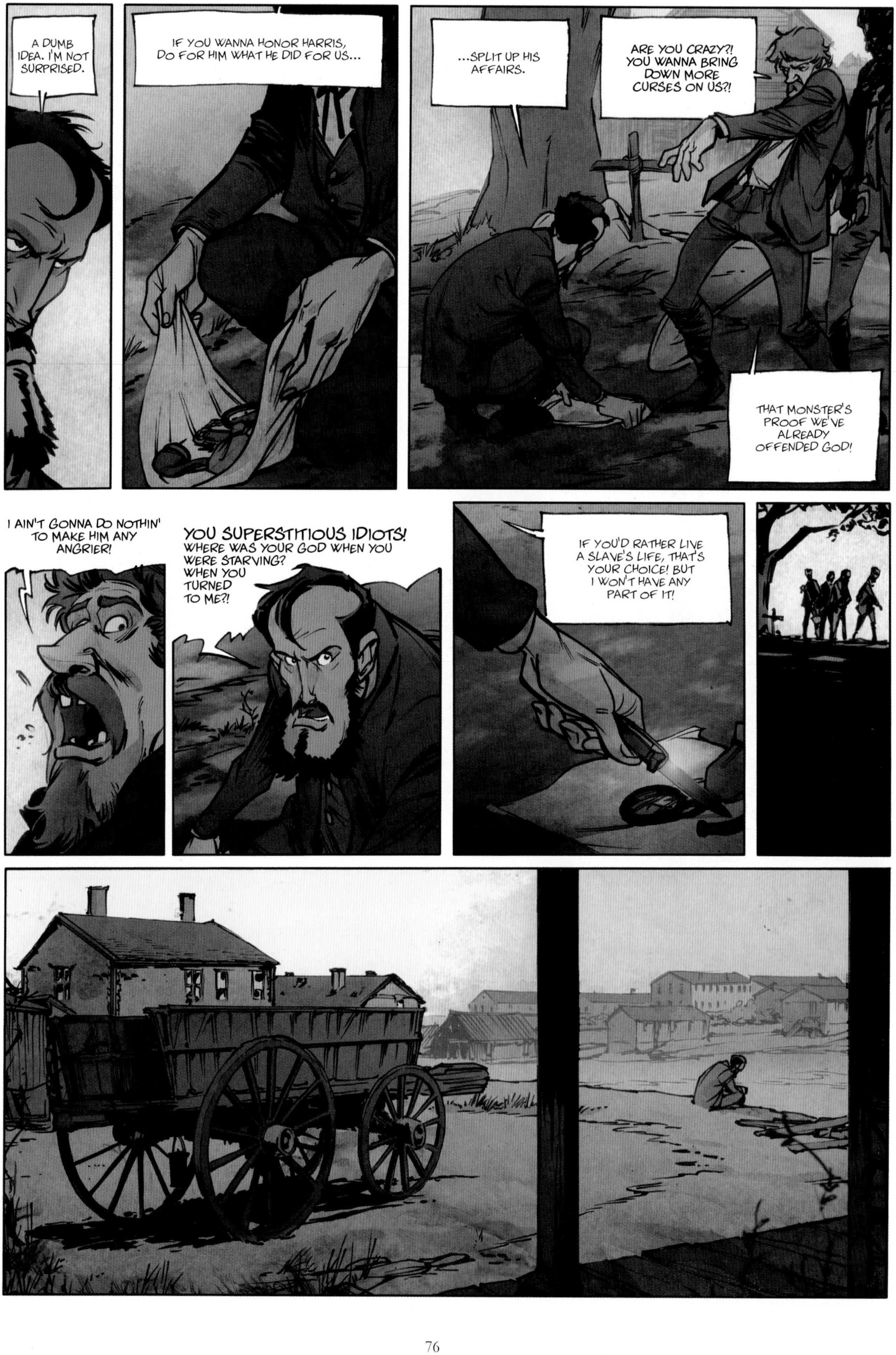
A DUMB IDEA. I'M NOT SURPRISED.
IF YOU WANNA HONOR HARRIS, DO FOR HIM WHAT HE DID FOR US...
...SPLIT UP HIS AFFAIRS.
ARE YOU CRAZY?! YOU WANNA BRING DOWN MORE CURSES ON US?!
THAT MONSTER'S PROOF WE'VE ALREADY OFFENDED GOD!
I AIN'T GONNA DO NOTHIN' TO MAKE HIM ANY ANGRIER!
YOU SUPERSTITIOUS IDIOTS! WHERE WAS YOUR GOD WHEN YOU WERE STARVING? WHEN YOU TURNED TO ME?!
IF YOU'D RATHER LIVE A SLAVE'S LIFE, THAT'S YOUR CHOICE! BUT I WON'T HAVE ANY PART OF IT!

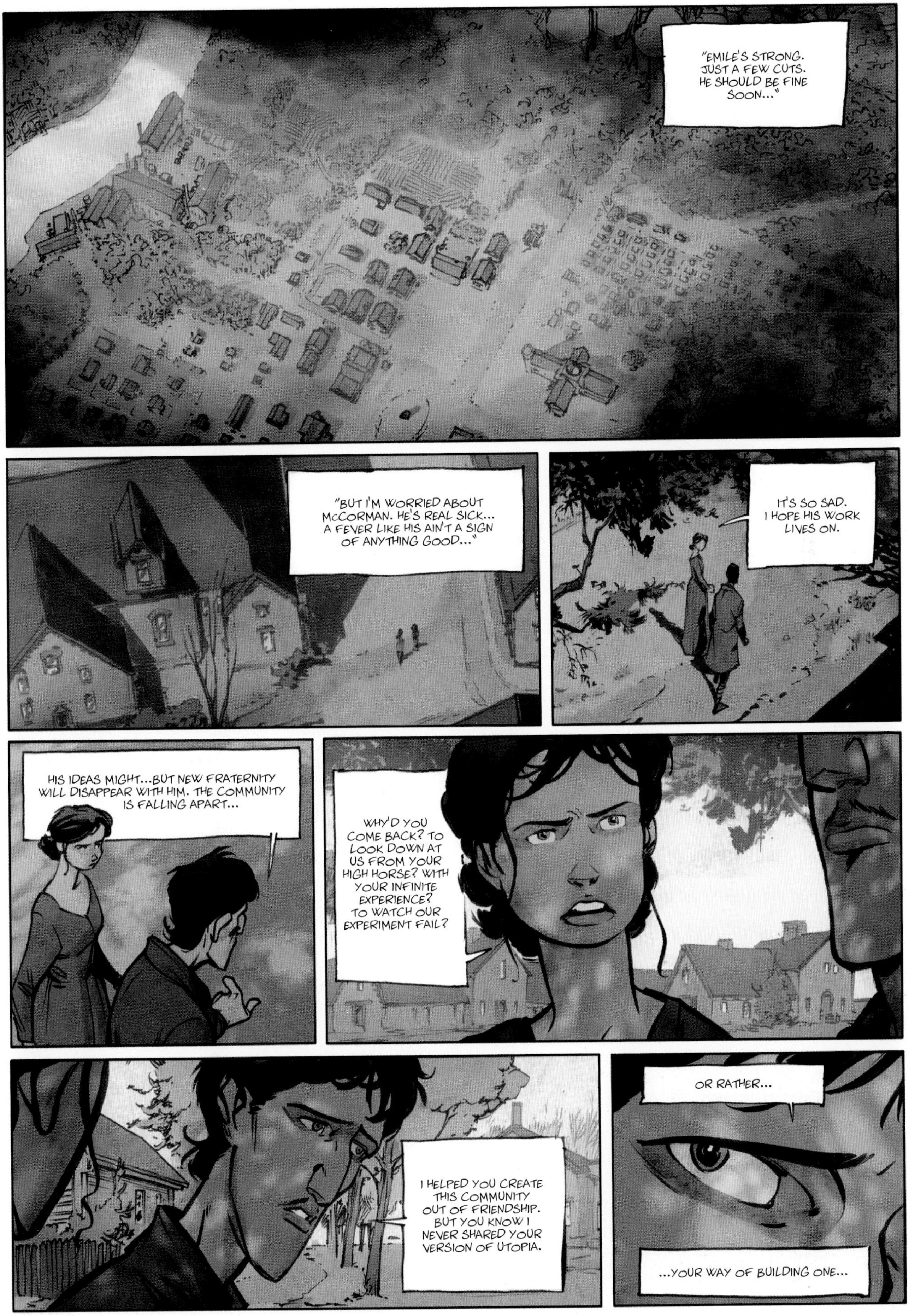
"EMILE'S STRONG. JUST A FEW CUTS. HE SHOULD BE FINE SOON..."
"BUT I'M WORRIED ABOUT McCORMAN. HE'S REAL SICK... A FEVER LIKE HIS AIN'T A SIGN OF ANYTHING GOOD..."
IT'S SO SAD. I HOPE HIS WORK LIVES ON.
HIS IDEAS MIGHT...BUT NEW FRATERNITY WILL DISAPPEAR WITH HIM. THE COMMUNITY IS FALLING APART...
WHY'D YOU COME BACK? TO LOOK DOWN AT US FROM YOUR HIGH HORSE? WITH YOUR INFINITE EXPERIENCE? TO WATCH OUR EXPERIMENT FAIL?
I HELPED YOU CREATE THIS COMMUNITY OUT OF FRIENDSHIP. BUT YOU KNOW I NEVER SHARED YOUR VERSION OF UTOPIA.
OR RATHER...
...YOUR WAY OF BUILDING ONE...

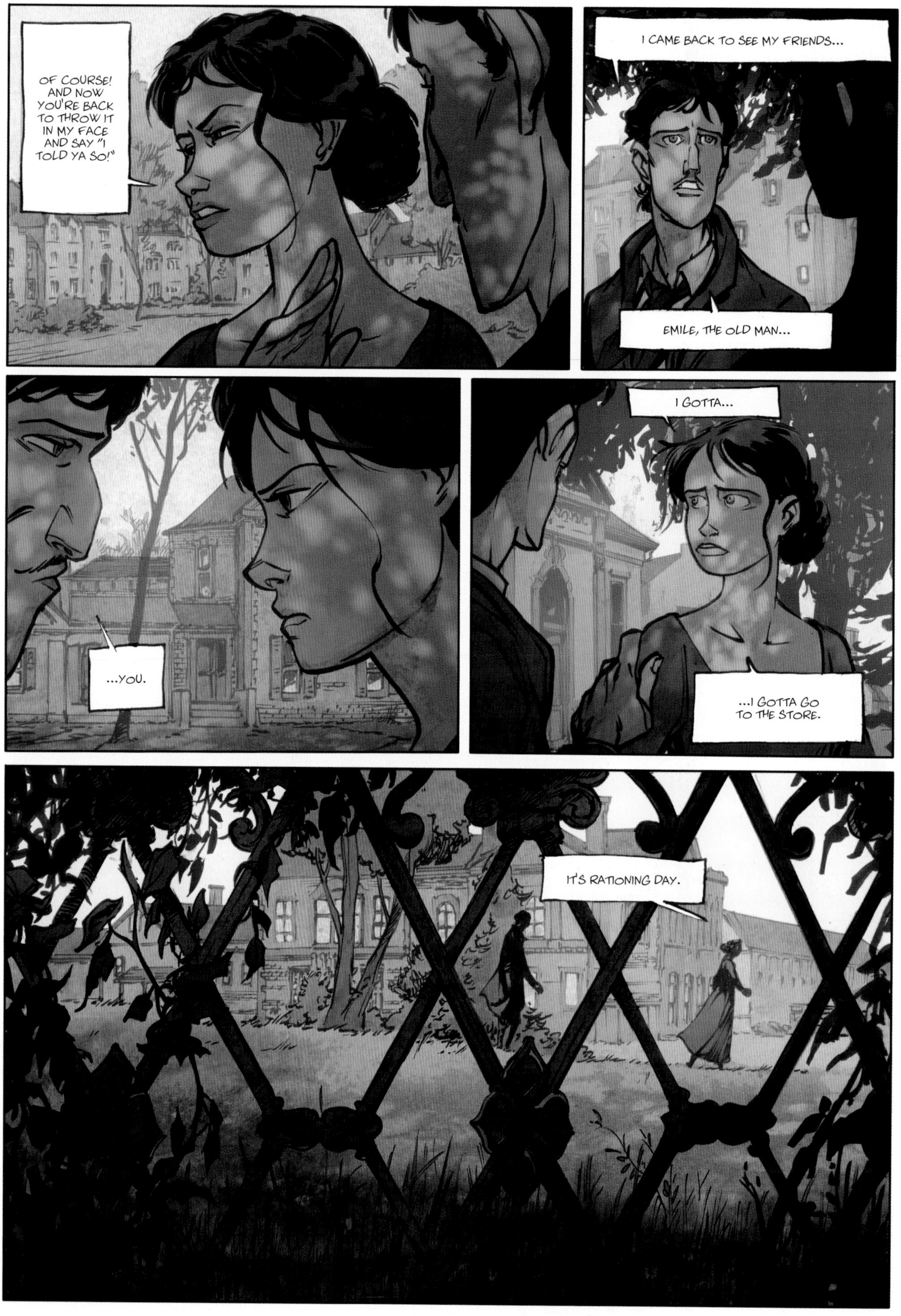

OF COURSE! AND NOW YOU'RE BACK TO THROW IT IN MY FACE AND SAY "I TOLD YA SO!"
I CAME BACK TO SEE MY FRIENDS...
EMILE, THE OLD MAN...
...YOU.
I GOTTA...
...I GOTTA GO TO THE STORE.
IT'S RATIONING DAY.

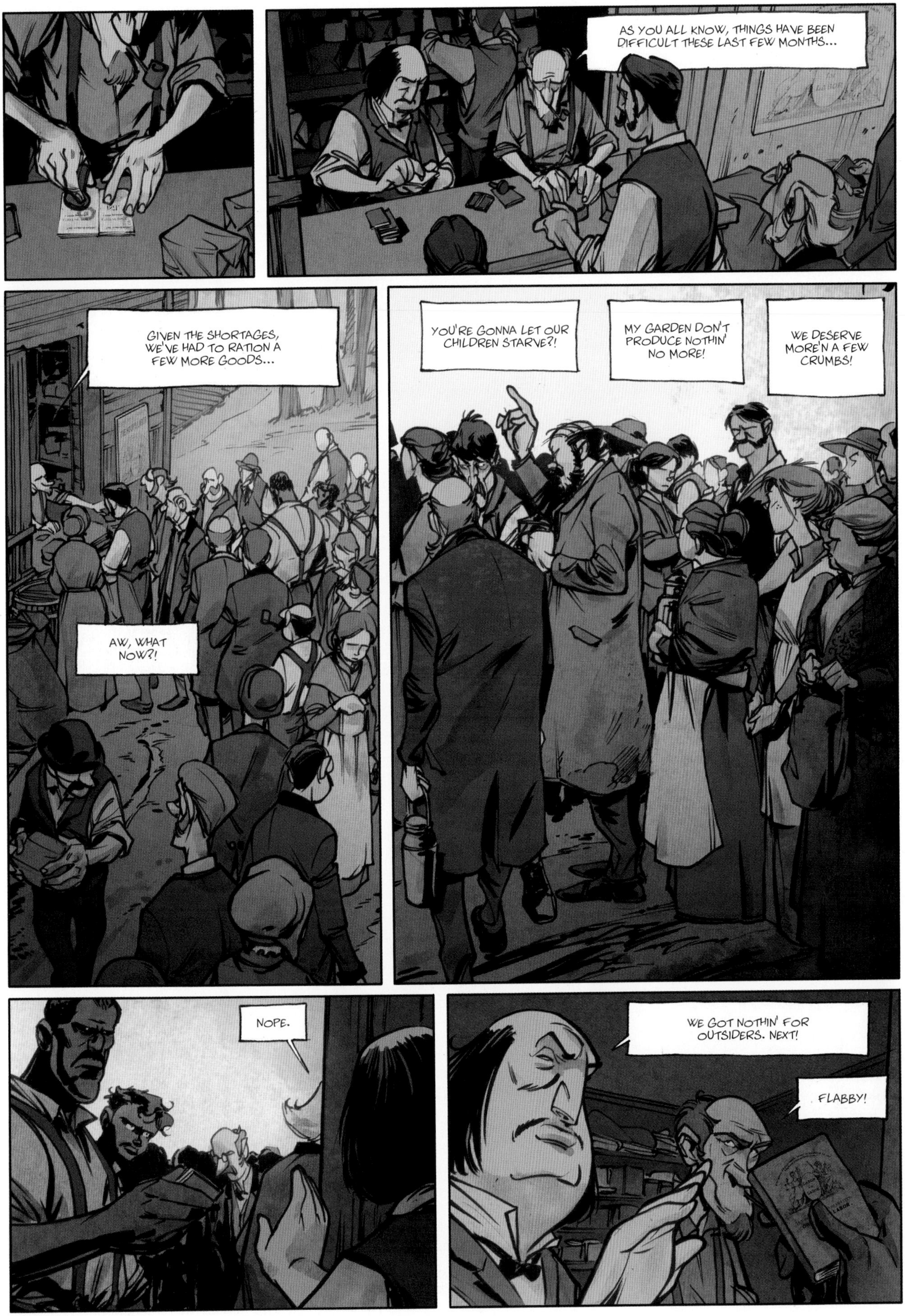
AS YOU ALL KNOW, THINGS HAVE BEEN DIFFICULT THESE LAST FEW MONTHS...
GIVEN THE SHORTAGES, WE'VE HAD TO RATION A FEW MORE GOODS...
AW, WHAT NOW?!
YOU'RE GONNA LET OUR CHILDREN STARVE?!
MY GARDEN DON'T PRODUCE NOTHIN' NO MORE!
WE DESERVE MORE'N A FEW CRUMBS!
NOPE.
WE GOT NOTHIN' FOR OUTSIDERS. NEXT!
FLABBY!

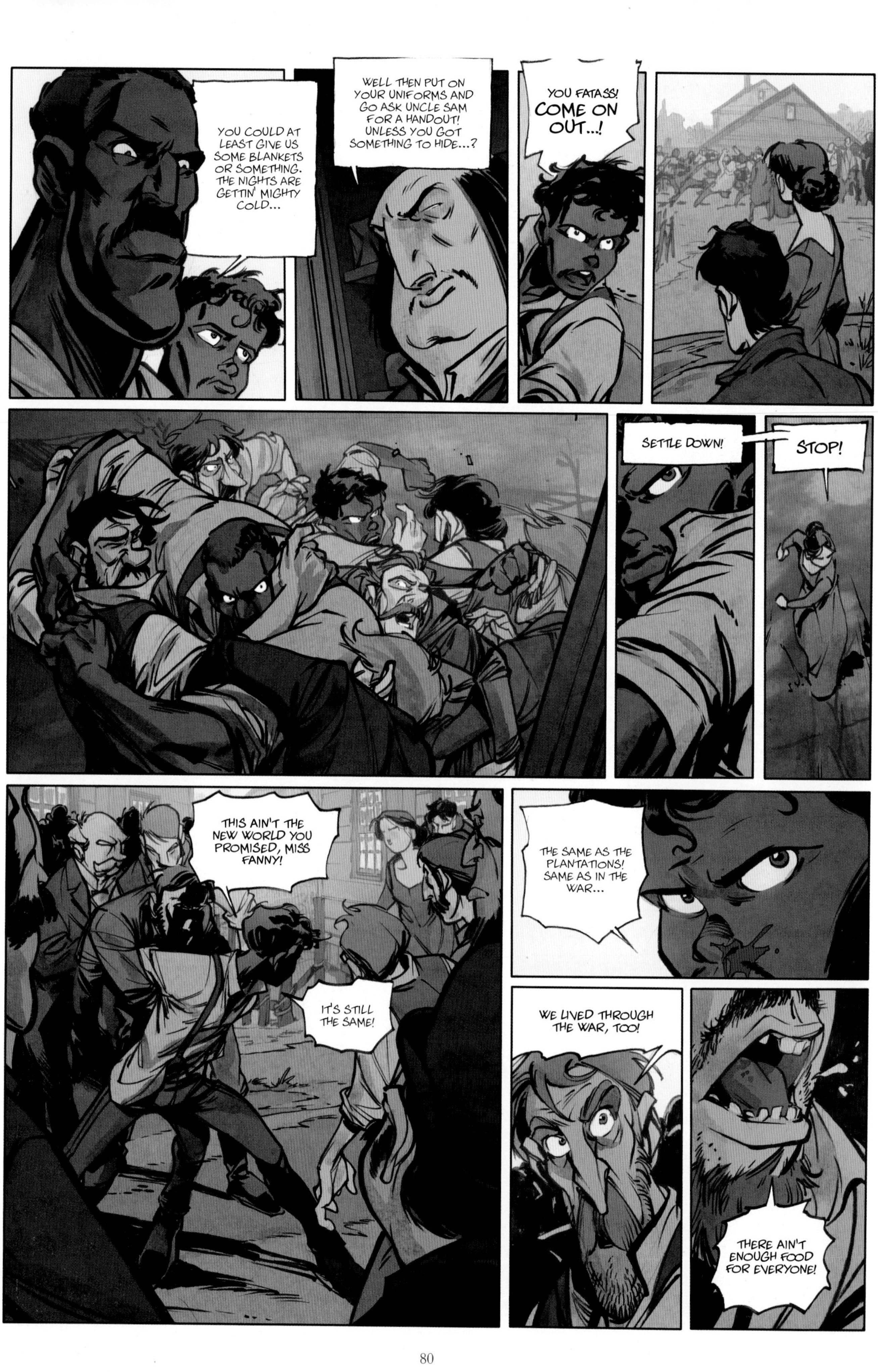
YOU COULD AT LEAST GIVE US SOME BLANKETS OR SOMETHING. THE NIGHTS ARE GETTIN' MIGHTY COLD...
WELL THEN PUT ON YOUR UNIFORMS AND GO ASK UNCLE SAM FOR A HANDOUT! UNLESS YOU GOT SOMETHING TO HIDE...?
YOU FATASS! COME ON OUT...!
SETTLE DOWN!
STOP!
THIS AIN'T THE NEW WORLD YOU PROMISED, MISS FANNY!
IT'S STILL THE SAME!
THE SAME AS THE PLANTATIONS! SAME AS IN THE WAR...
WE LIVED THROUGH THE WAR, TOO!
THERE AIN'T ENOUGH FOOD FOR EVERYONE!

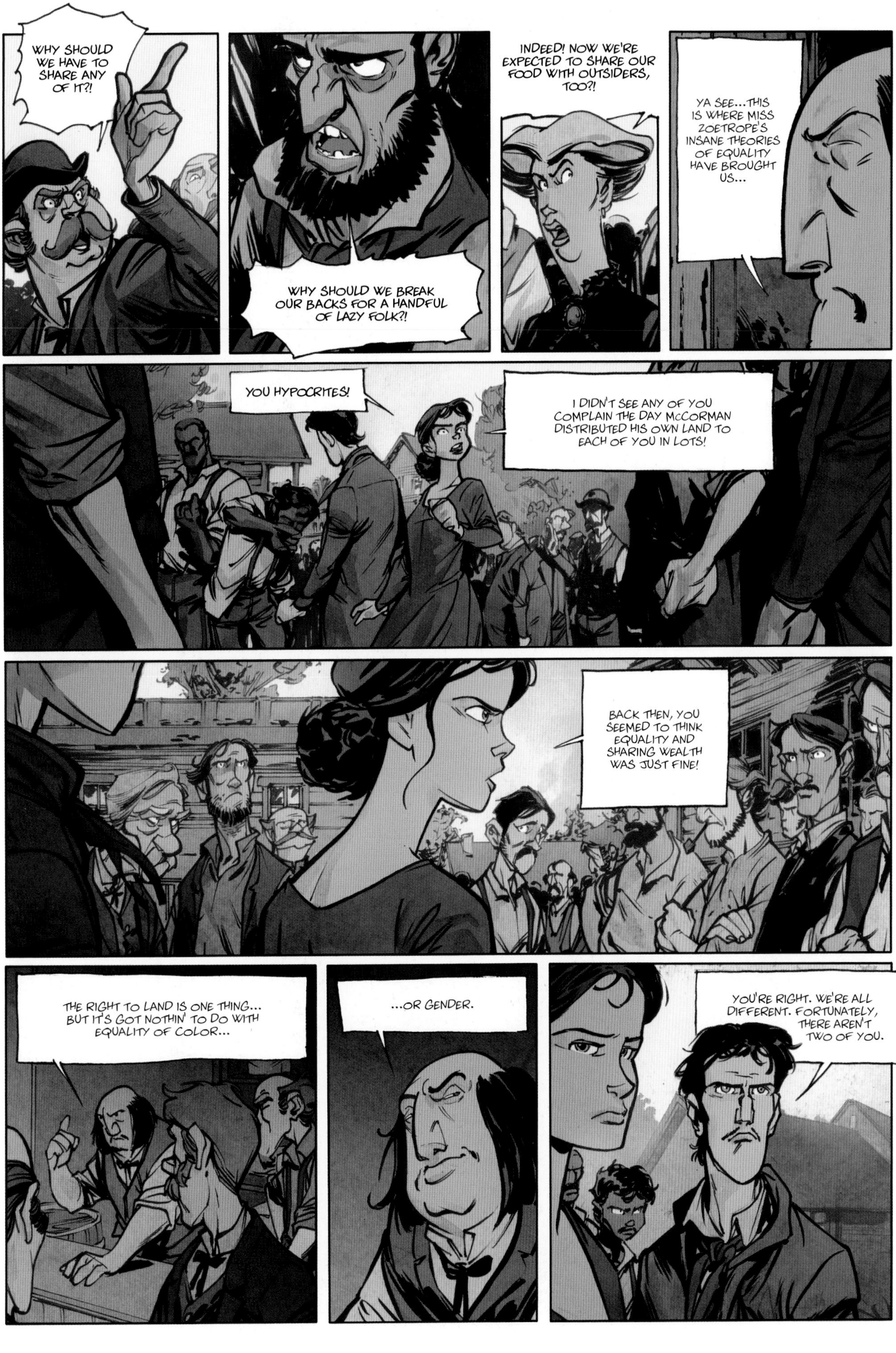
WHY SHOULD WE HAVE TO SHARE ANY OF IT?!
WHY SHOULD WE BREAK OUR BACKS FOR A HANDFUL OF LAZY FOLK?!
INDEED! NOW WE'RE EXPECTED TO SHARE OUR FOOD WITH OUTSIDERS, TOO?!
YA SEE... THIS IS WHERE MISS ZOETROPE'S INSANE THEORIES OF EQUALITY HAVE BROUGHT US...
YOU HYPOCRITES!
I DIDN'T SEE ANY OF YOU COMPLAIN THE DAY McCORMAN DISTRIBUTED HIS OWN LAND TO EACH OF YOU IN LOTS!
BACK THEN, YOU SEEMED TO THINK EQUALITY AND SHARING WEALTH WAS JUST FINE!
THE RIGHT TO LAND IS ONE THING... BUT IT'S GOT NOTHIN' TO DO WITH EQUALITY OF COLOR...
...OR GENDER.
YOU'RE RIGHT. WE'RE ALL DIFFERENT. FORTUNATELY, THERE AREN'T TWO OF YOU.

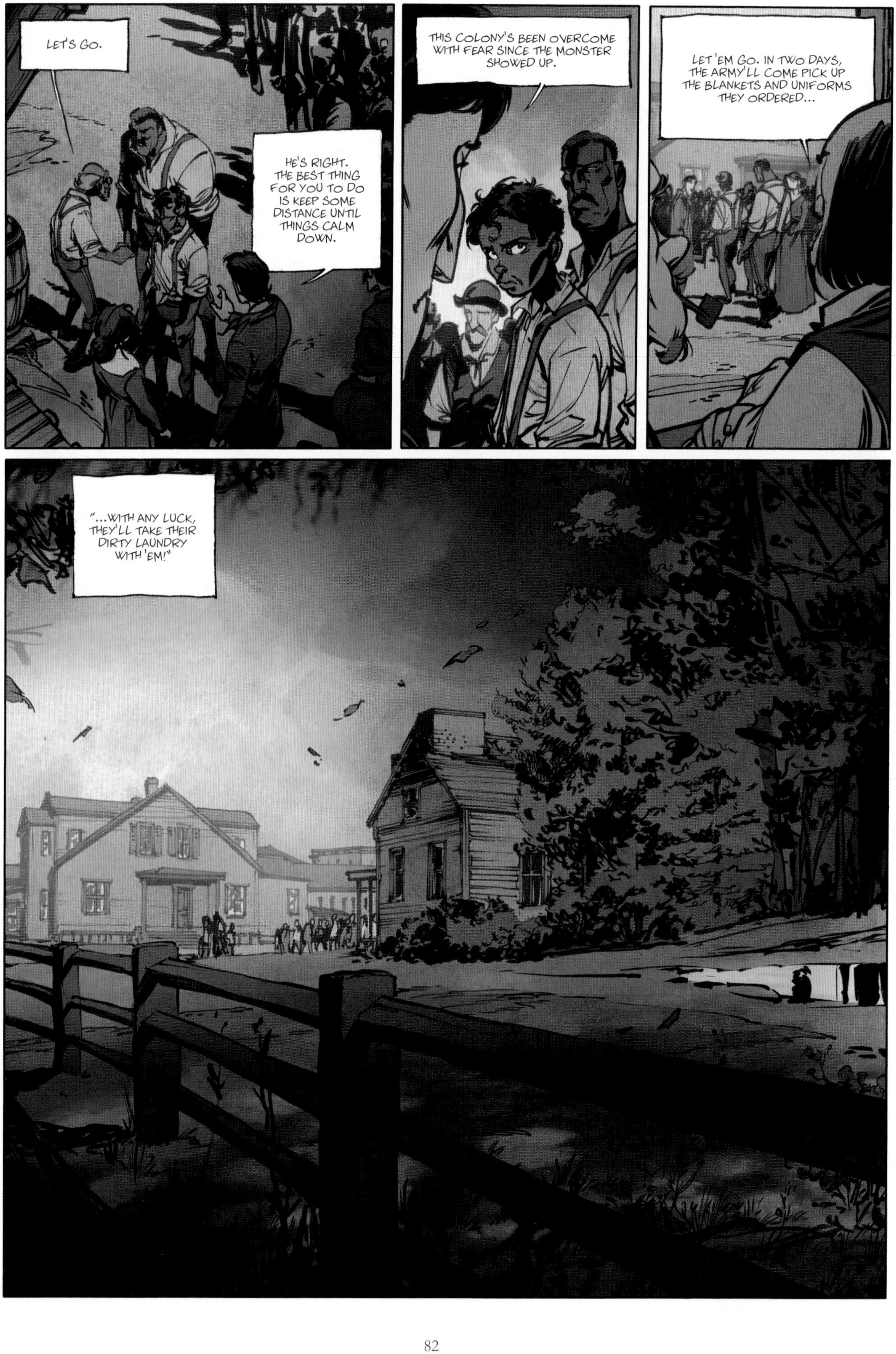
LET'S GO.
HE'S RIGHT. THE BEST THING FOR YOU TO DO IS KEEP SOME DISTANCE UNTIL THINGS CALM DOWN.
THIS COLONY'S BEEN OVERCOME WITH FEAR SINCE THE MONSTER SHOWED UP.
LET 'EM GO. IN TWO DAYS, THE ARMY'LL COME PICK UP THE BLANKETS AND UNIFORMS THEY ORDERED...
"...WITH ANY LUCK, THEY'LL TAKE THEIR DIRTY LAUNDRY WITH 'EM!"

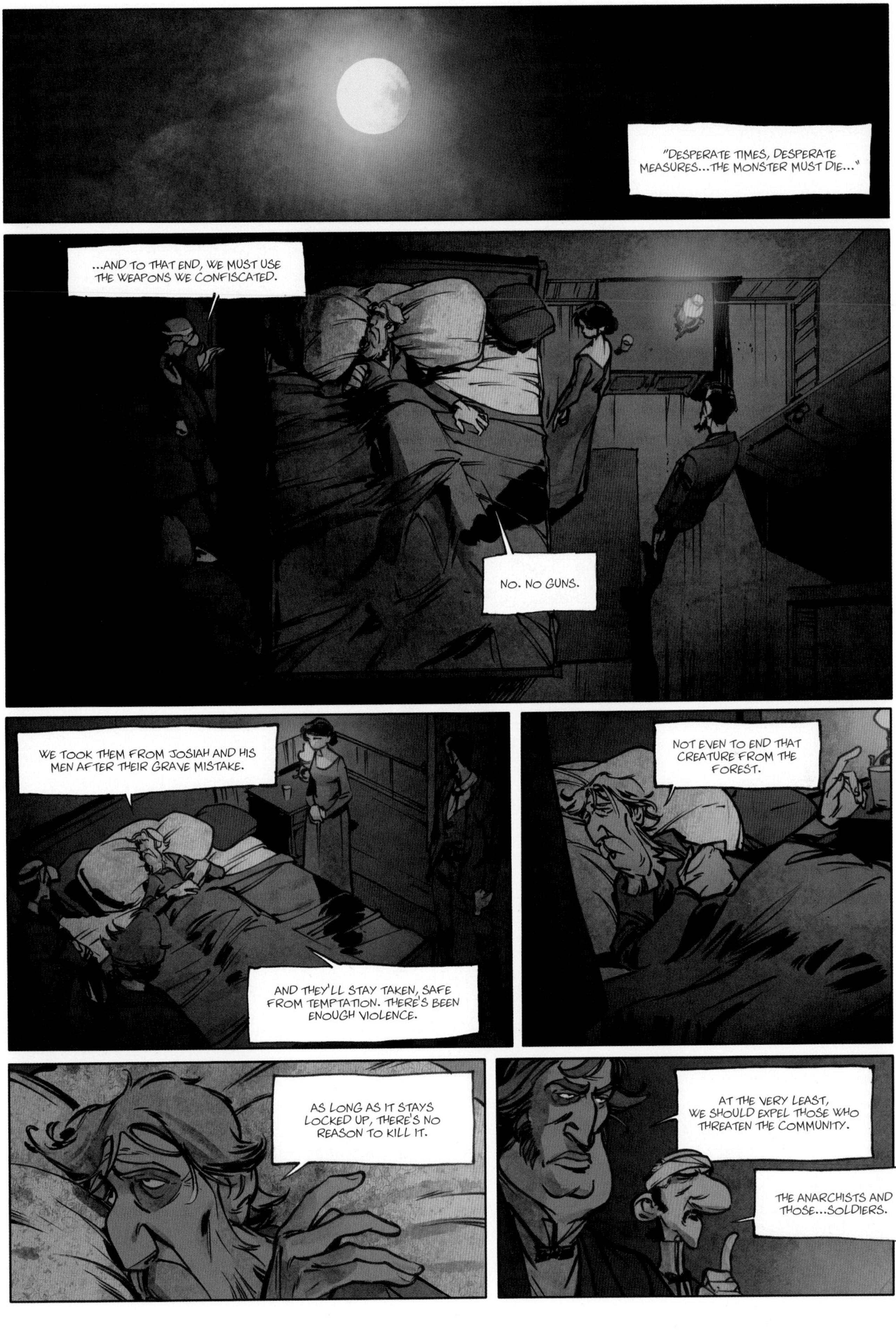
"DESPERATE TIMES, DESPERATE MEASURES... THE MONSTER MUST DIE..."
...AND TO THAT END, WE MUST USE THE WEAPONS WE CONFISCATED.
NO. NO GUNS.
WE TOOK THEM FROM JOSIAH AND HIS MEN AFTER THEIR GRAVE MISTAKE.
AND THEY'LL STAY TAKEN, SAFE FROM TEMPTATION. THERE'S BEEN ENOUGH VIOLENCE.
NOT EVEN TO END THAT CREATURE FROM THE FOREST.
AS LONG AS IT STAYS LOCKED UP, THERE'S NO REASON TO KILL IT.
AT THE VERY LEAST, WE SHOULD EXPEL THOSE WHO THREATEN THE COMMUNITY.
THE ANARCHISTS AND THOSE... SOLDIERS.

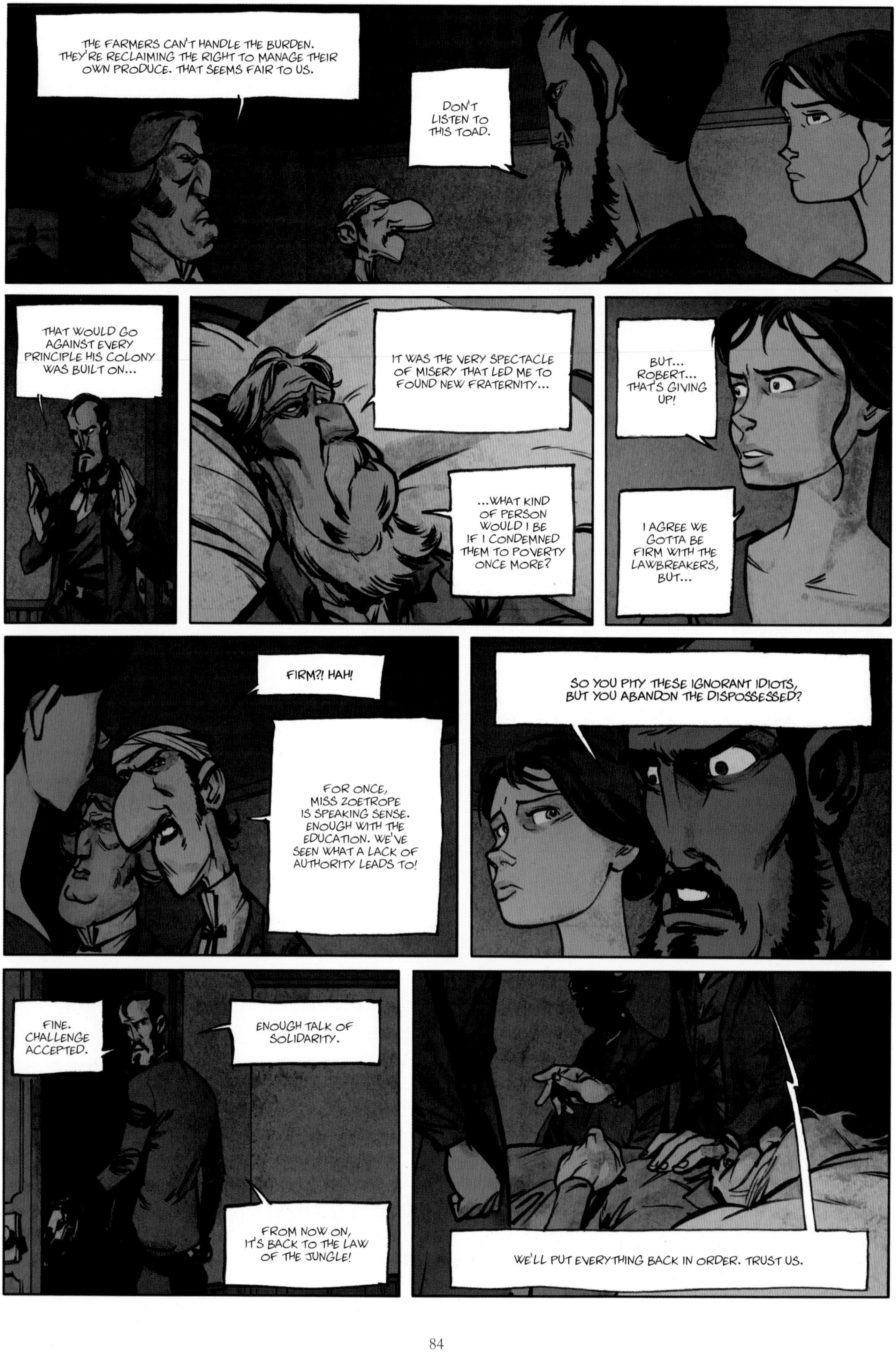
THE FARMERS CAN'T HANDLE THE BURDEN. THEY'RE RECLAIMING THE RIGHT TO MANAGE THEIR OWN PRODUCE. THAT SEEMS FAIR TO US.
DON'T LISTEN TO THIS TOAD.
THAT WOULD GO AGAINST EVERY PRINCIPLE HIS COLONY WAS BUILT ON...
IT WAS THE VERY SPECTACLE OF MISERY THAT LED ME TO FOUND NEW FRATERNITY...
...WHAT KIND OF PERSON WOULD I BE IF I CONDEMNED THEM TO POVERTY ONCE MORE?
BUT... ROBERT... THAT'S GIVING UP!
I AGREE WE GOTTA BE FIRM WITH THE LAWBREAKERS, BUT...
FIRM?! HAH!
FOR ONCE, MISS ZOETROPE IS SPEAKING SENSE. ENOUGH WITH THE EDUCATION. WE'VE SEEN WHAT A LACK OF AUTHORITY LEADS TO!
SO YOU PITY THESE IGNORANT IDIOTS, BUT YOU ABANDON THE DISPOSSESSED?
FINE. CHALLENGE ACCEPTED.
ENOUGH TALK OF SOLIDARITY.
FROM NOW ON, IT'S BACK TO THE LAW OF THE JUNGLE!
WE'LL PUT EVERYTHING BACK IN ORDER. TRUST US.

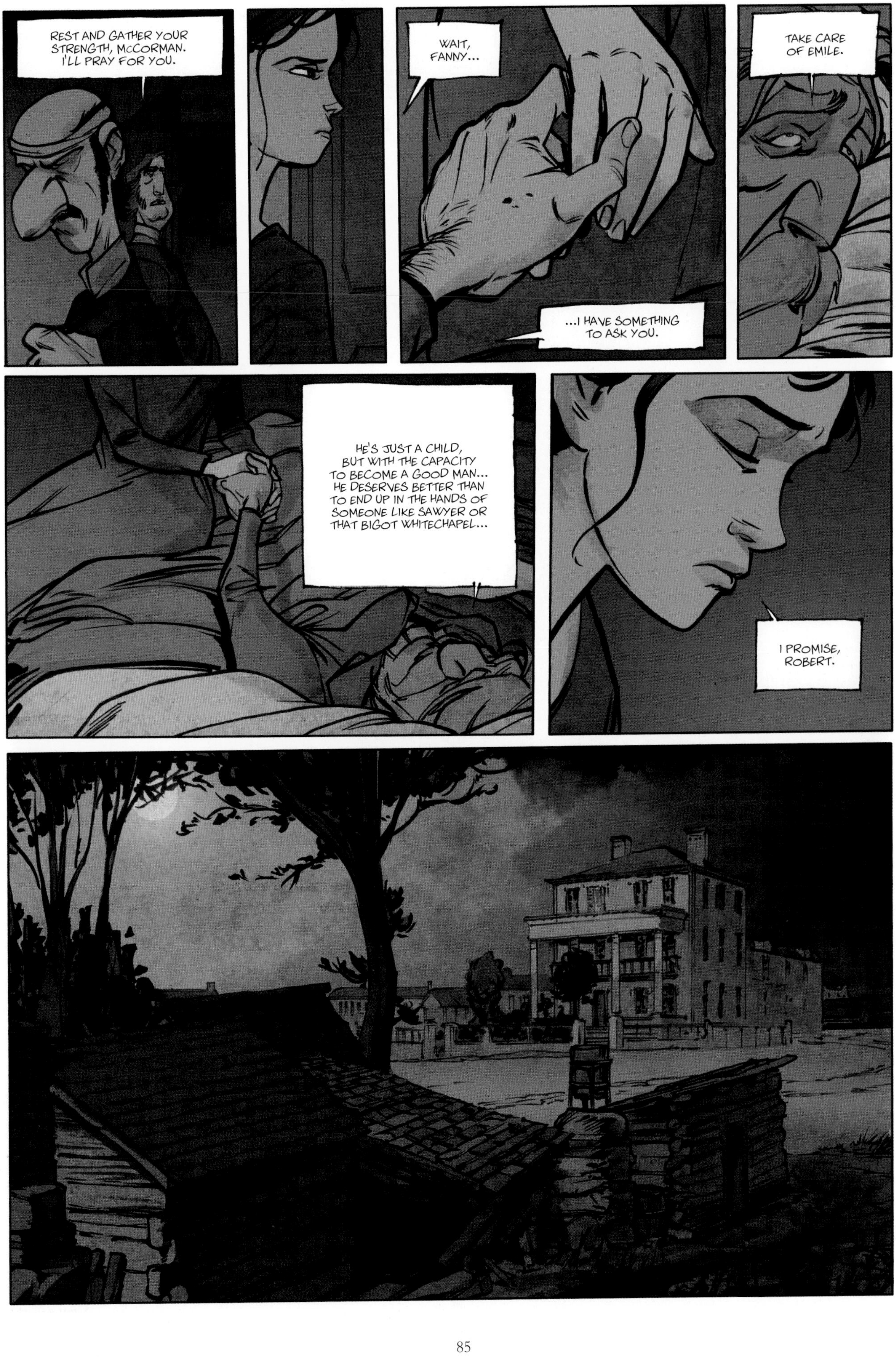
REST AND GATHER YOUR STRENGTH, McCORMAN. I'LL PRAY FOR YOU.
WAIT, FANNY...
...I HAVE SOMETHING TO ASK YOU.
TAKE CARE OF EMILE.
HE'S JUST A CHILD, BUT WITH THE CAPACITY TO BECOME A GOOD MAN... HE DESERVES BETTER THAN TO END UP IN THE HANDS OF SOMEONE LIKE SAWYER OR THAT BIGOT WHITECHAPEL...
I PROMISE, ROBERT.

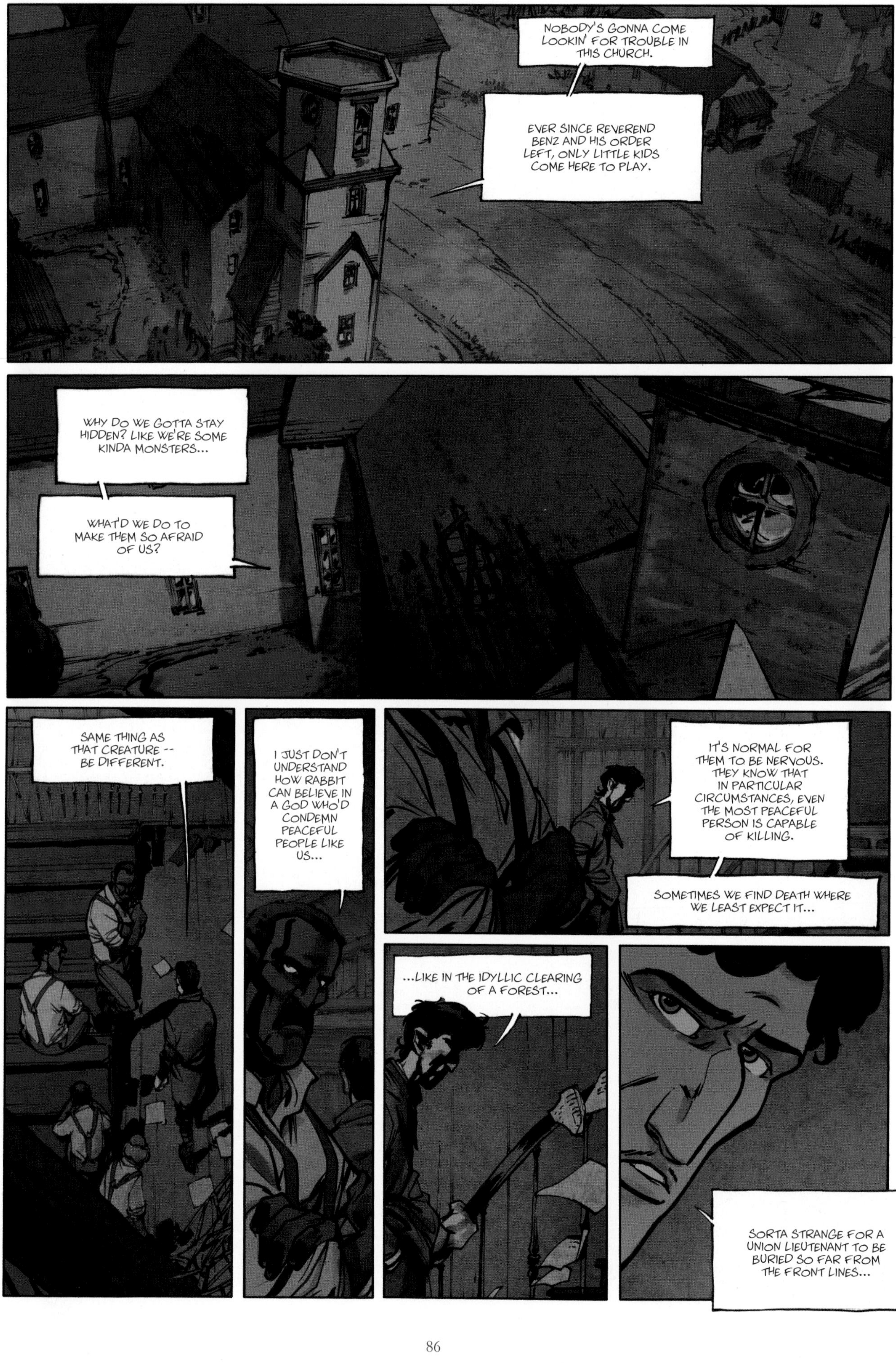
NOBODY'S GONNA COME LOOKIN' FOR TROUBLE IN THIS CHURCH.
EVER SINCE REVEREND BENZ AND HIS ORDER LEFT, ONLY LITTLE KIDS COME HERE TO PLAY.
WHY DO WE GOTTA STAY HIDDEN? LIKE WE'RE SOME KINDA MONSTERS...
WHAT'D WE DO TO MAKE THEM SO AFRAID OF US?
SAME THING AS THAT CREATURE -- BE DIFFERENT.
I JUST DON'T UNDERSTAND HOW RABBIT CAN BELIEVE IN A GOD WHO'D CONDEMN PEACEFUL PEOPLE LIKE US...
IT'S NORMAL FOR THEM TO BE NERVOUS. THEY KNOW THAT IN PARTICULAR CIRCUMSTANCES, EVEN THE MOST PEACEFUL PERSON IS CAPABLE OF KILLING.
SOMETIMES WE FIND DEATH WHERE WE LEAST EXPECT IT...
...LIKE IN THE IDYLLIC CLEARING OF A FOREST...
SORTA STRANGE FOR A UNION LIEUTENANT TO BE BURIED SO FAR FROM THE FRONT LINES...

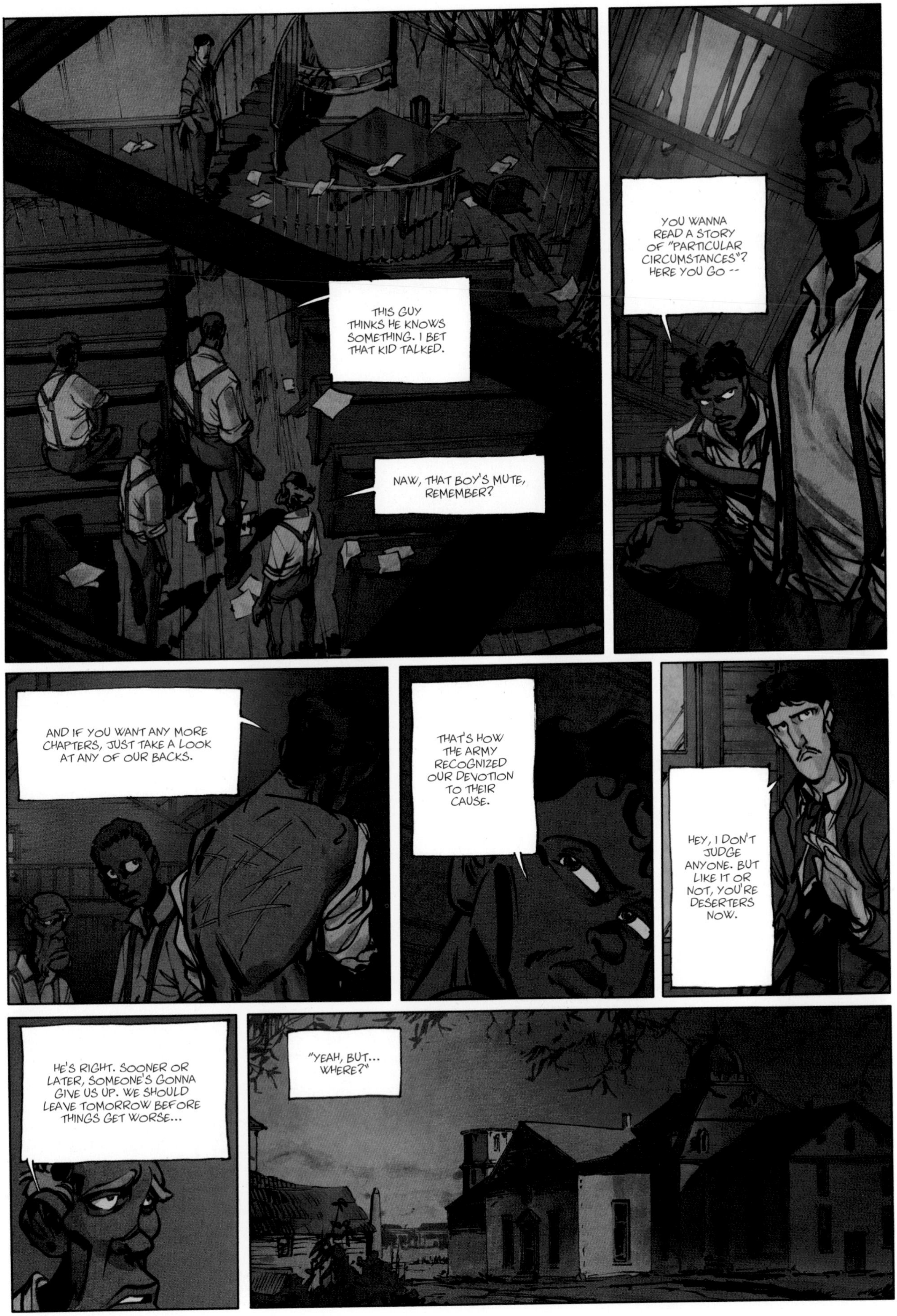
THIS GUY THINKS HE KNOWS SOMETHING. I BET THAT KID TALKED.
NAW, THAT BOY'S MUTE, REMEMBER?
YOU WANNA READ A STORY OF "PARTICULAR CIRCUMSTANCES"? HERE YOU GO --
AND IF YOU WANT ANY MORE CHAPTERS, JUST TAKE A LOOK AT ANY OF OUR BACKS.
THAT'S HOW THE ARMY RECOGNIZED OUR DEVOTION TO THEIR CAUSE.
HEY, I DON'T JUDGE ANYONE. BUT LIKE IT OR NOT, YOU'RE DESERTERS NOW.
HE'S RIGHT. SOONER OR LATER, SOMEONE'S GONNA GIVE US UP. WE SHOULD LEAVE TOMORROW BEFORE THINGS GET WORSE...
"YEAH, BUT... WHERE?"

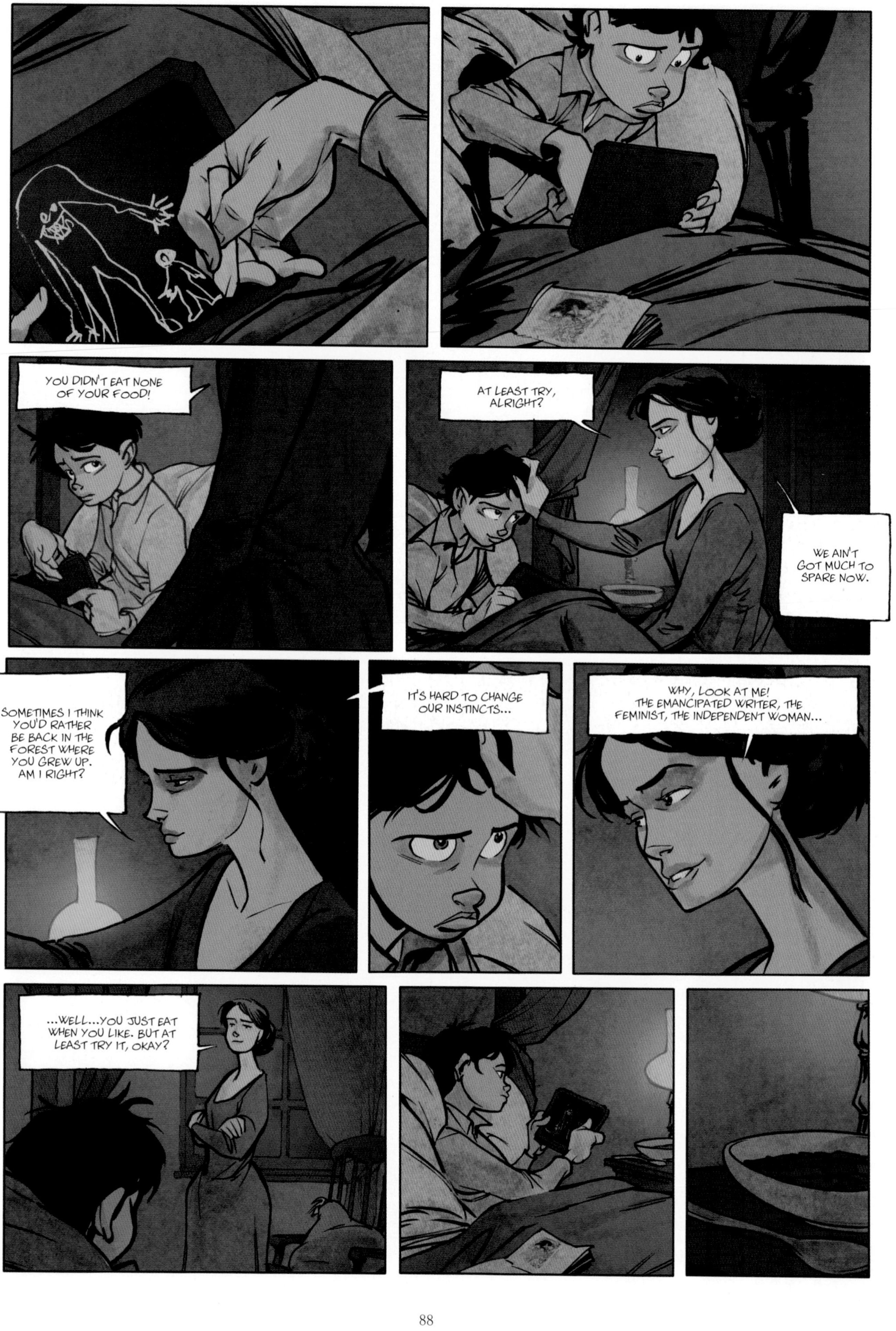
YOU DIDN'T EAT NONE OF YOUR FOOD!
AT LEAST TRY, ALRIGHT?
WE AIN'T GOT MUCH TO SPARE NOW.
SOMETIMES I THINK YOU'D RATHER BE BACK IN THE FOREST WHERE YOU GREW UP. AM I RIGHT?
IT'S HARD TO CHANGE OUR INSTINCTS...
WHY, LOOK AT ME! THE EMANCIPATED WRITER, THE FEMINIST, THE INDEPENDENT WOMAN...
...WELL...YOU JUST EAT WHEN YOU LIKE. BUT AT LEAST TRY IT, OKAY?

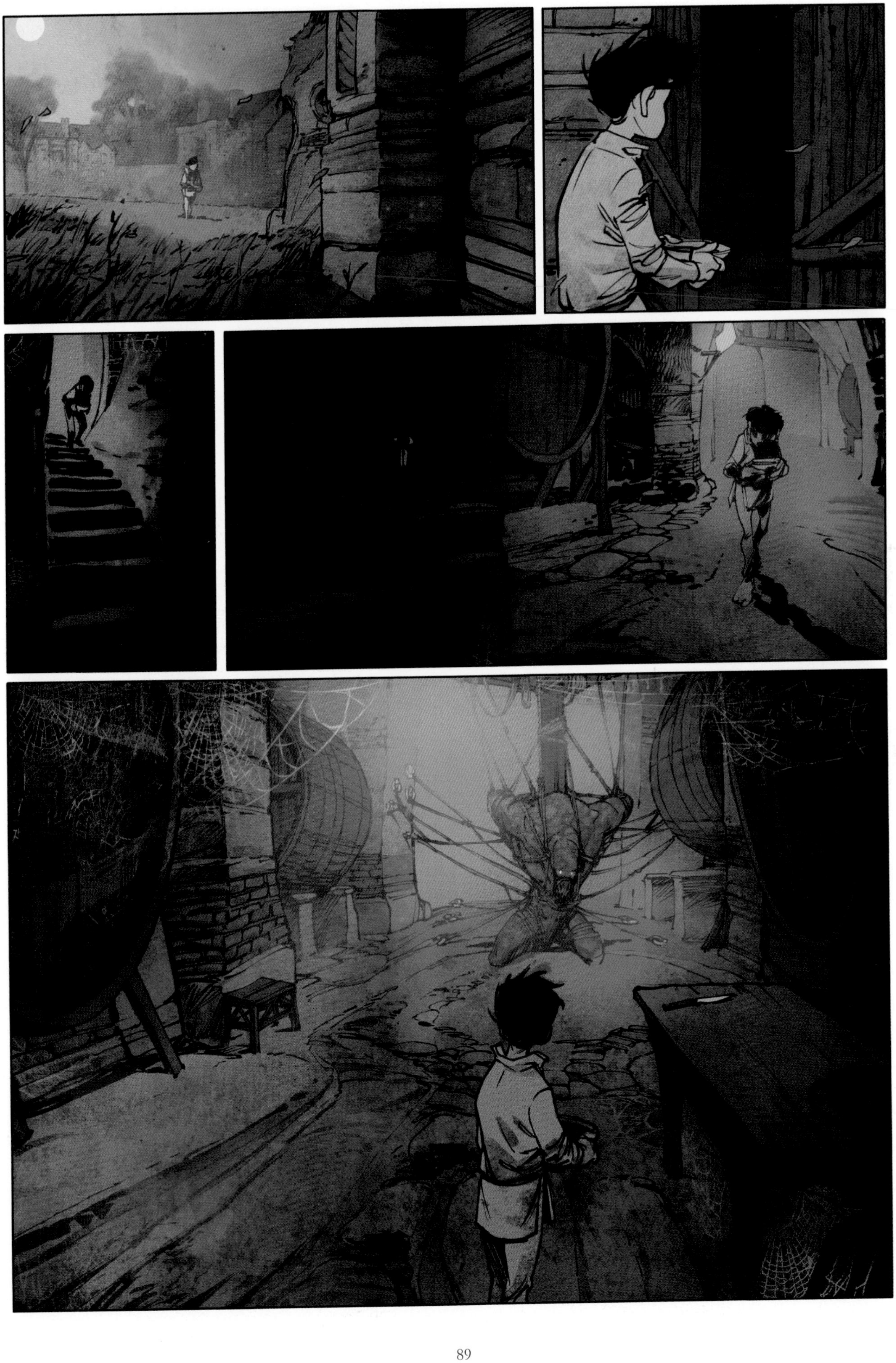

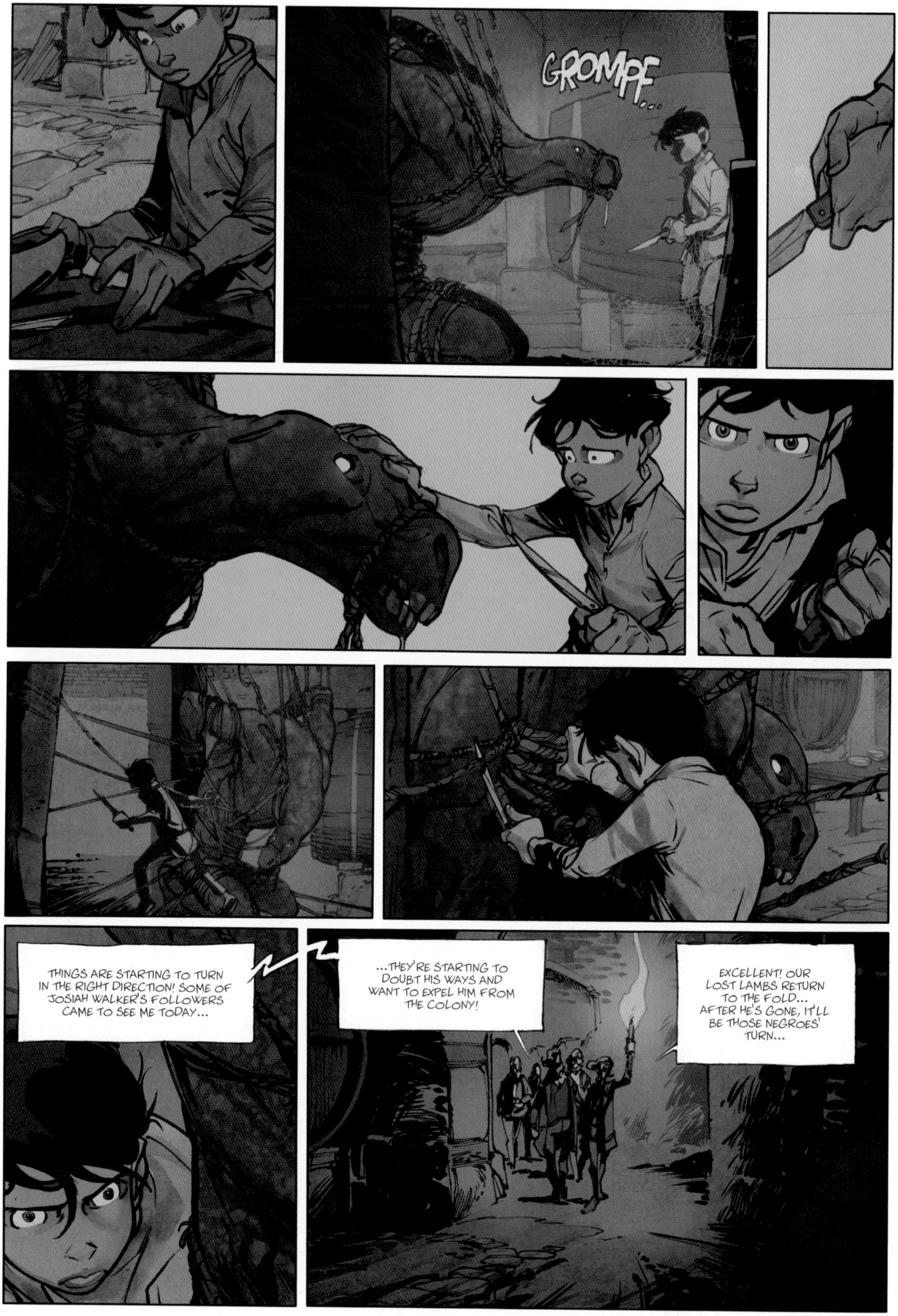
GROMPF...
THINGS ARE STARTING TO TURN IN THE RIGHT DIRECTION! SOME OF JOSIAH WALKER'S FOLLOWERS CAME TO SEE ME TODAY...
...THEY'RE STARTING TO DOUBT HIS WAYS AND WANT TO EXPEL HIM FROM THE COLONY!
EXCELLENT! OUR LOST LAMBS RETURN TO THE FOLD... AFTER HE'S GONE, IT'LL BE THOSE NEGROES' TURN...

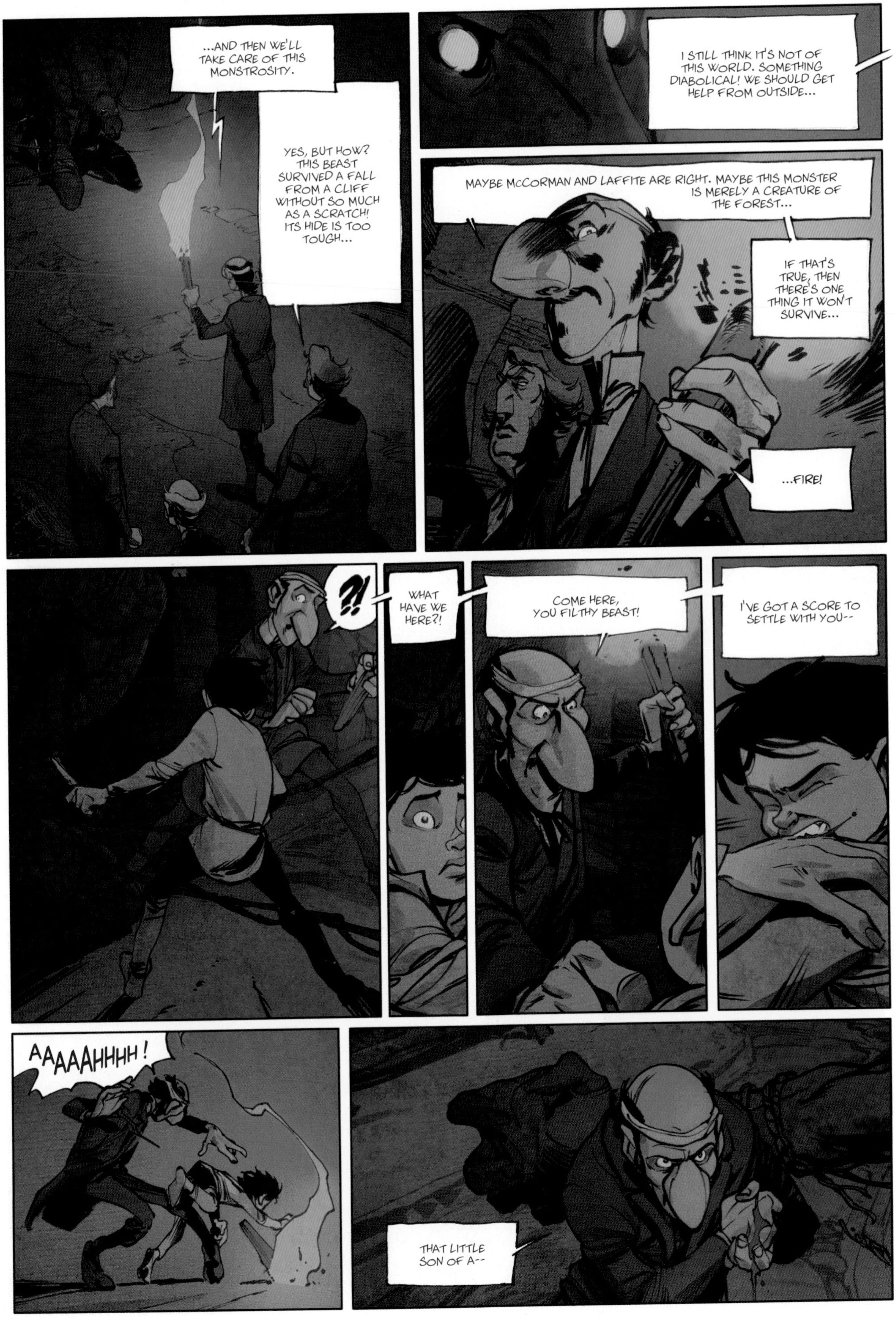
...AND THEN WE'LL TAKE CARE OF THIS MONSTROSITY.
YES, BUT HOW? THIS BEAST SURVIVED A FALL FROM A CLIFF WITHOUT SO MUCH AS A SCRATCH! ITS HIDE IS TOO TOUGH...
I STILL THINK IT'S NOT OF THIS WORLD. SOMETHING DIABOLICAL! WE SHOULD GET HELP FROM OUTSIDE...
MAYBE McCORMAN AND LAFFITE ARE RIGHT. MAYBE THIS MONSTER IS MERELY A CREATURE OF THE FOREST...
IF THAT'S TRUE, THEN THERE'S ONE THING IT WON'T SURVIVE...
...FIRE!
?!
WHAT HAVE WE HERE?!
COME HERE, YOU FILTHY BEAST!
I'VE GOT A SCORE TO SETTLE WITH YOU--
AAAAAHHHH!
THAT LITTLE SON OF A--

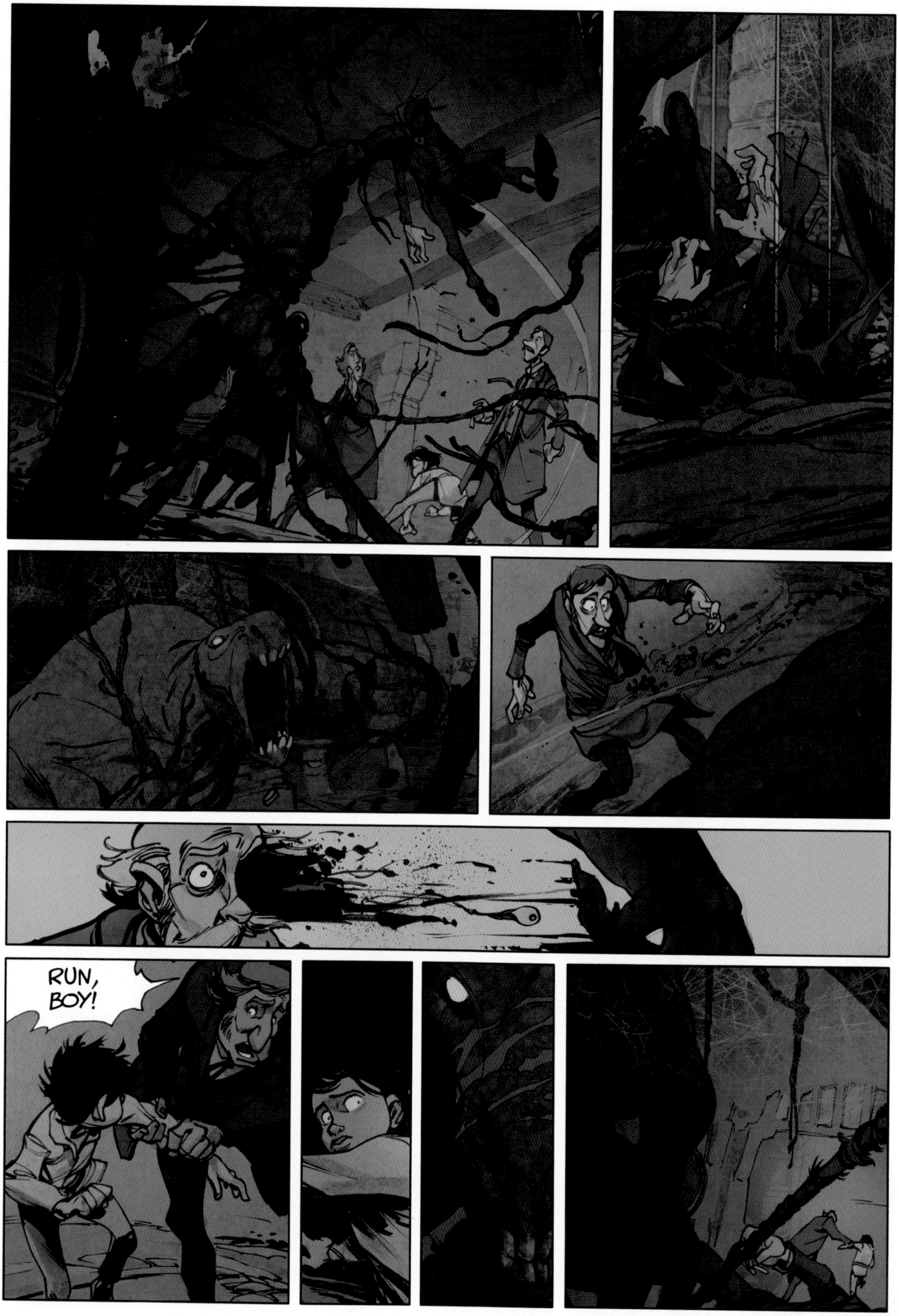
RUN, BOY!

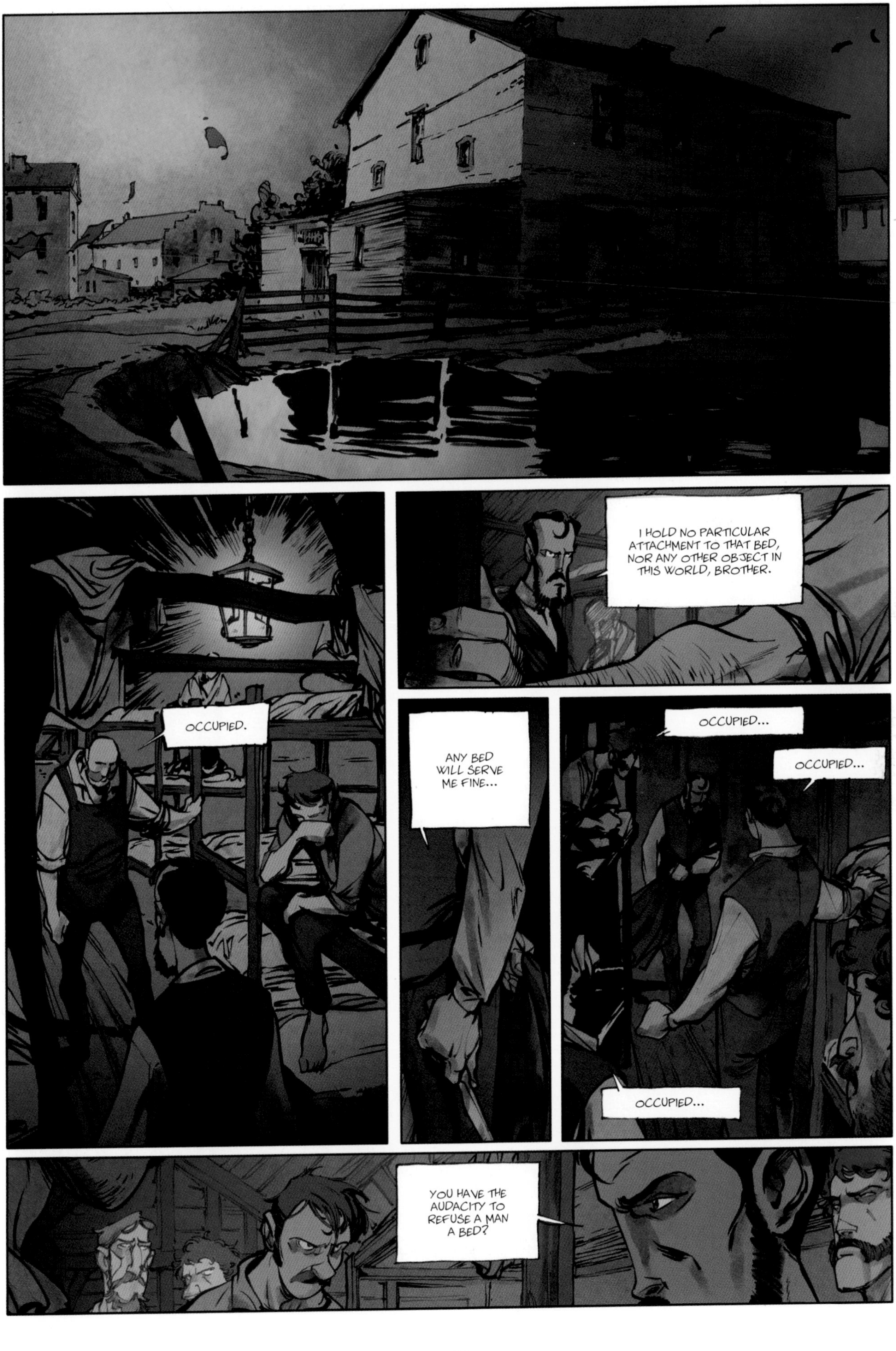
I HOLD NO PARTICULAR ATTACHMENT TO THAT BED, NOR ANY OTHER OBJECT IN THIS WORLD, BROTHER.
OCCUPIED.
ANY BED WILL SERVE ME FINE...
OCCUPIED...
OCCUPIED...
OCCUPIED...
YOU HAVE THE AUDACITY TO REFUSE A MAN A BED?

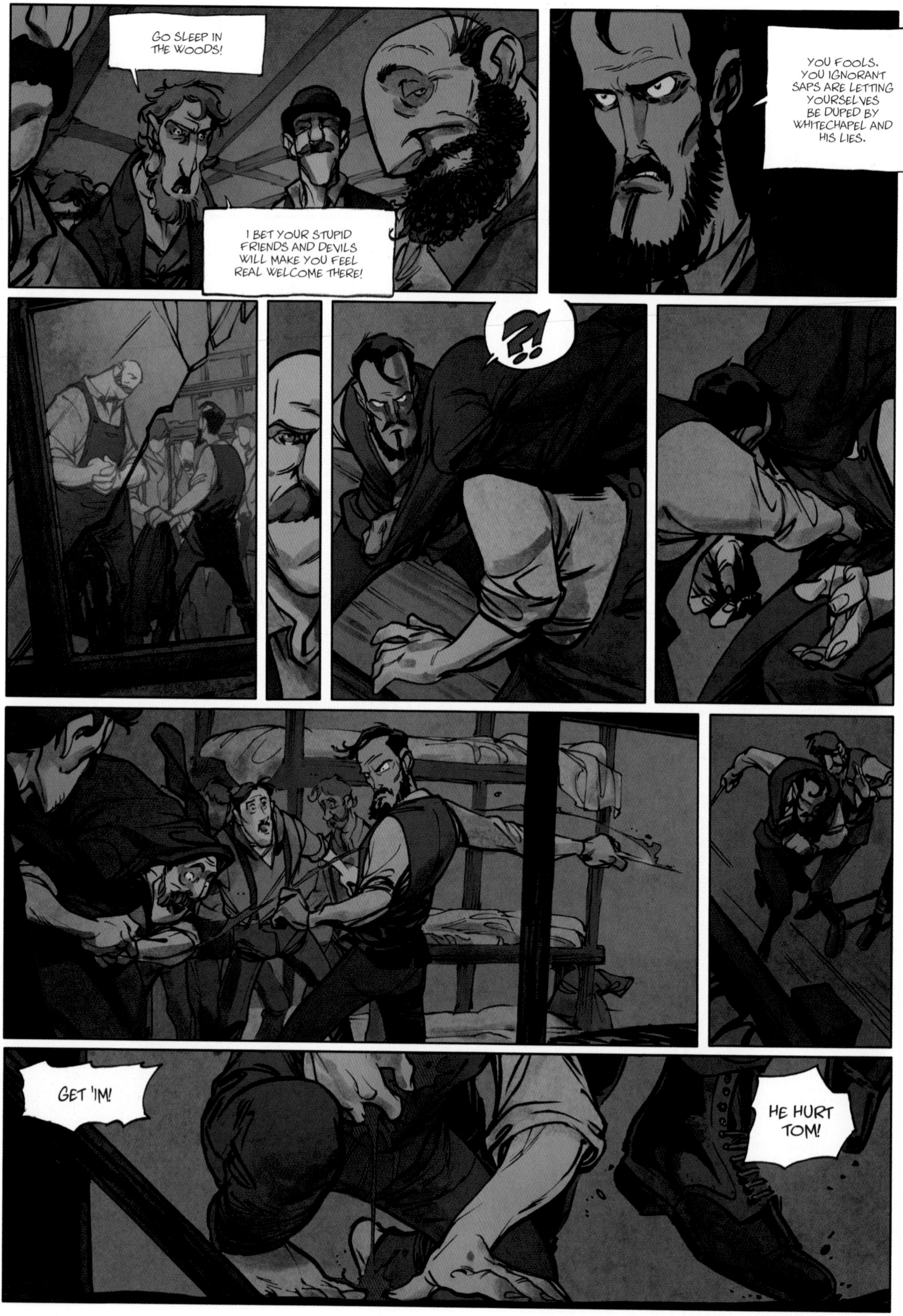
GO SLEEP IN THE WOODS!
I BET YOUR STUPID FRIENDS AND DEVILS WILL MAKE YOU FEEL REAL WELCOME THERE!
YOU FOOLS. YOU IGNORANT SAPS ARE LETTING YOURSELVES BE DUPED BY WHITECHAPEL AND HIS LIES.
?!
GET 'IM!
HE HURT TOM!

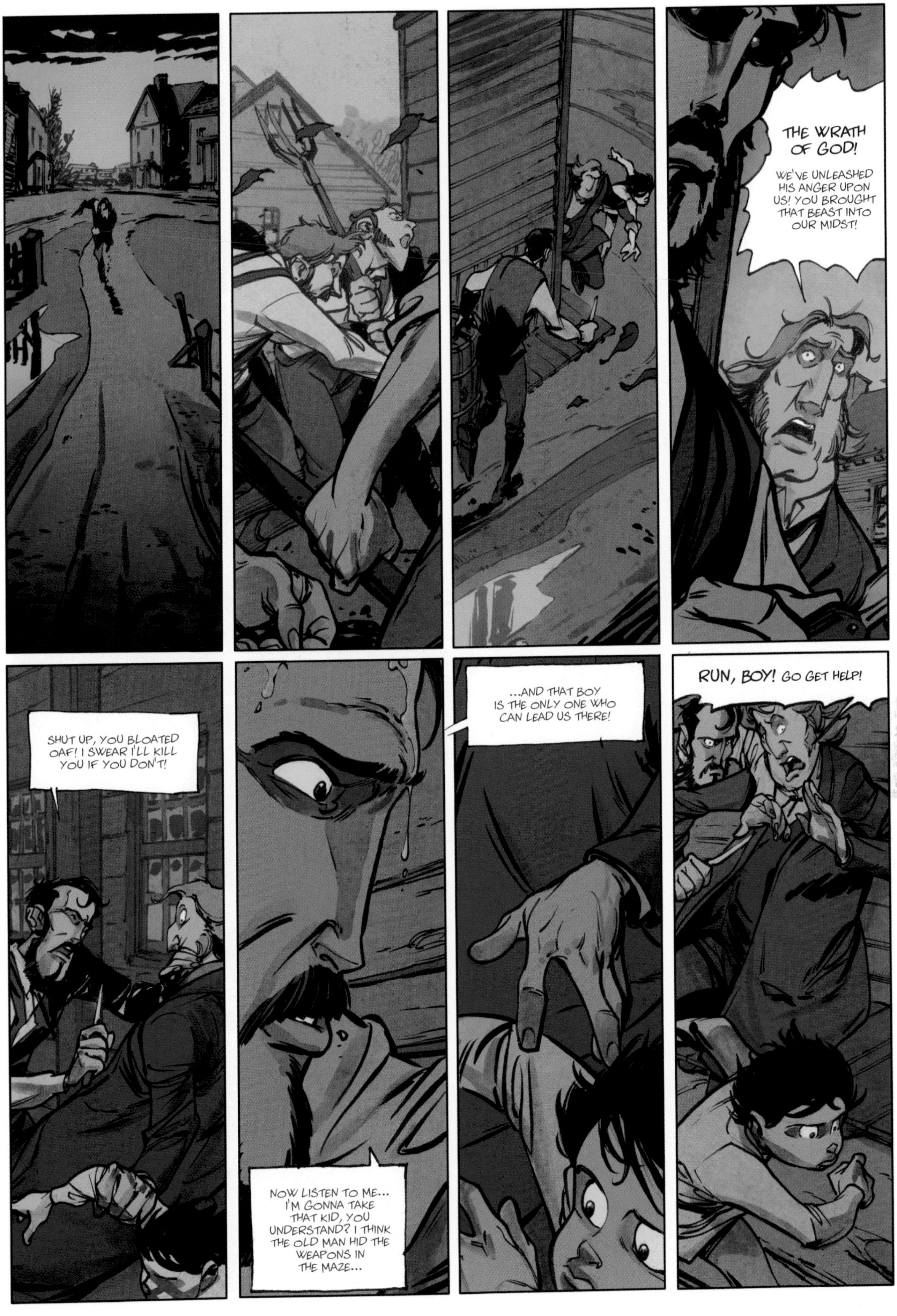
THE WRATH OF GOD!
WE'VE UNLEASHED HIS ANGER UPON US! YOU BROUGHT THAT BEAST INTO OUR MIDST!
SHUT UP, YOU BLOATED OAF! I SWEAR I'LL KILL YOU IF YOU DON'T!
NOW LISTEN TO ME... I'M GONNA TAKE THAT KID, YOU UNDERSTAND? I THINK THE OLD MAN HID THE WEAPONS IN THE MAZE...
...AND THAT BOY IS THE ONLY ONE WHO CAN LEAD US THERE!
RUN, BOY! GO GET HELP!

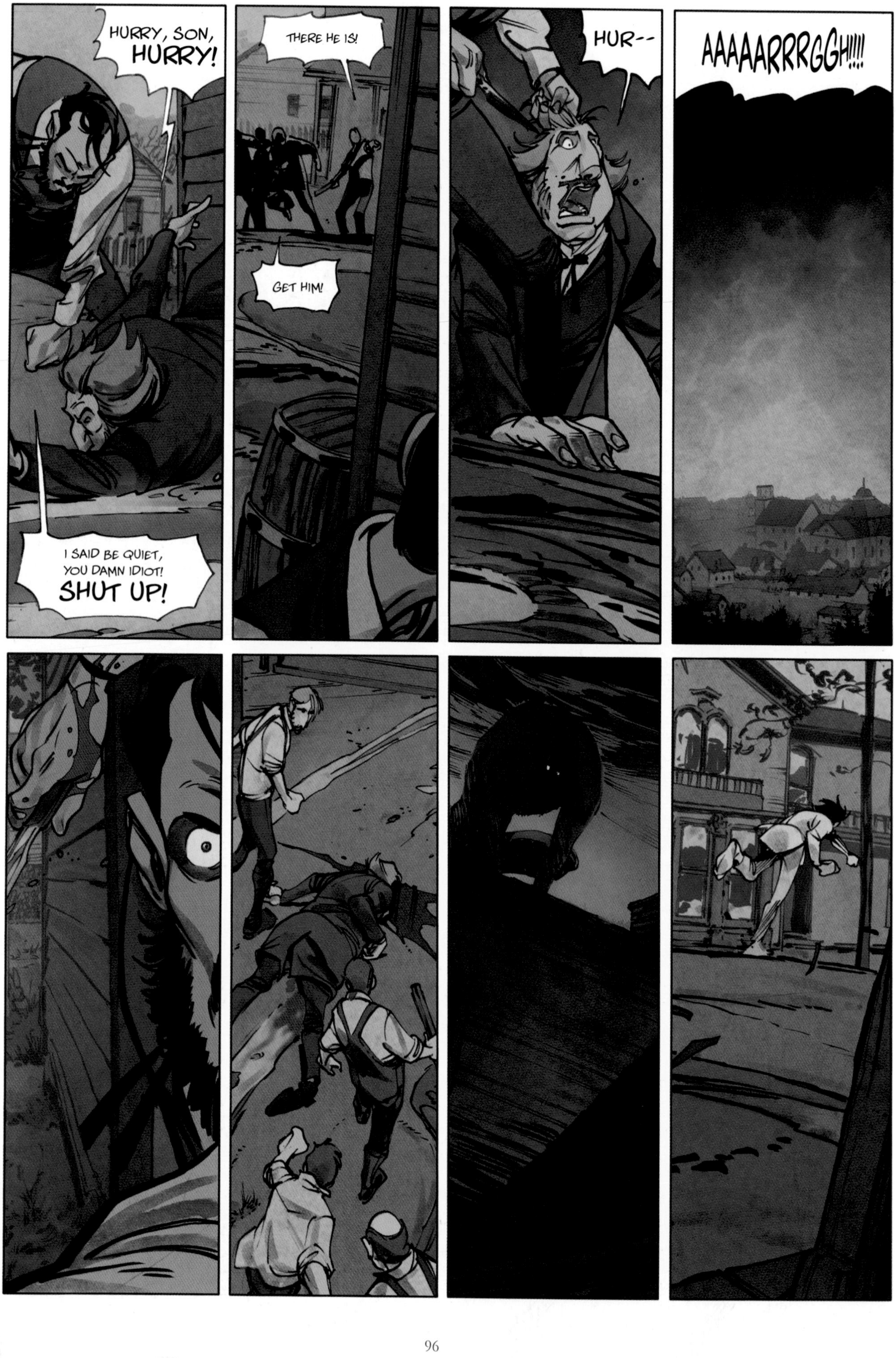
HURRY, SON, HURRY!
I SAID BE QUIET, YOU DAMN IDIOT! SHUT UP!
THERE HE IS!
GET HIM!
HUR--
AAAAARRRGGH!!!!

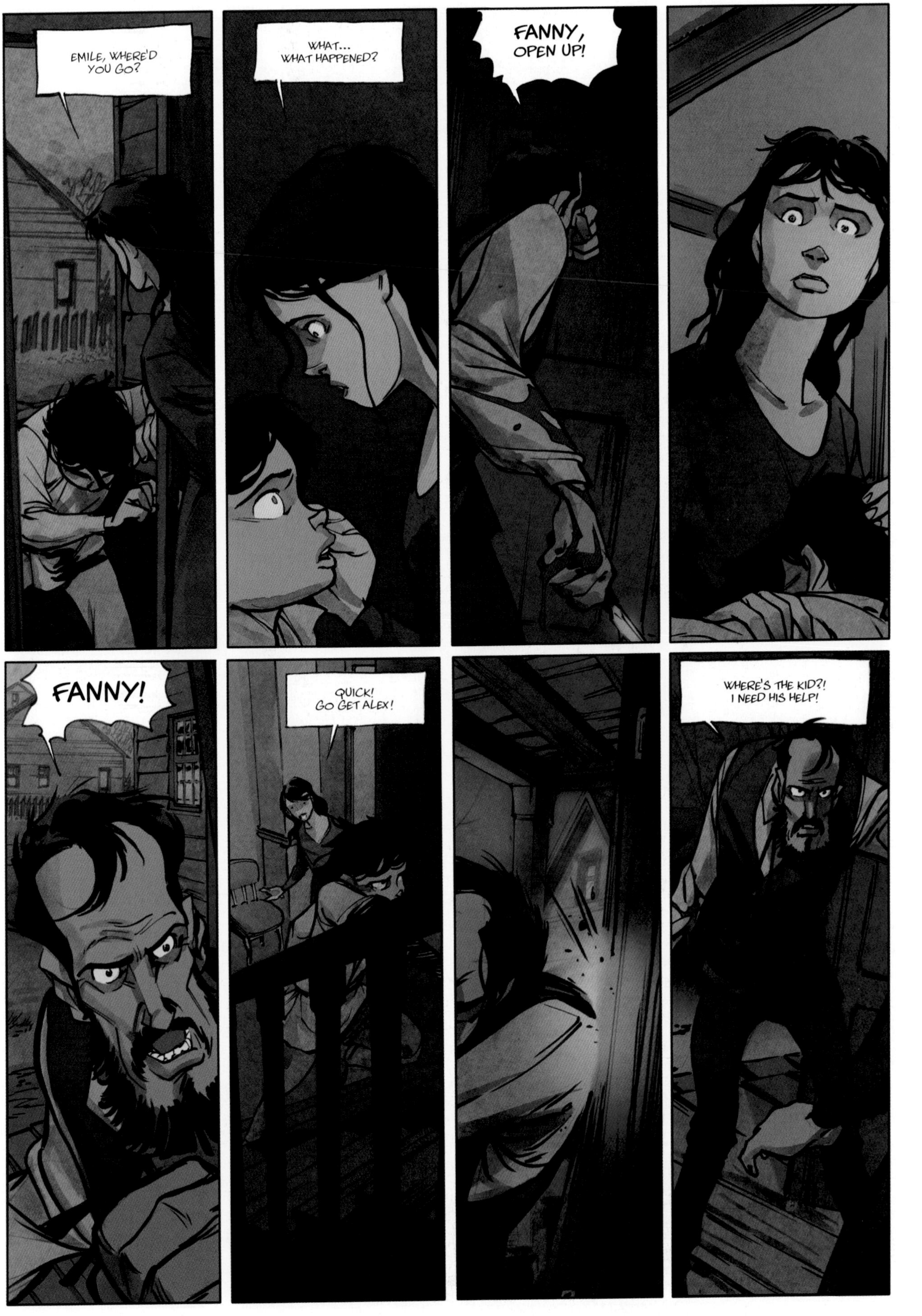
EMILE, WHERE'D YOU GO?
WHAT... WHAT HAPPENED?
FANNY, OPEN UP!
FANNY!
QUICK! GO GET ALEX!
WHERE'S THE KID?! I NEED HIS HELP!

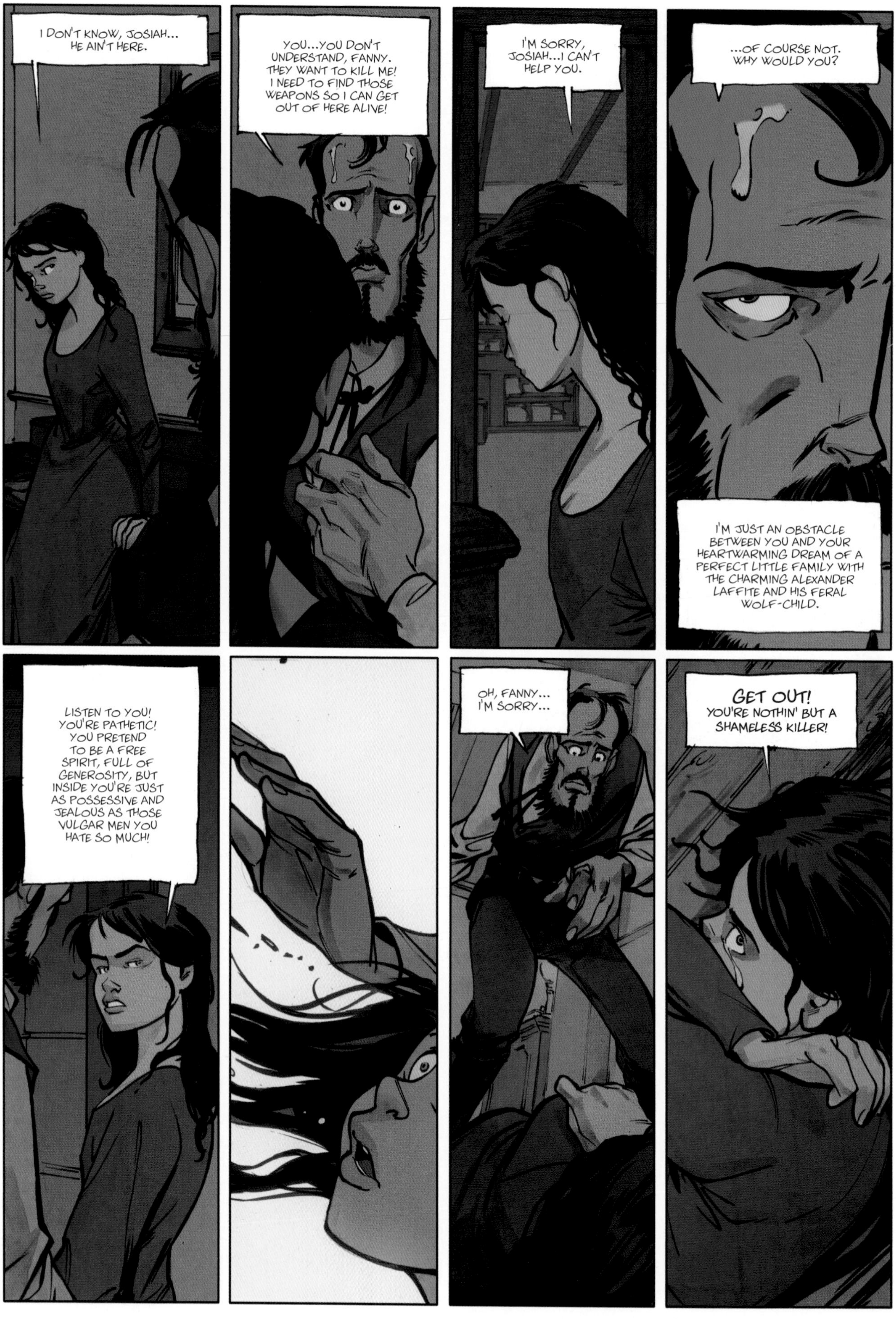
I DON'T KNOW, JOSIAH... HE AIN'T HERE.
YOU...YOU DON'T UNDERSTAND, FANNY. THEY WANT TO KILL ME! I NEED TO FIND THOSE WEAPONS SO I CAN GET OUT OF HERE ALIVE!
I'M SORRY, JOSIAH...I CAN'T HELP YOU.
...OF COURSE NOT. WHY WOULD YOU?
I'M JUST AN OBSTACLE BETWEEN YOU AND YOUR HEARTWARMING DREAM OF A PERFECT LITTLE FAMILY WITH THE CHARMING ALEXANDER LAFFITE AND HIS FERAL WOLF-CHILD.
LISTEN TO YOU! YOU'RE PATHETIC! YOU PRETEND TO BE A FREE SPIRIT, FULL OF GENEROSITY, BUT INSIDE YOU'RE JUST AS POSSESSIVE AND JEALOUS AS THOSE VULGAR MEN YOU HATE SO MUCH!
OH, FANNY... I'M SORRY...
GET OUT! YOU'RE NOTHIN' BUT A SHAMELESS KILLER!

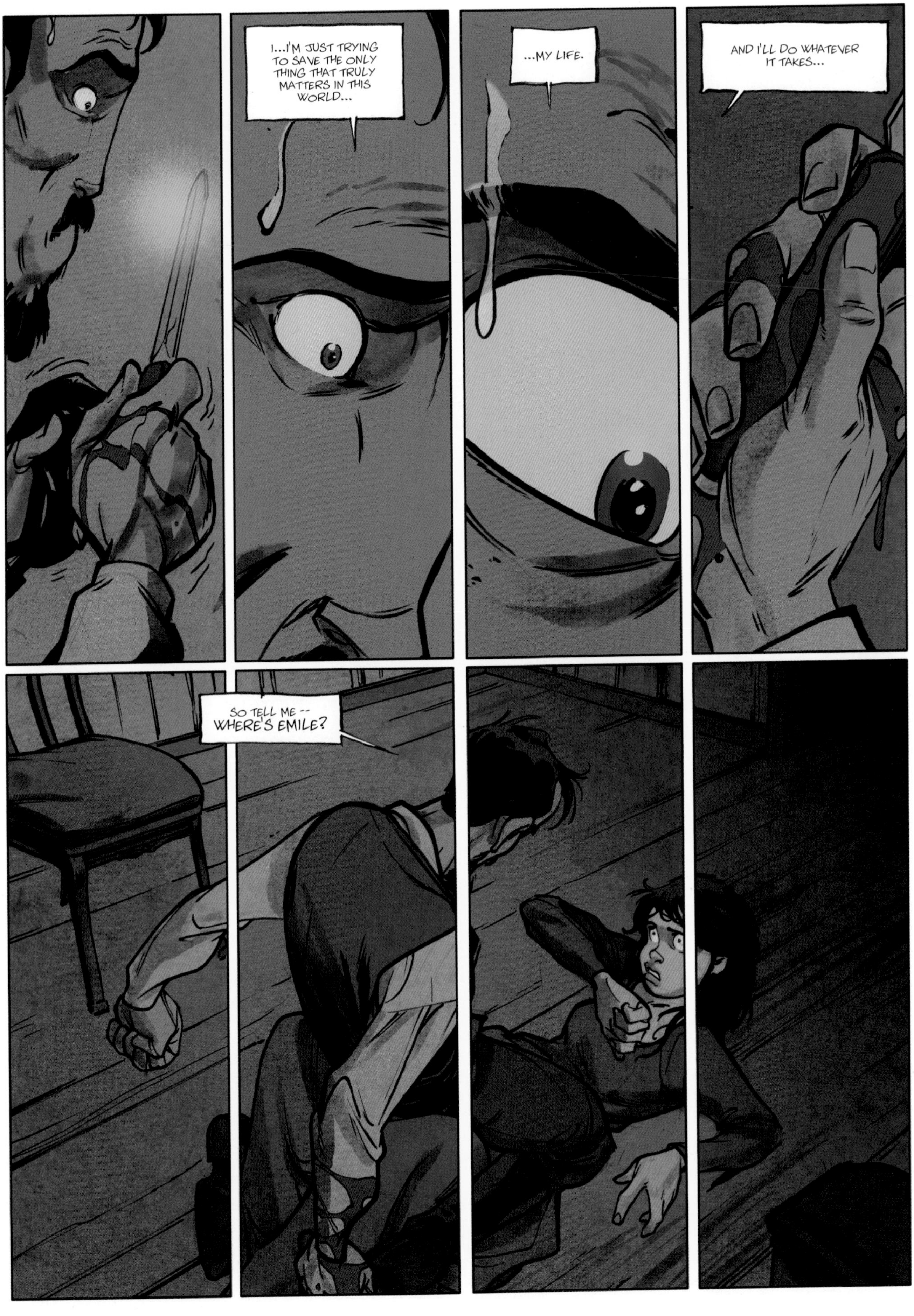

I...I'M JUST TRYING TO SAVE THE ONLY THING THAT TRULY MATTERS IN THIS WORLD...
...MY LIFE.
AND I'LL DO WHATEVER IT TAKES...
SO TELL ME -- WHERE'S EMILE?

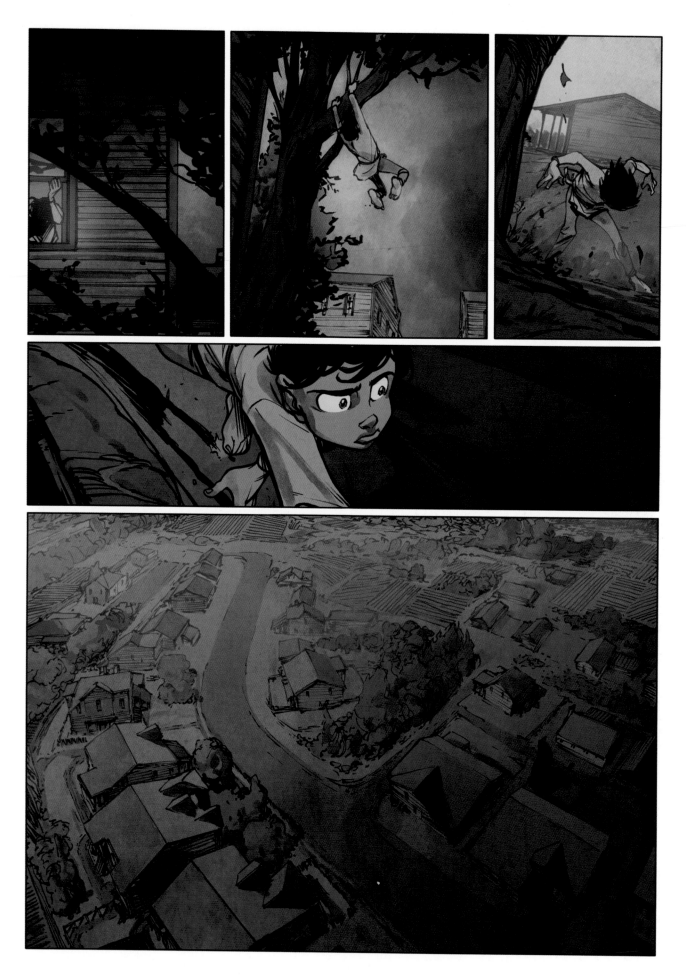

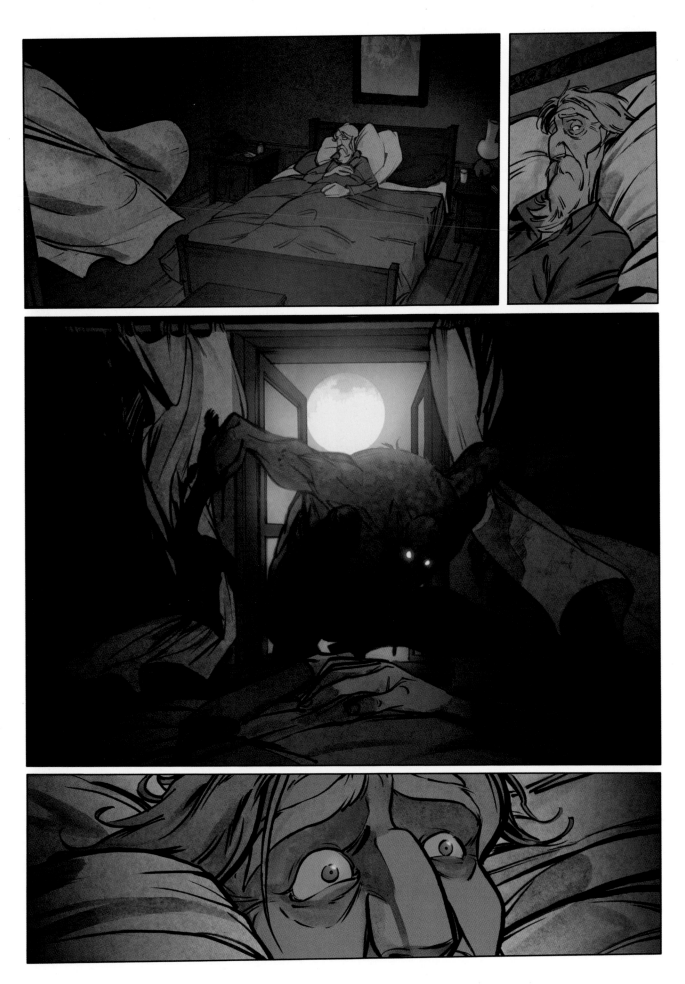

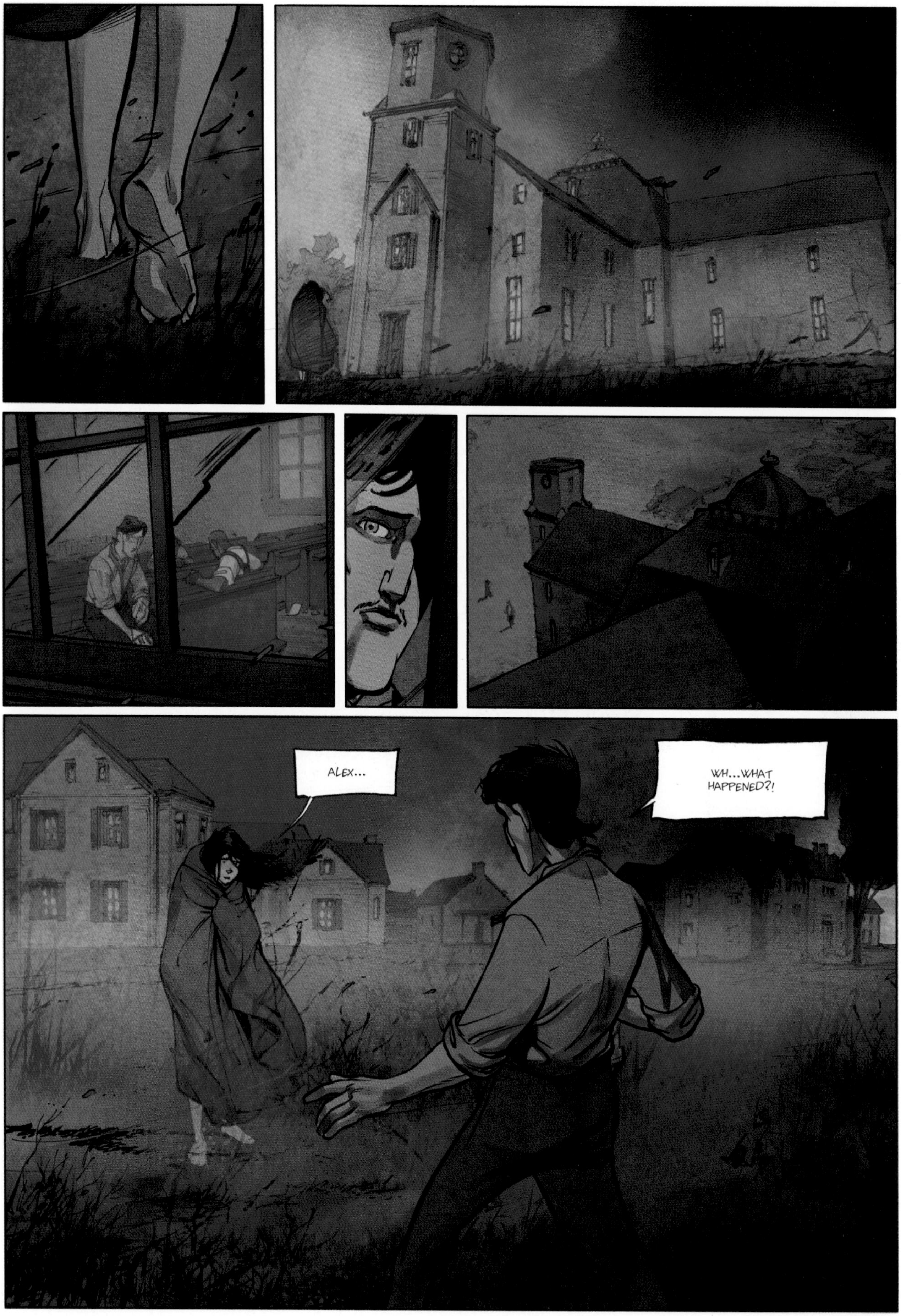
ALEX...
WH...WHAT HAPPENED?!

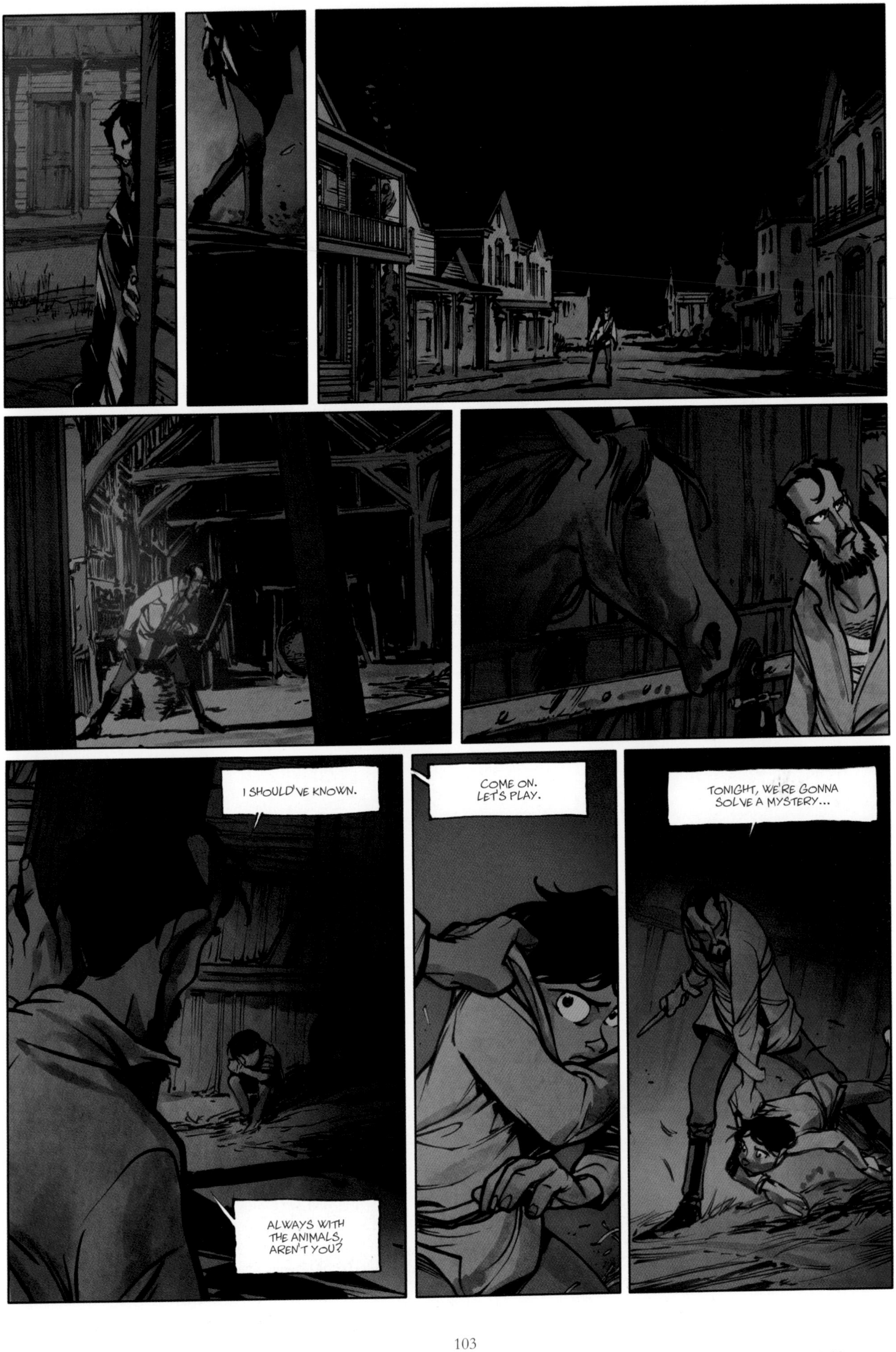
I SHOULD'VE KNOWN.
ALWAYS WITH THE ANIMALS, AREN'T YOU?
COME ON. LET'S PLAY.
TONIGHT, WE'RE GONNA SOLVE A MYSTERY...

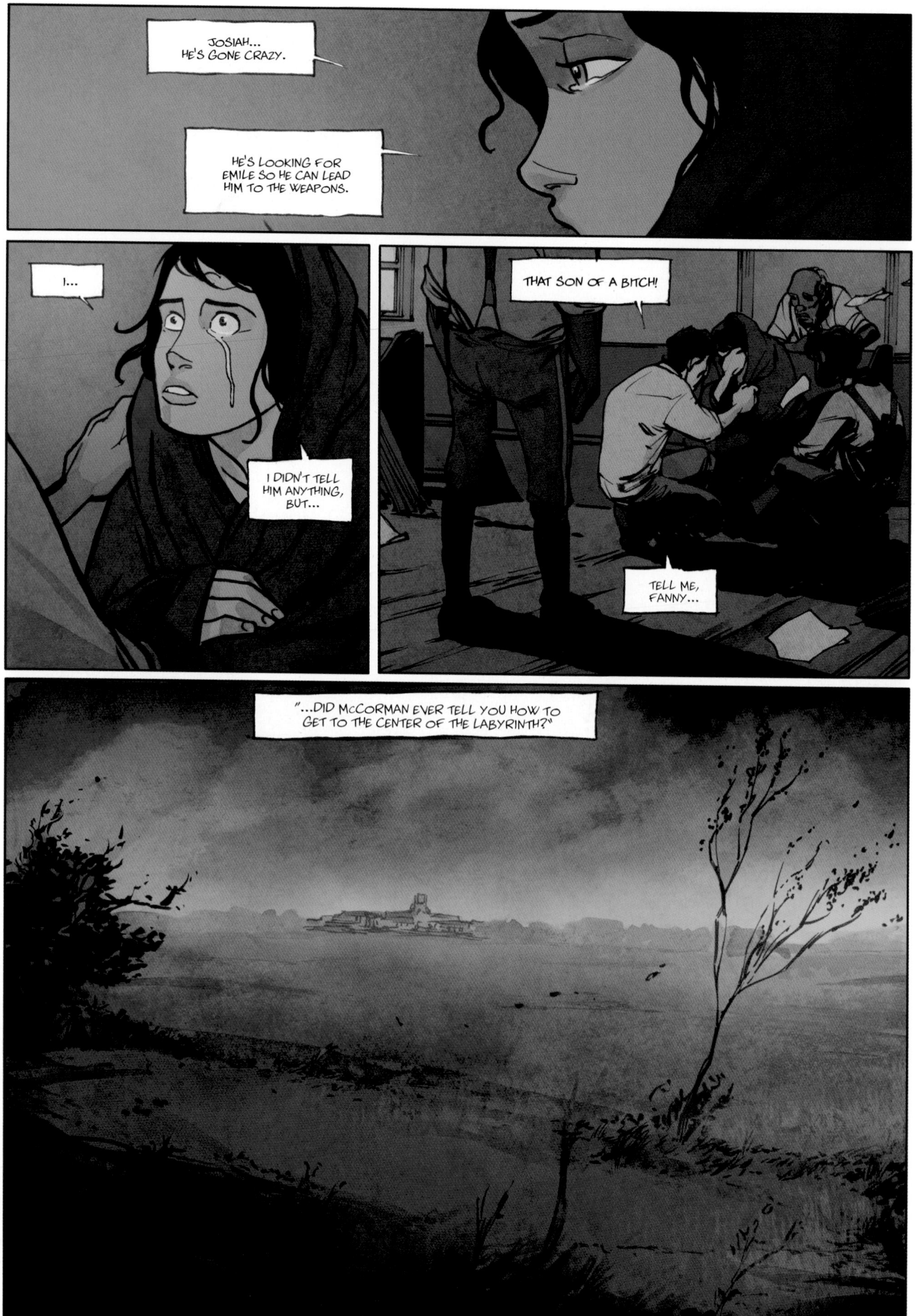
JOSIAH... HE'S GONE CRAZY.
HE'S LOOKING FOR EMILE SO HE CAN LEAD HIM TO THE WEAPONS.
I...
I DIDN'T TELL HIM ANYTHING, BUT...
THAT SON OF A BITCH!
TELL ME, FANNY...
"...DID McCORMAN EVER TELL YOU HOW TO GET TO THE CENTER OF THE LABYRINTH?"

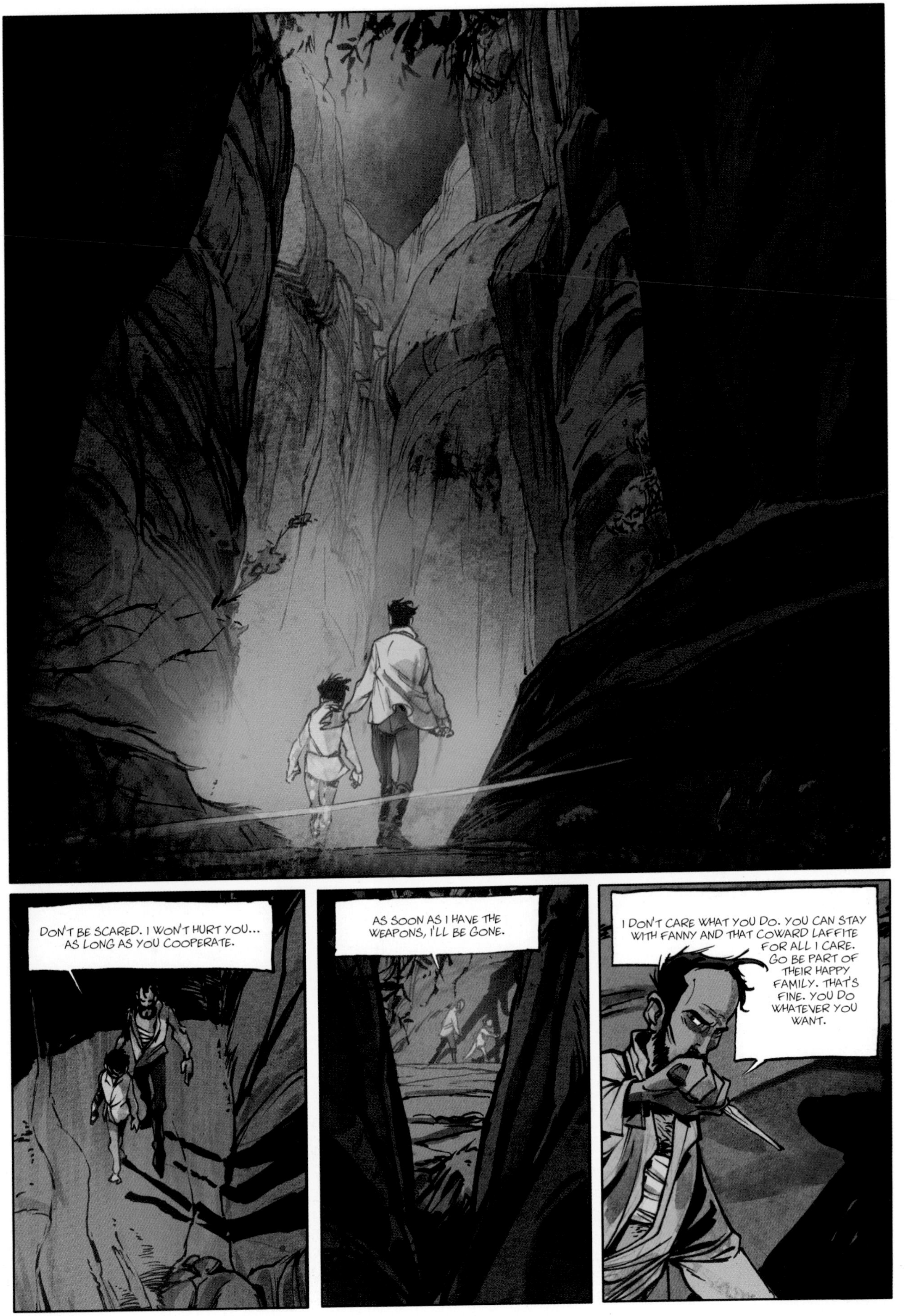
DON'T BE SCARED. I WON'T HURT YOU... AS LONG AS YOU COOPERATE.
AS SOON AS I HAVE THE WEAPONS, I'LL BE GONE.
I DON'T CARE WHAT YOU DO. YOU CAN STAY WITH FANNY AND THAT COWARD LAFFITE FOR ALL I CARE. GO BE PART OF THEIR HAPPY FAMILY. THAT'S FINE. YOU DO WHATEVER YOU WANT.

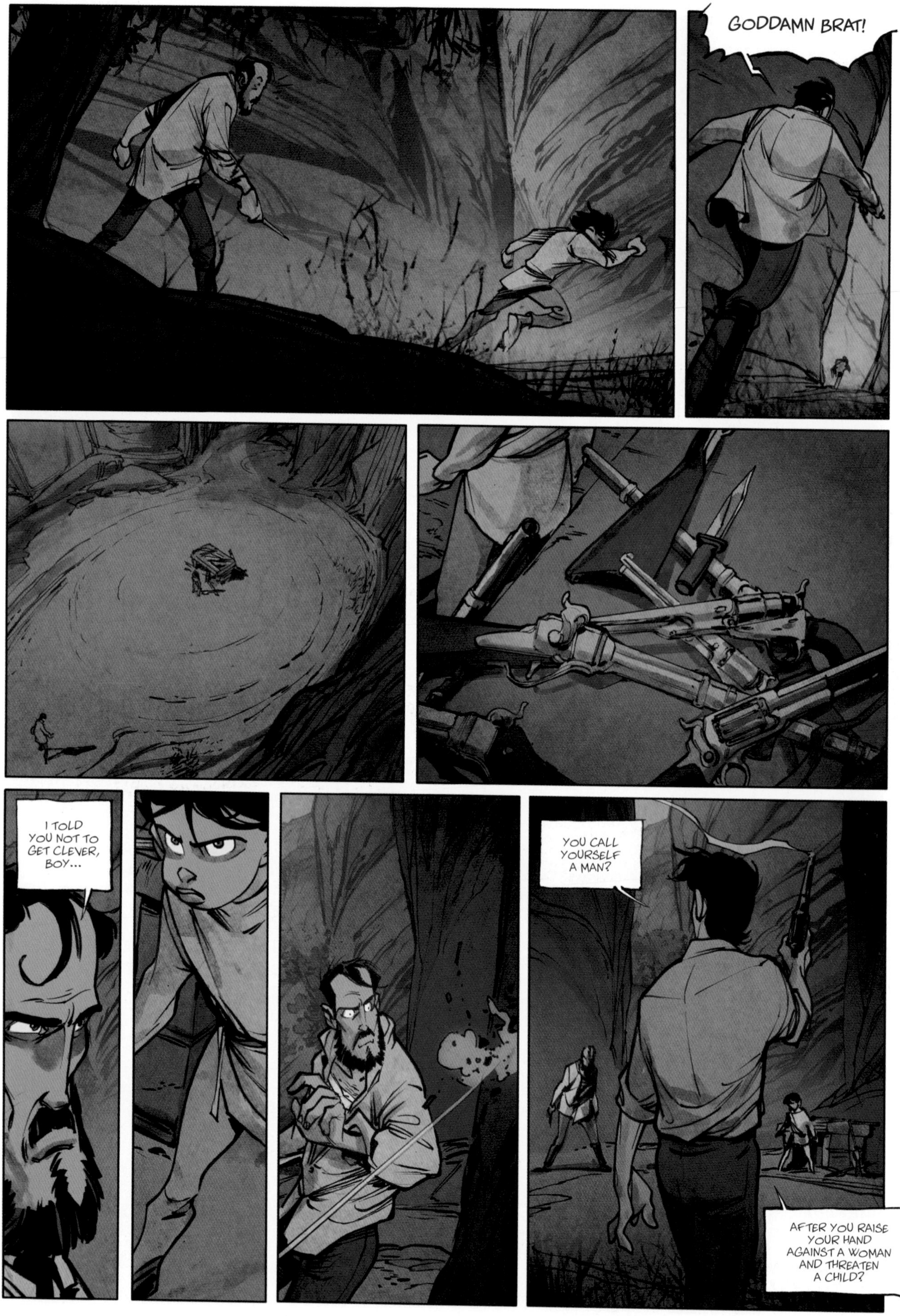
GODDAMN BRAT!
I TOLD YOU NOT TO GET CLEVER, BOY...
YOU CALL YOURSELF A MAN?
AFTER YOU RAISE YOUR HAND AGAINST A WOMAN AND THREATEN A CHILD?

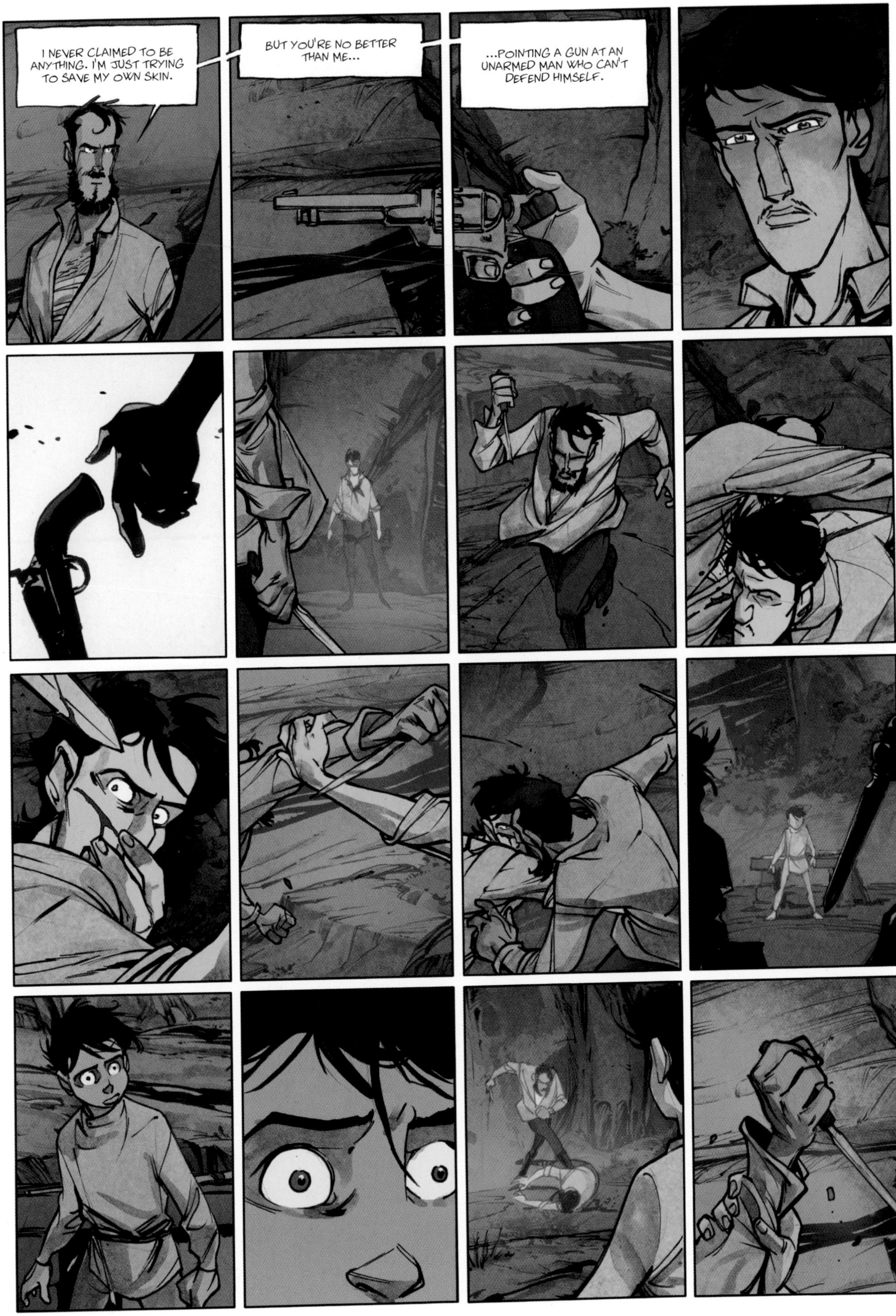
I NEVER CLAIMED TO BE ANYTHING. I'M JUST TRYING TO SAVE MY OWN SKIN.
BUT YOU'RE NO BETTER THAN ME...
...POINTING A GUN AT AN UNARMED MAN WHO CAN'T DEFEND HIMSELF.

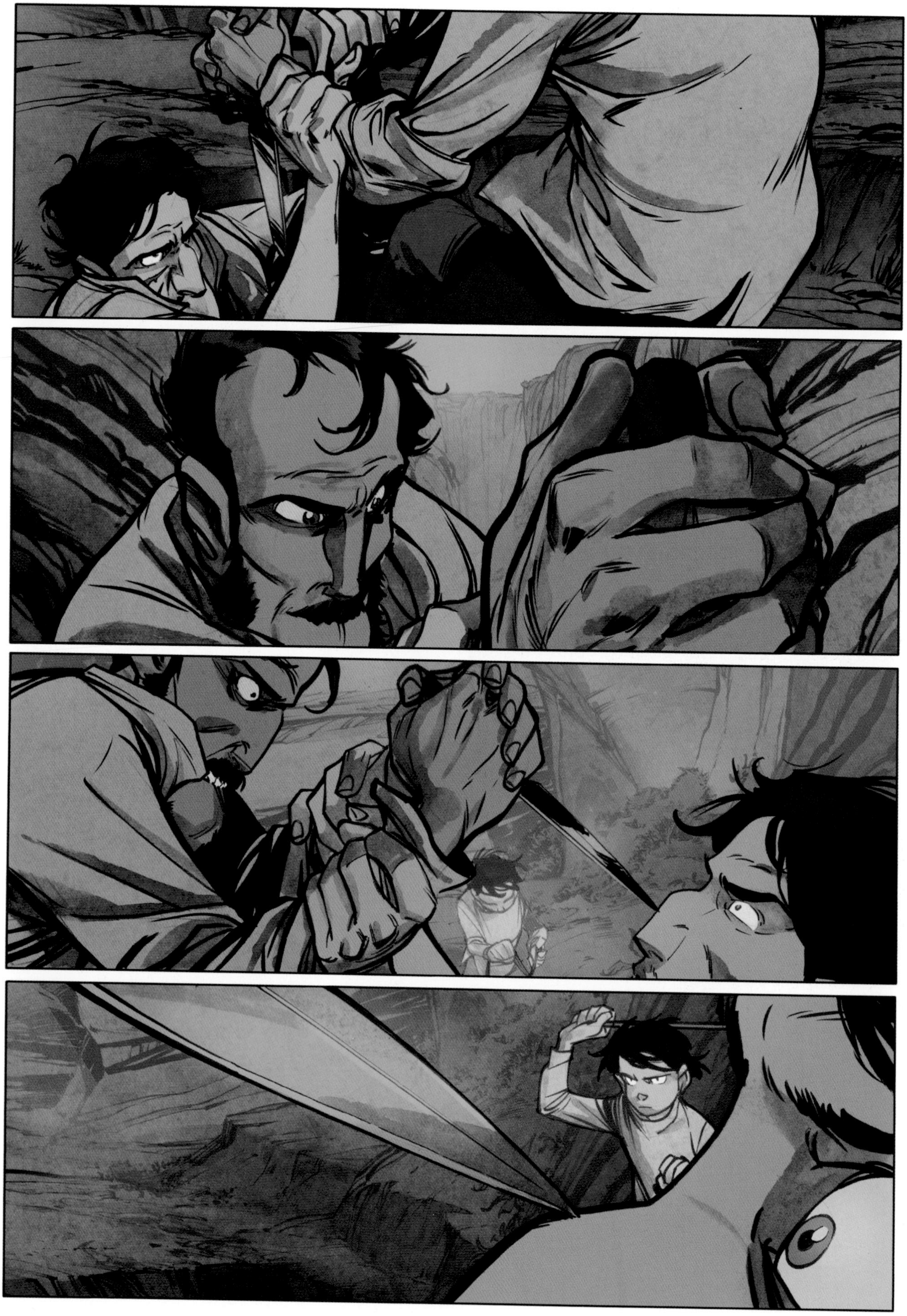

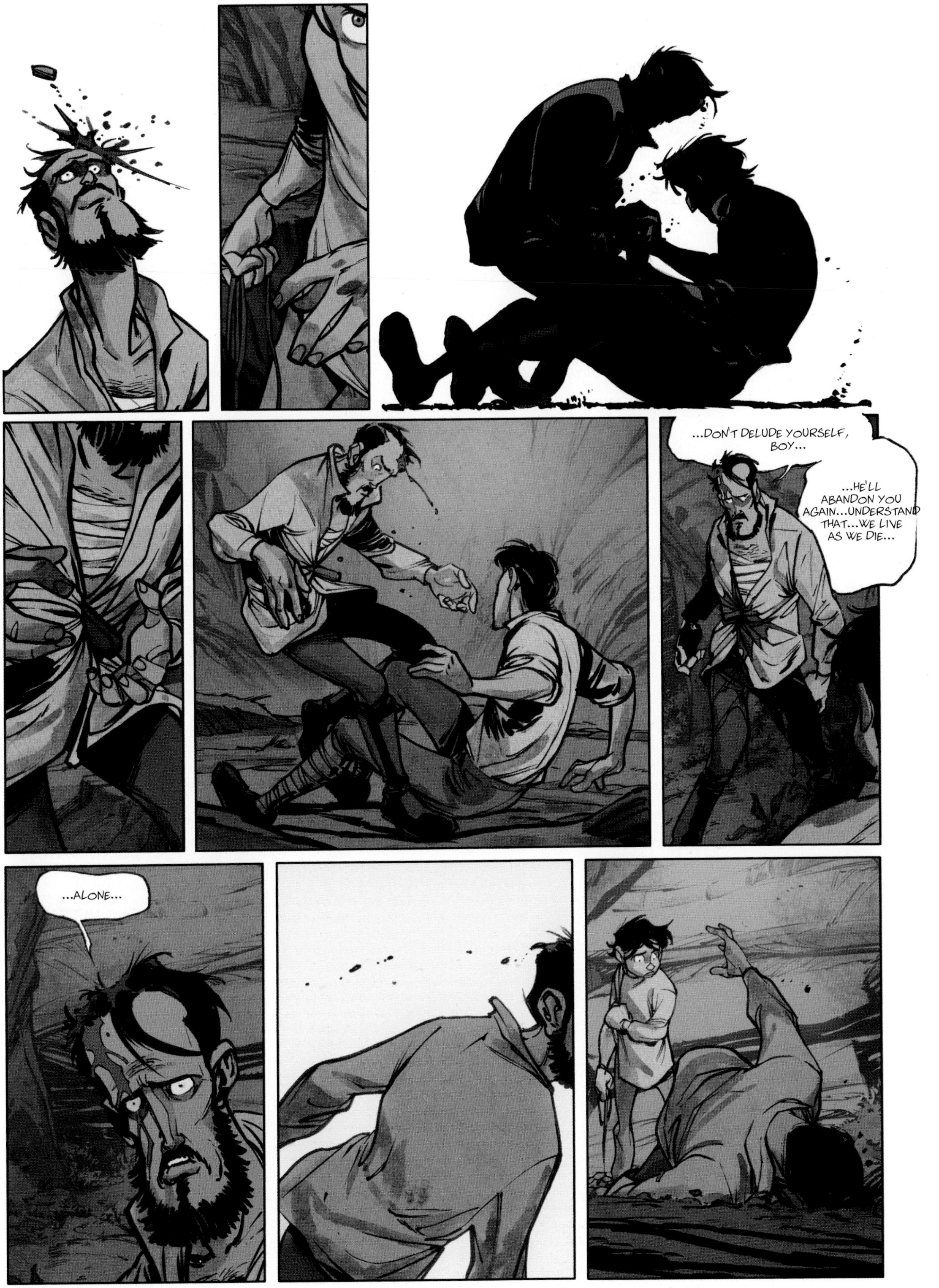
...DON'T DELUDE YOURSELF, BOY...
...HE'LL ABANDON YOU AGAIN...UNDERSTAND THAT...WE LIVE AS WE DIE...
...ALONE...

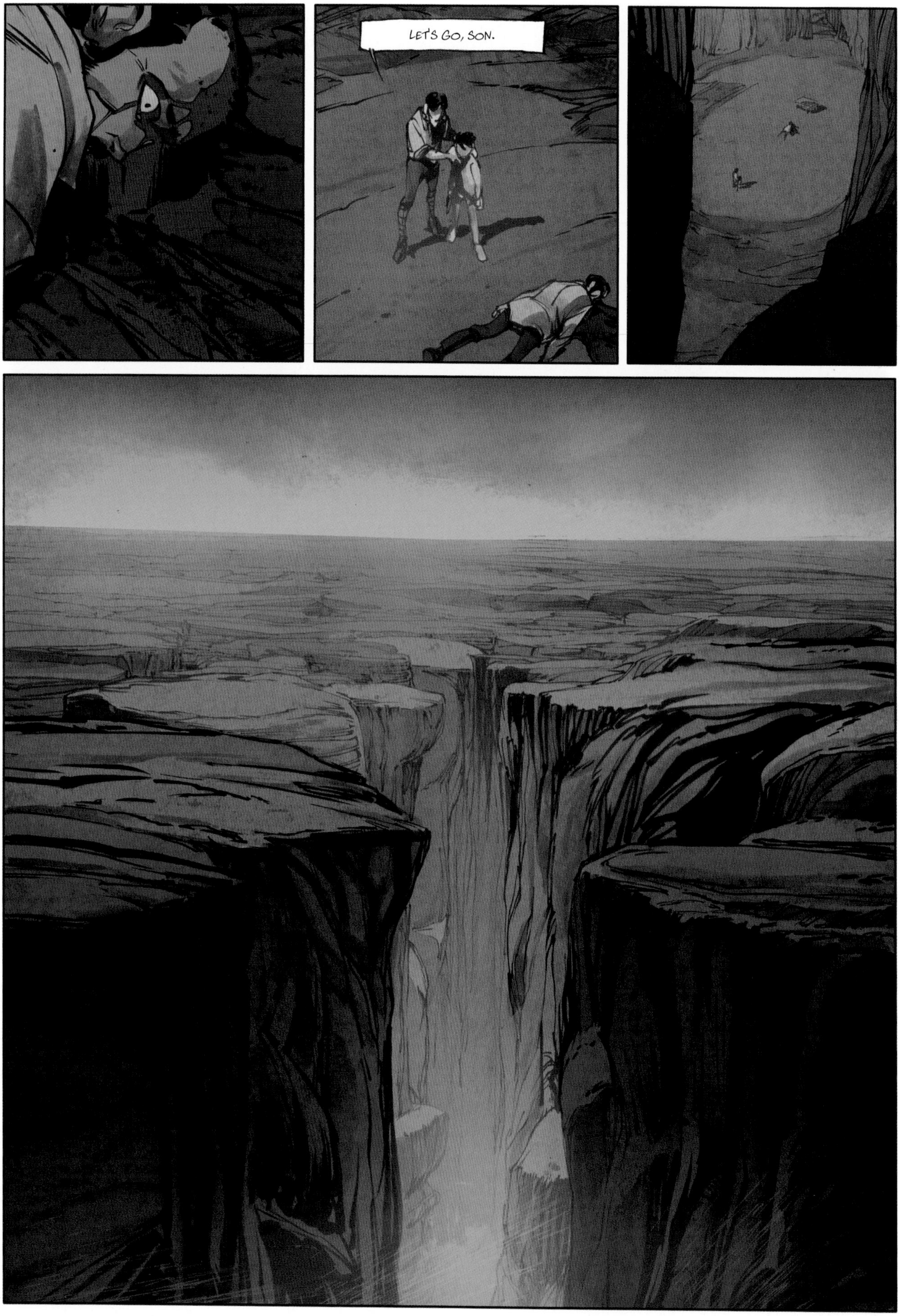
LET'S GO, SON.

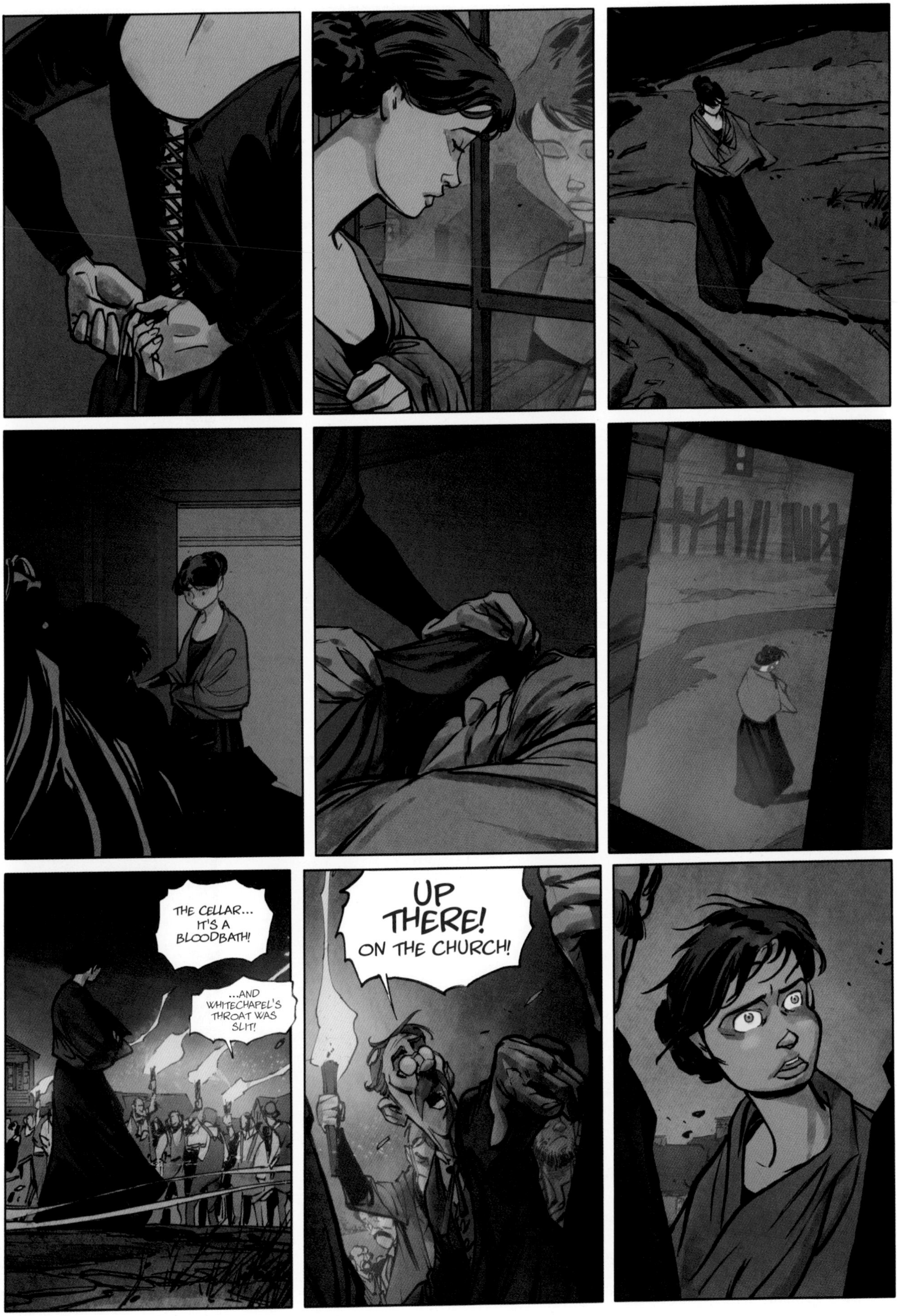
THE CELLAR... IT'S A BLOODBATH!
...AND WHITECHAPEL'S THROAT WAS SLIT!
UP THERE! ON THE CHURCH!

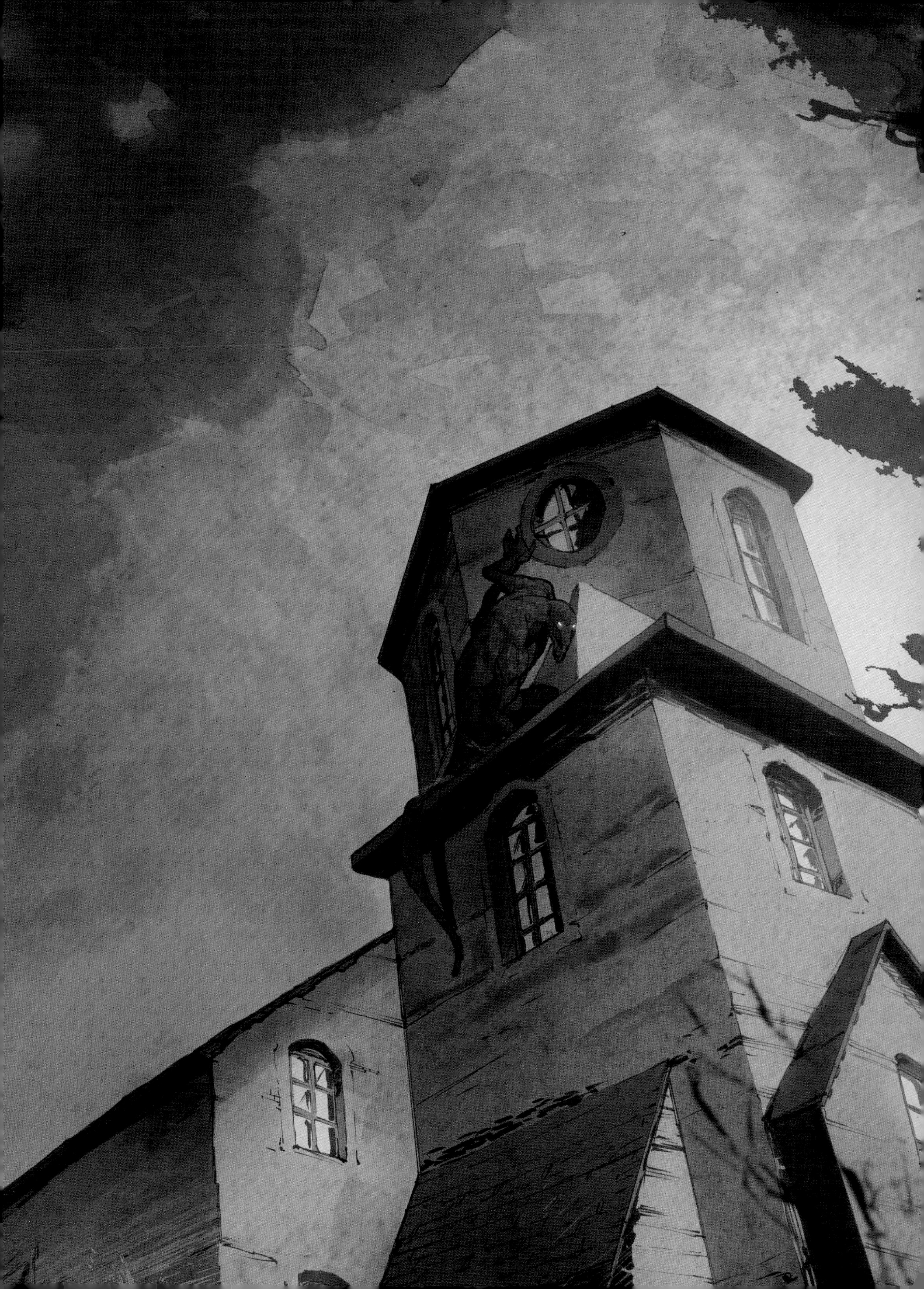

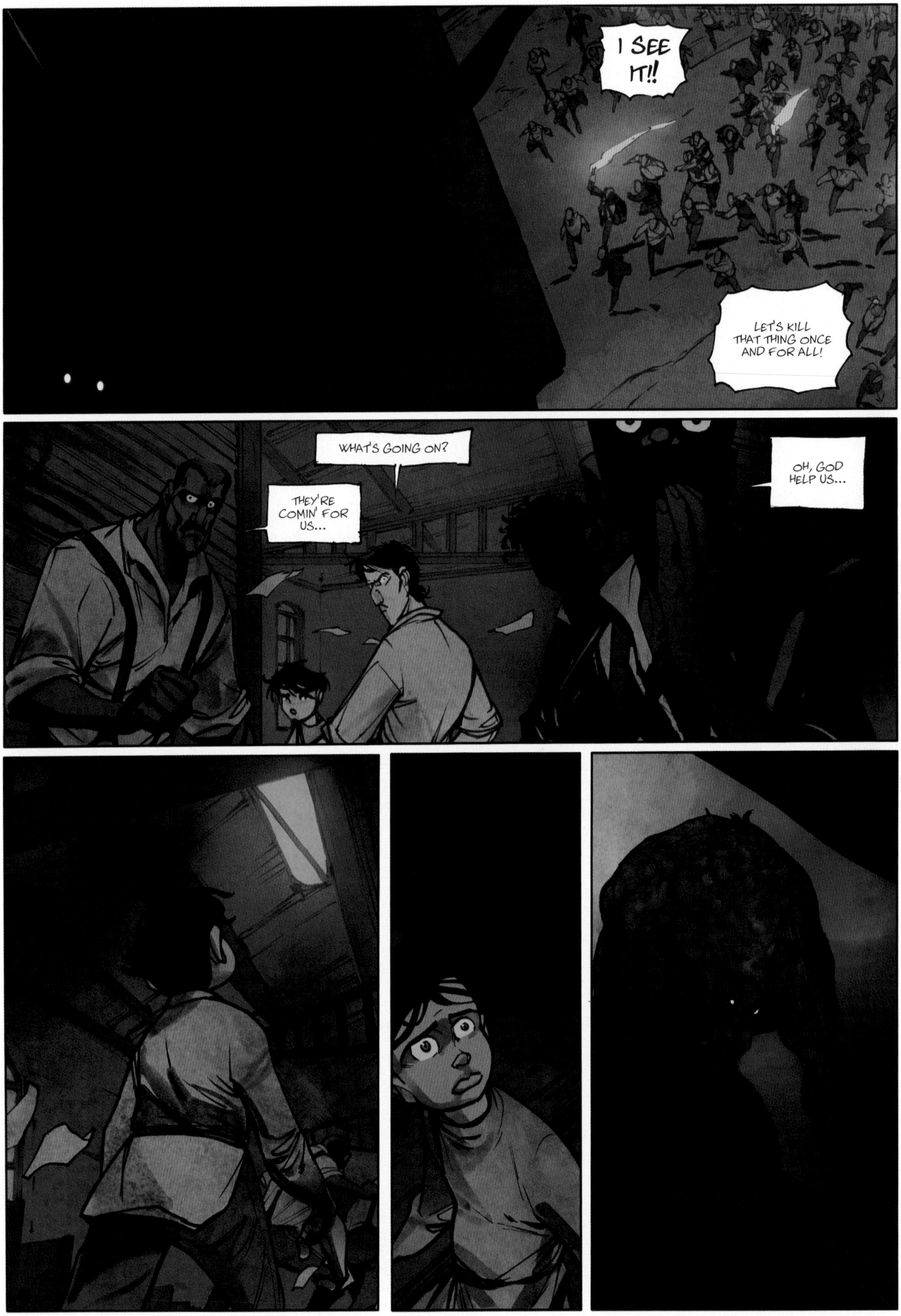
I SEE IT!!
LET'S KILL THAT THING ONCE AND FOR ALL!
THEY'RE COMIN' FOR US...
WHAT'S GOING ON?
OH, GOD HELP US...

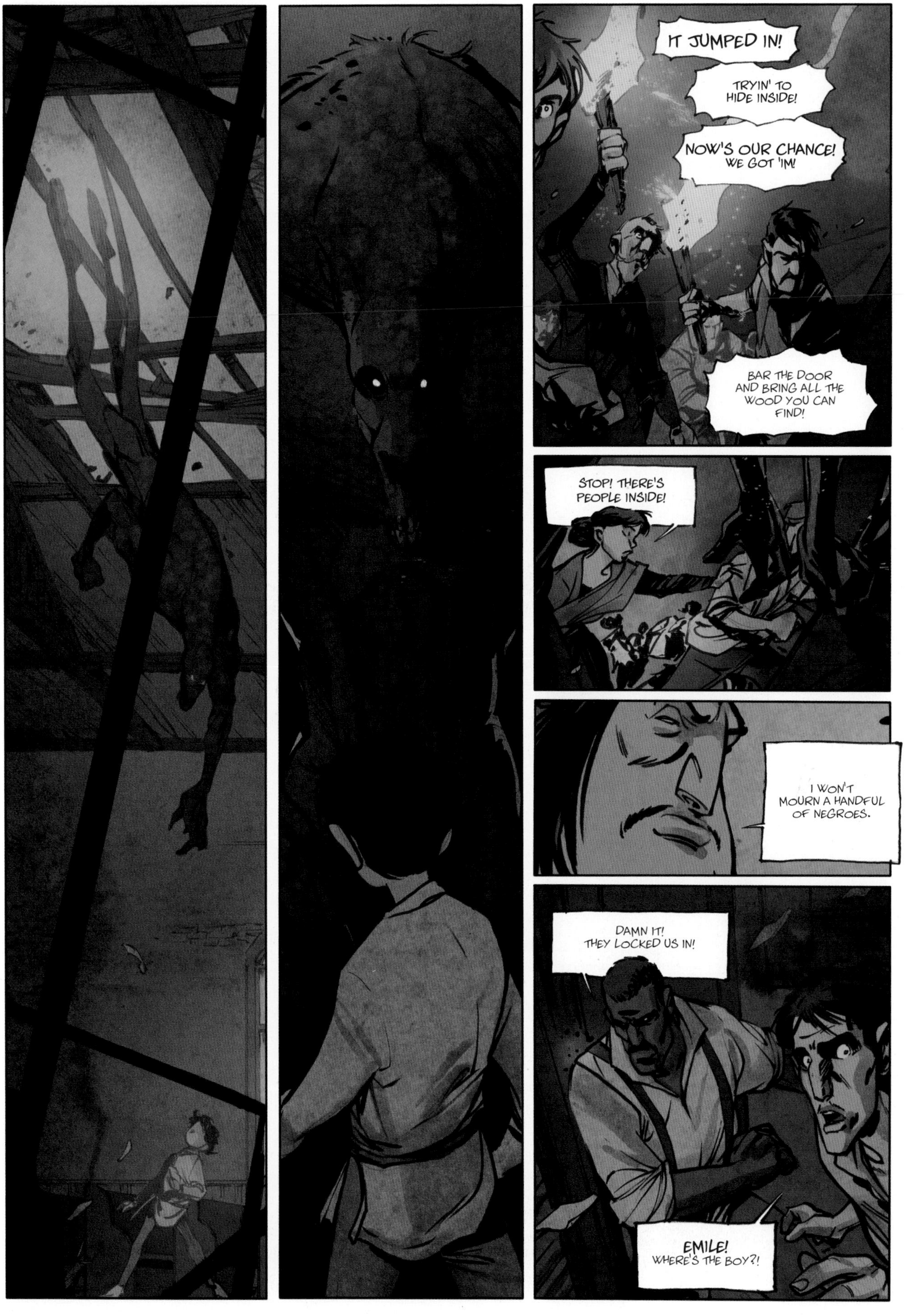

IT JUMPED IN!
TRYIN' TO HIDE INSIDE!
NOW'S OUR CHANCE! WE GOT 'IM!
BAR THE DOOR AND BRING ALL THE WOOD YOU CAN FIND!
STOP! THERE'S PEOPLE INSIDE!
I WON'T MOURN A HANDFUL OF NEGROES.
DAMN IT! THEY LOCKED US IN!
EMILE! WHERE'S THE BOY?!

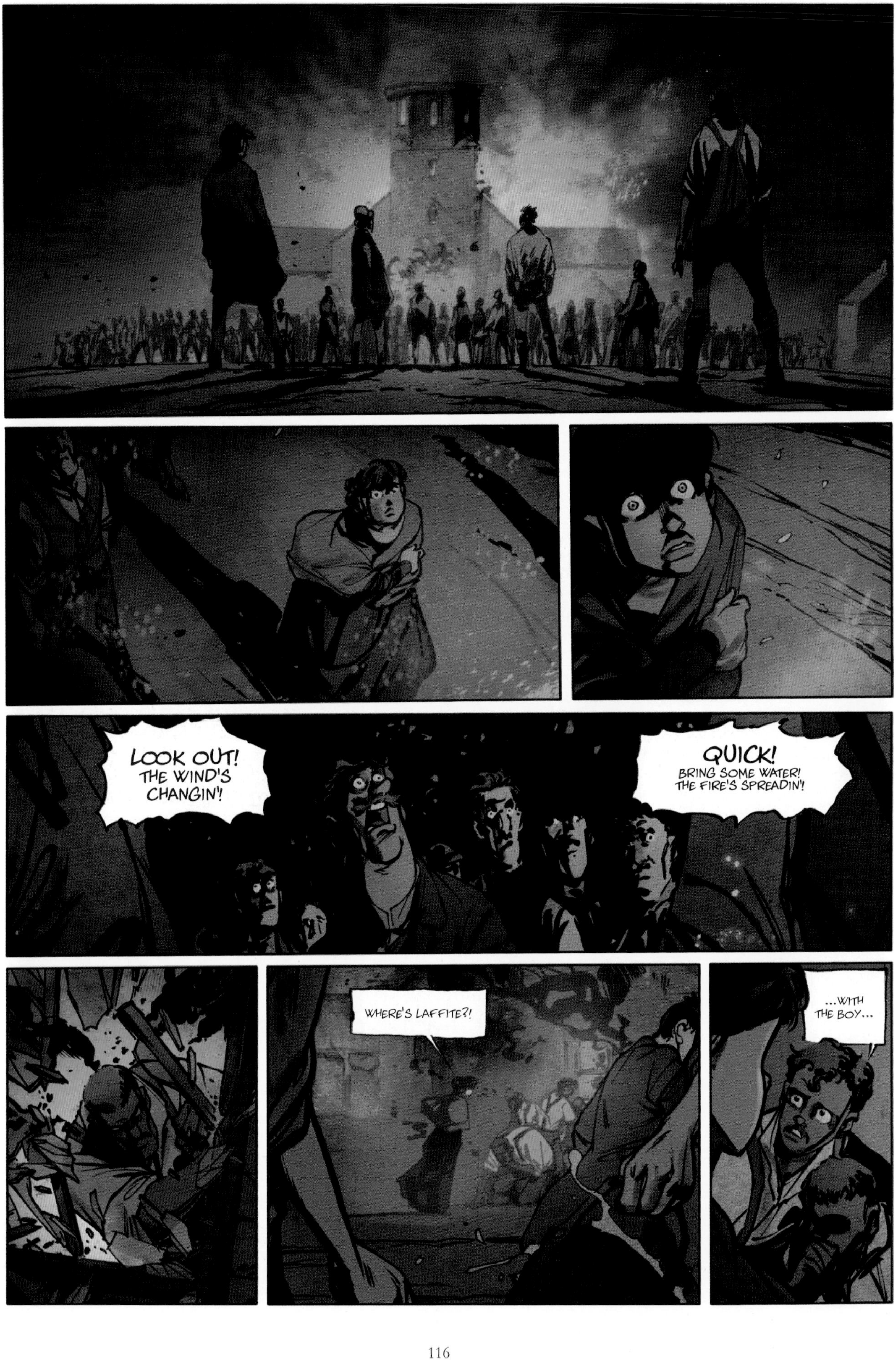
LOOK OUT! THE WIND'S CHANGIN'!
QUICK! BRING SOME WATER! THE FIRE'S SPREADIN'!
WHERE'S LAFFITE?!
...WITH THE BOY...

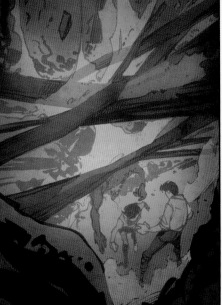

LEAVE HIM, EMILE! WE GOTTA GET OUT OF HERE!

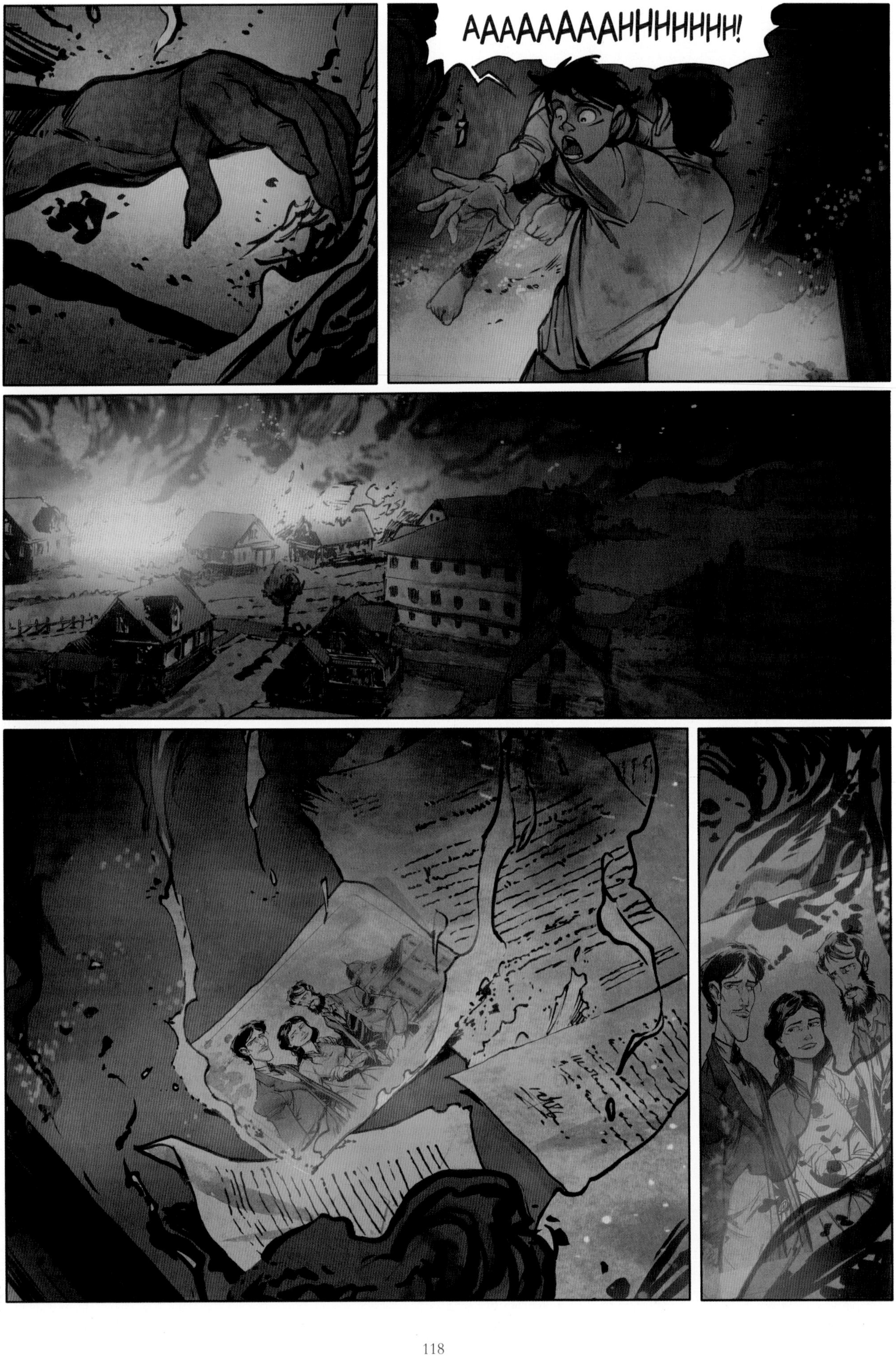
AAAAAAAAHHHHHHH!

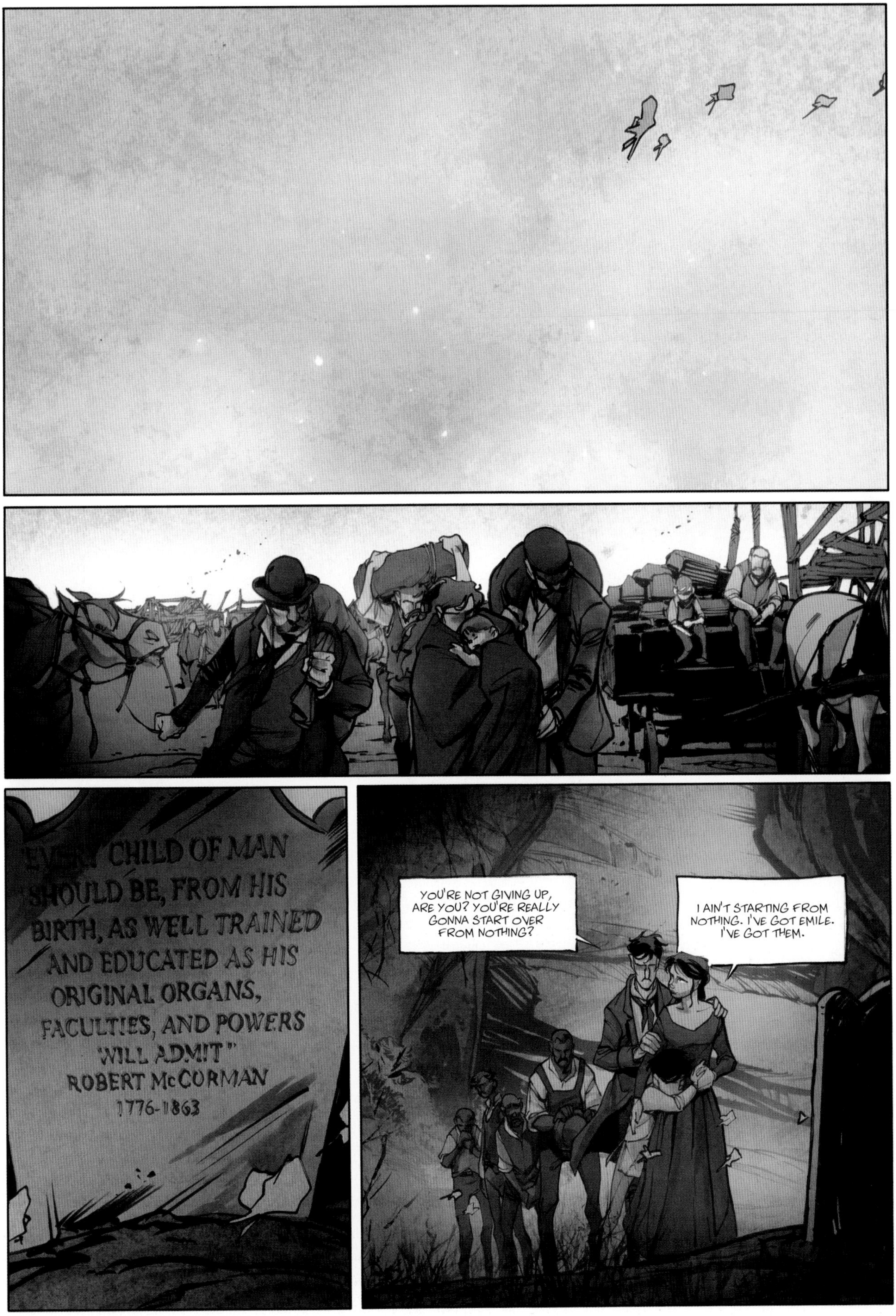
EVERY CHILD OF MAN SHOULD BE, FROM HIS BIRTH, AS WELL TRAINED AND EDUCATED AS HIS ORIGINAL ORGANS, FACULTIES, AND POWERS WILL ADMIT"
ROBERT McCORMAN
1776-1863
YOU'RE NOT GIVING UP, ARE YOU? YOU'RE REALLY GONNA START OVER FROM NOTHING?
I AIN'T STARTING FROM NOTHING. I'VE GOT EMILE. I'VE GOT THEM.

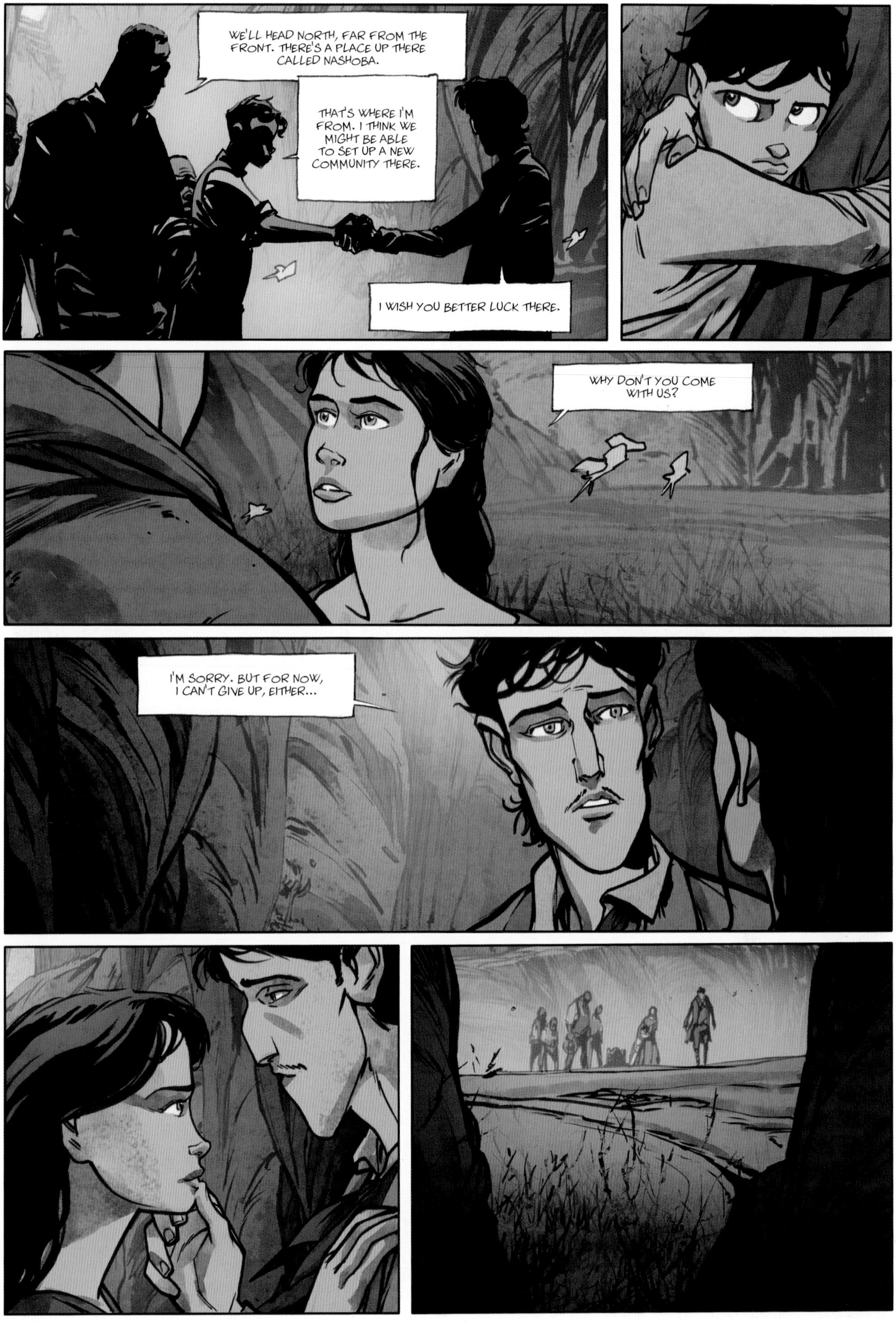
WE'LL HEAD NORTH, FAR FROM THE FRONT. THERE'S A PLACE UP THERE CALLED NASHOBA.
THAT'S WHERE I'M FROM. I THINK WE MIGHT BE ABLE TO SET UP A NEW COMMUNITY THERE.
I WISH YOU BETTER LUCK THERE.
WHY DON'T YOU COME WITH US?
I'M SORRY. BUT FOR NOW, I CAN'T GIVE UP, EITHER...

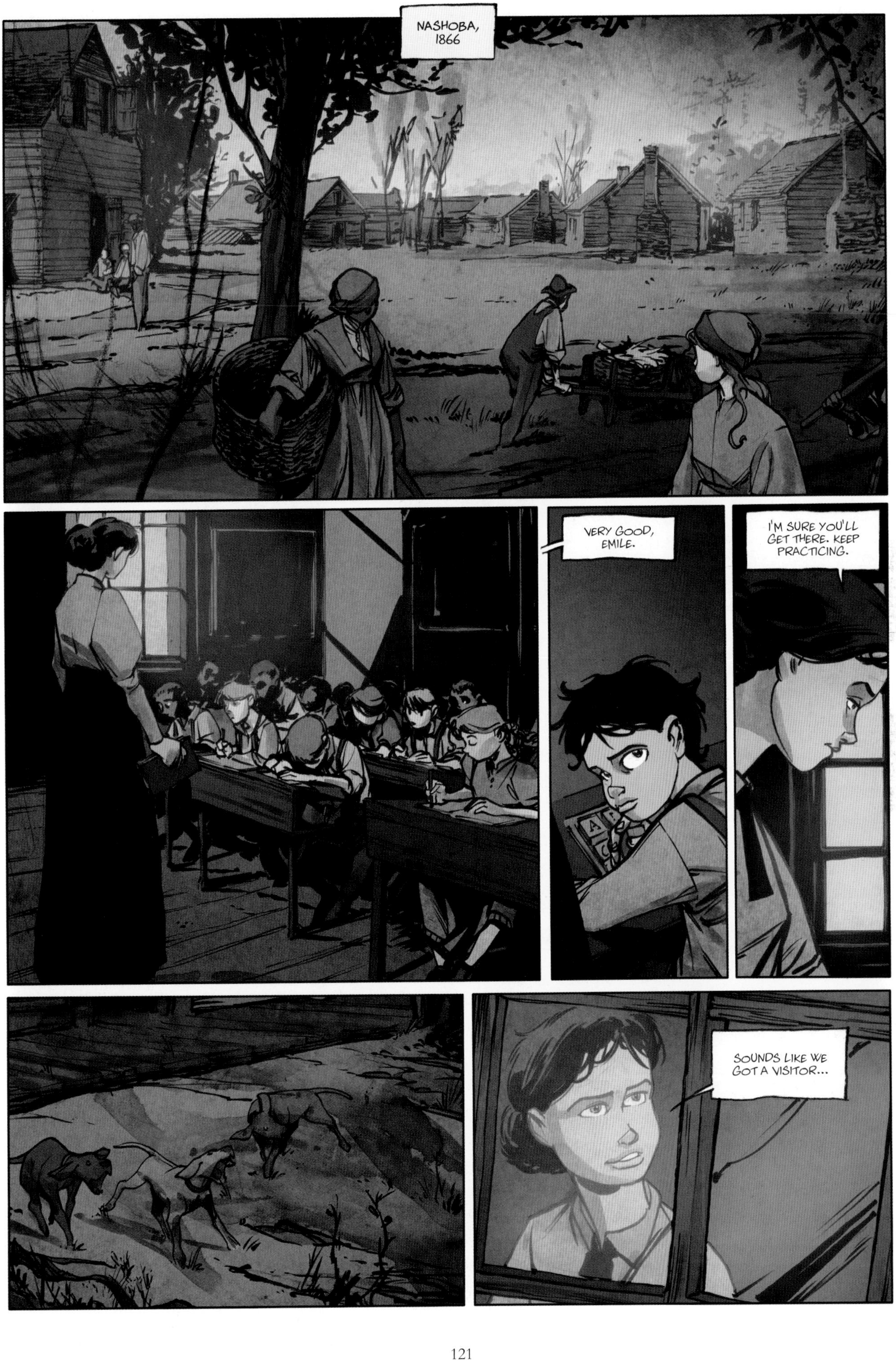
NASHOBA, 1866
VERY GOOD, EMILE.
I'M SURE YOU'LL GET THERE. KEEP PRACTICING.
SOUNDS LIKE WE GOT A VISITOR...

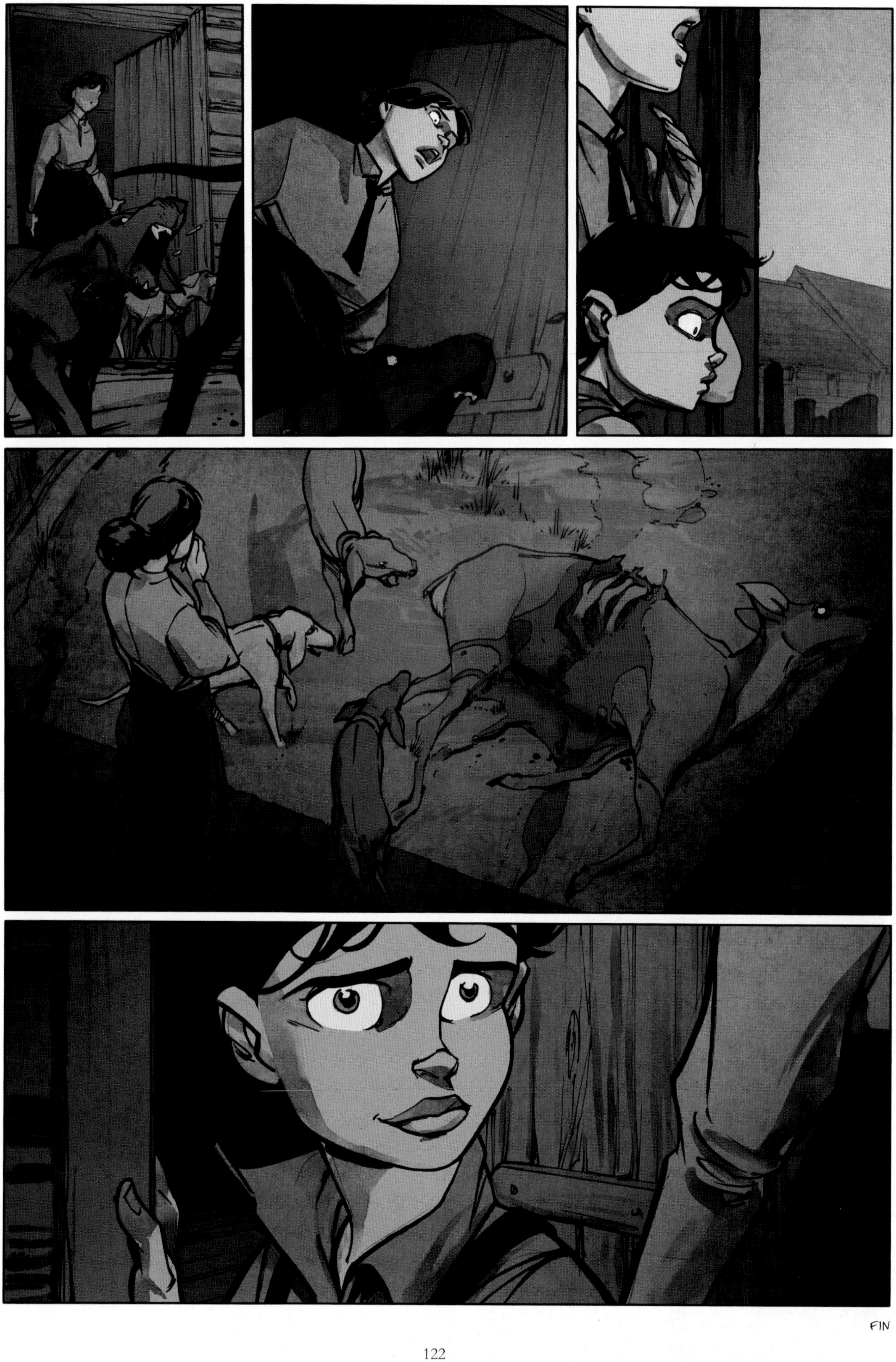

FIN

FraTerNiTy

BONUS

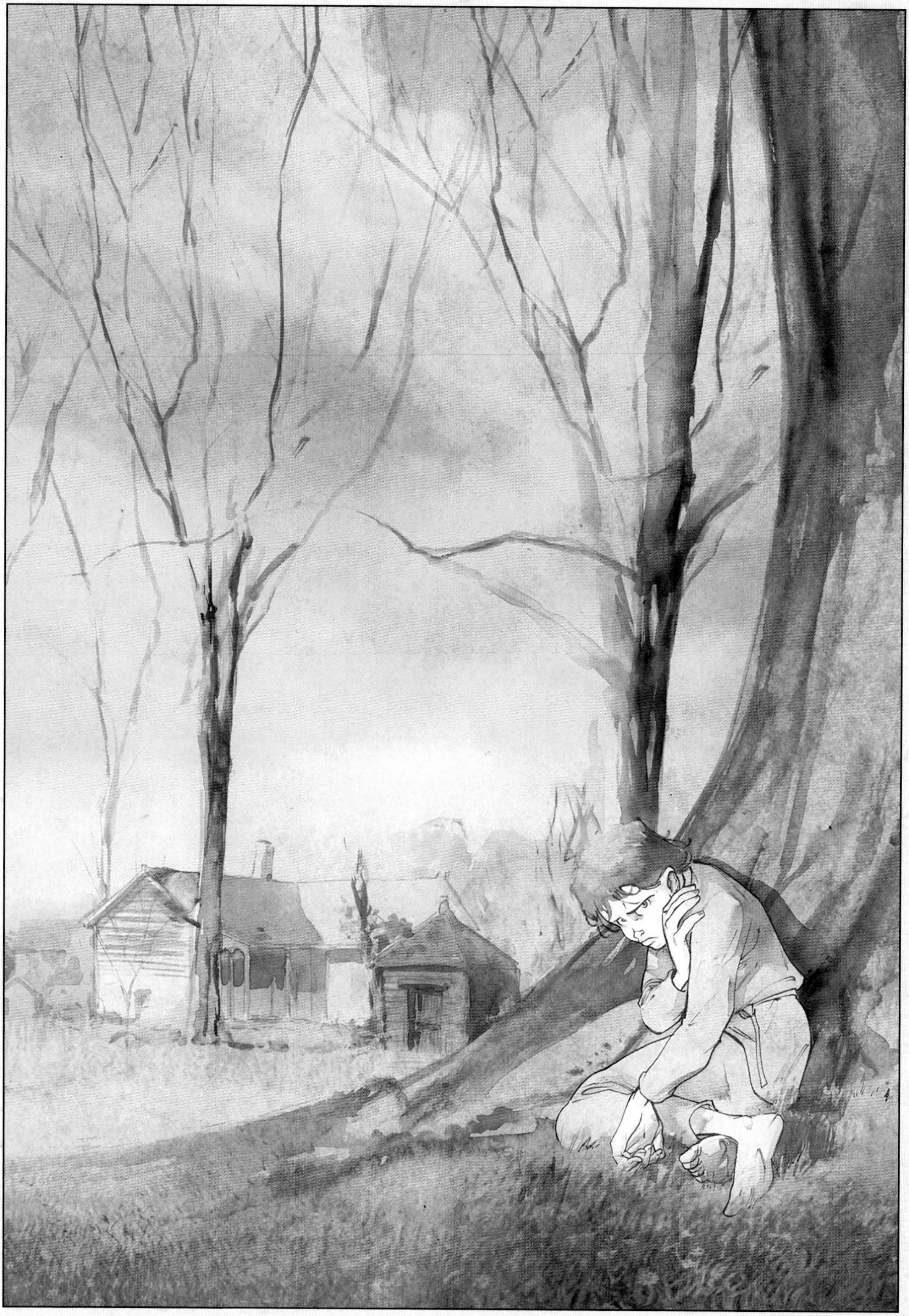

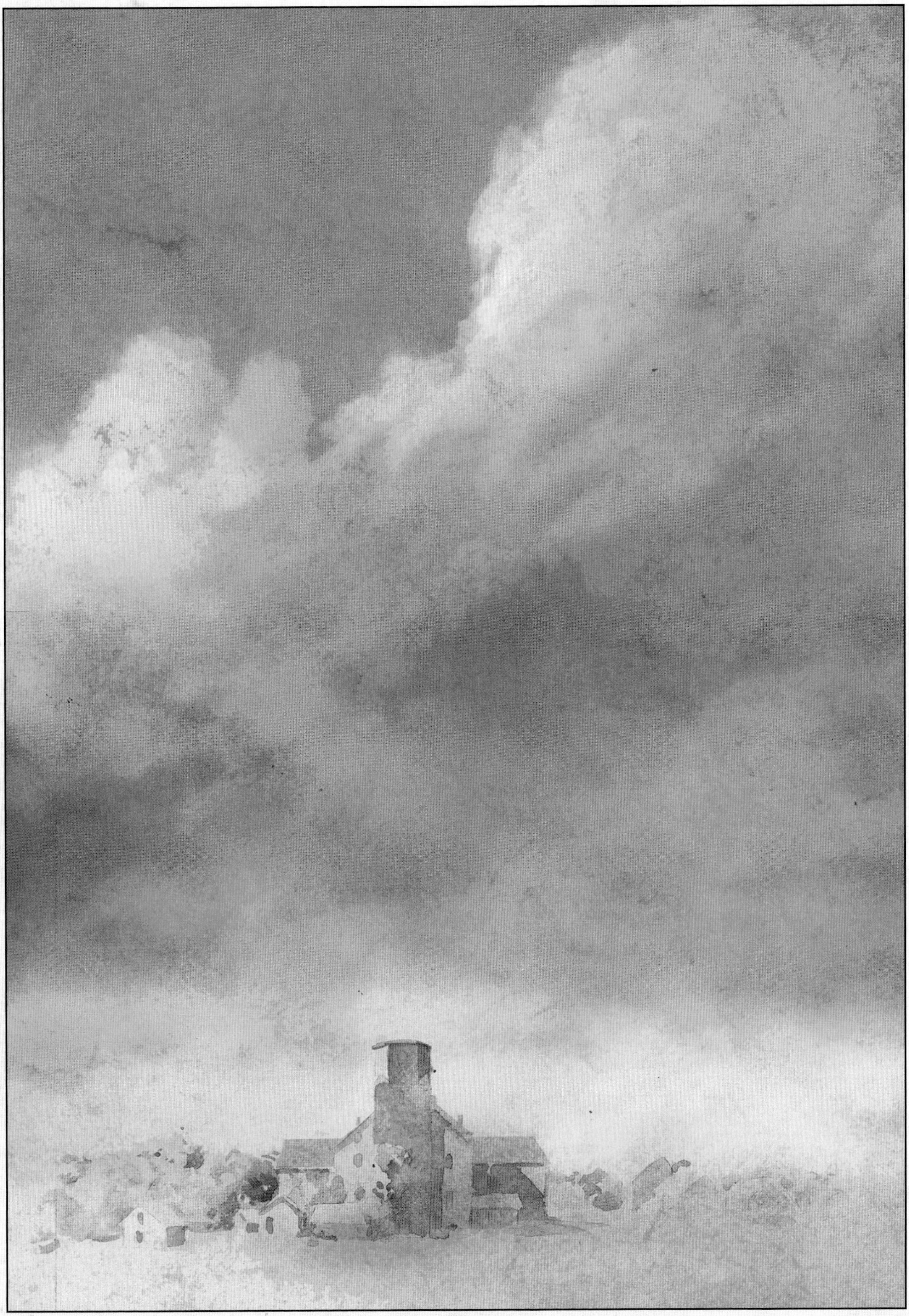

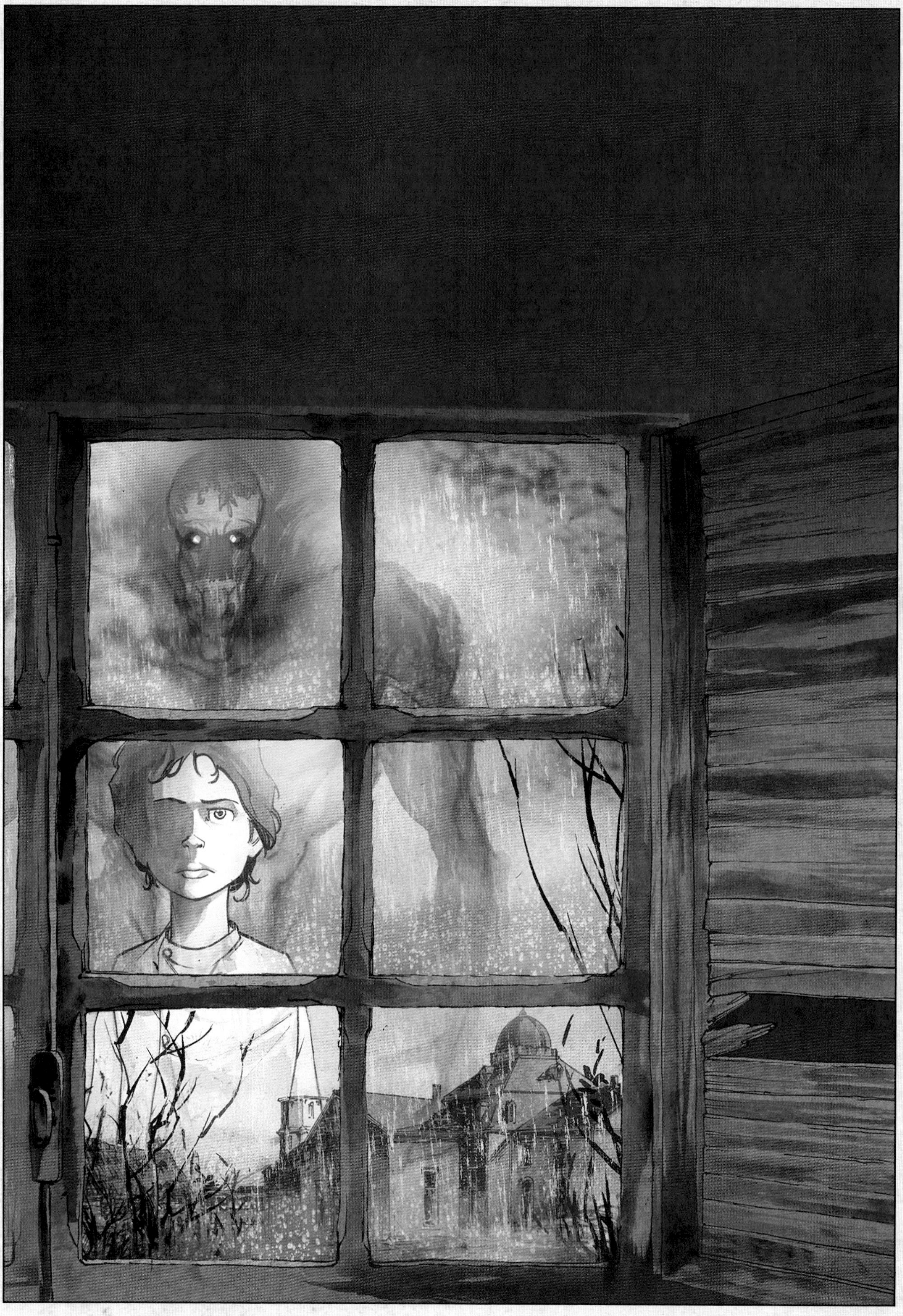

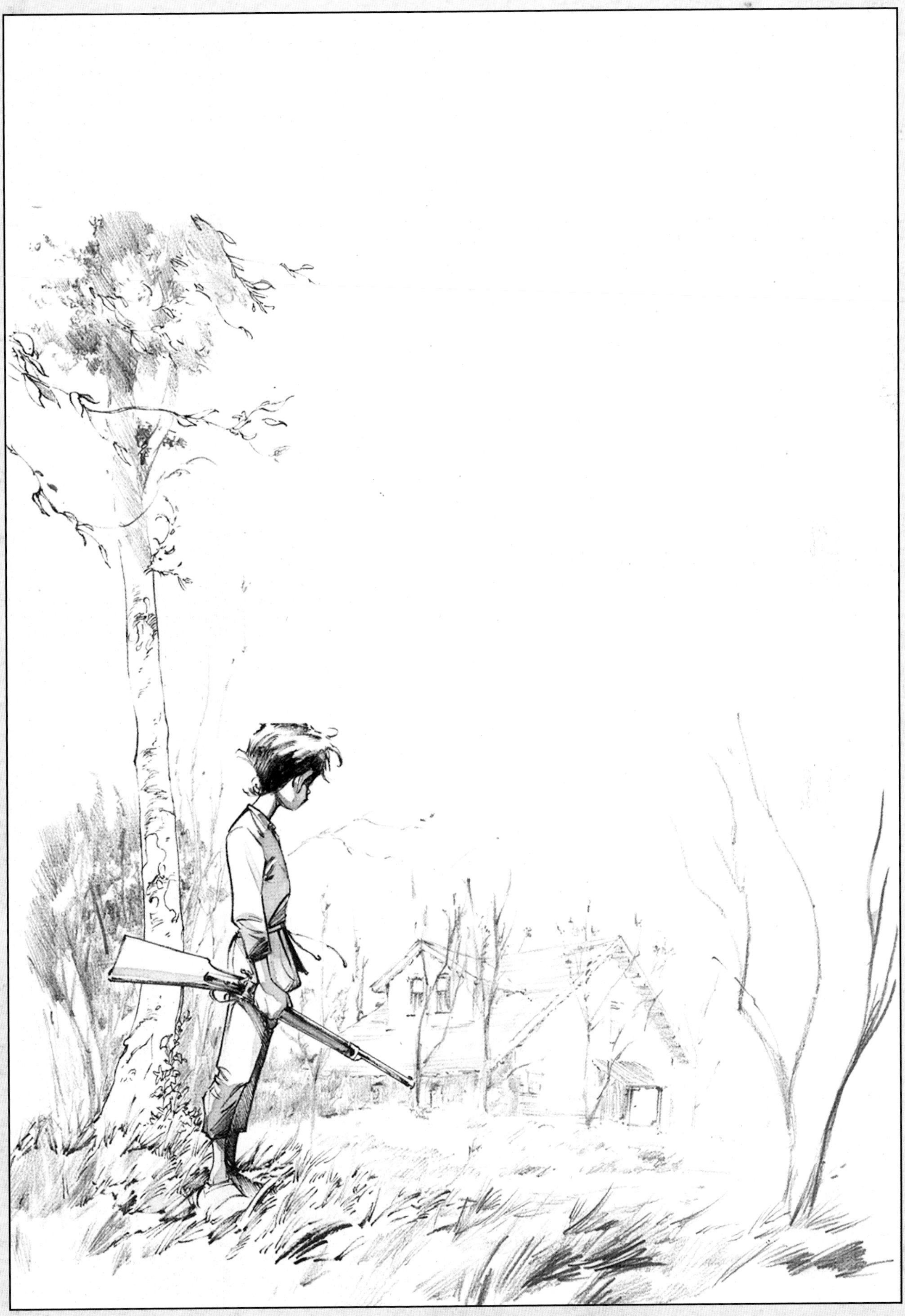

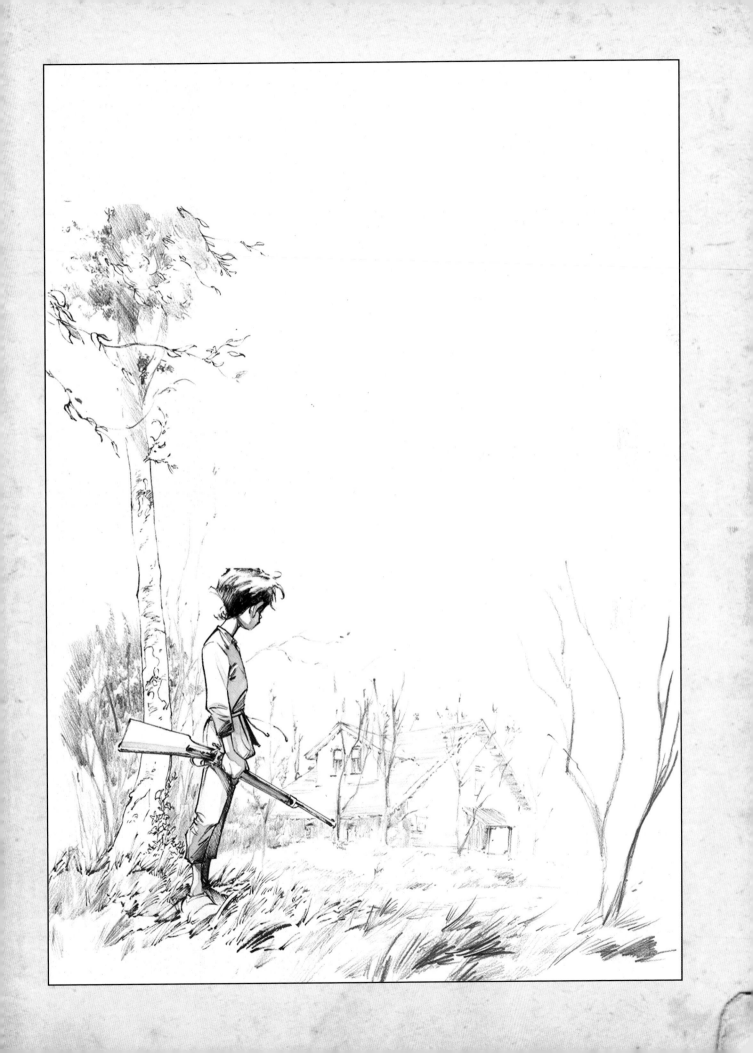

JUAN DÍAZ CANALES was born in Madrid, Spain, in 1972, where he began reading comics at a very early age. He soon discovered cartoons as well and decided that is what he would do for a living. At the age of eighteen, he began studying animation, and at the age of twenty-four, he founded his own studio called Tridente Animation. There, he first met artist/animator Juanjo Guarnido, with whom he created his first graphic novel series, *Blacksad*. The anthropomorphic animal-noir detective series was immensely popular, winning numerous awards and being translated into numerous languages. Since then, he has continued to write and supervise animation projects for TV and feature films while also writing the official continuing adventures of *Corto Maltese*.

JOSÉ-LUIS MUNUERA was born in Lorca, Spain, in 1972, where he was weaned on primarily humorous Franco-Belgian comics that made their way over the Pyrenees. After studying at the Beaux-Arts in Grenada, he realized that editorial tastes had started to turn toward American comics, Japanese manga, and a more realistic aesthetic quite different from the more innate, humorous style of his initial inspiration, *Spirou and Fantasio*. Judged "too French" by his peers, he went on a pilgrimage to Angoulême where he landed his first title, *The Potamoks*, eventually followed by the comic adaptation of DreamWorks's *The Road to Eldorado*. Around that time, he met writer/editor J.D. Morvan, who invited him on board the ongoing series *Sillage* and its many spin-offs, which soon led full circle to working on the continuation of *Spirou and Fantasio*. He currently illustrates the series *Zorglub*, chronicling the misadventures of the popular villain/antihero from the *Spirou* universe.